Series editors' preface

Why do people study the past? How are they making sense of the remnants of the past they encounter in archives, libraries and interviews? And how do people then write the past? At a time when most professional historians are willing to accept that any such writing depends on authorial perspective, narrative strategy and cultural context, a thorough understanding of the history of historiography is widely regarded as the precondition of doing and reading history. Undergraduate and postgraduate courses increasingly include the compulsory study of the philosophy of history and historical theory. *Writing History* presents a book series that focuses on the practical application of theory in historical writing. It publishes accessibly written overviews of particular fields of history. Rather than focus upon abstract theory, the books in this series explain key concepts and demonstrate the ways in which they have informed practical work. Theoretical perspectives, acknowledged and unacknowledged, have shaped actual works of history. Each book in the series relates historical texts and their producers to the social conditions of their existence. As such, *Writing History* goes beyond a focus on historical works in themselves. In a variety of ways, each volume analyses texts within their institutional arrangement and as part of a wider social discourse.

Postcolonial history, which emerged from the *Subaltern Studies* group in India, founded in 1982, has been one of the most successful forms of history from below on a global level. Its impact could be felt not only across historical studies in the developing world, especially in Latin America, but reached right into the metropoles of history-writing in North America and Europe. It resulted in a fundamental critique of a Western-centric progressive idea of history, according to which the West set the pace for a universal historical development, which the rest of the world could only follow. Instead, postcolonial scholars championed the idea of multiple modernities and the hybridization of cultures as a consequence of the imperialization of the world. Postcolonialism explored the manifold ways in which empire led to both resistance and complicity among the colonized. They stressed local experiences without losing sight of those locations being set in wider universal narratives. Like other history-from-below movements, postcolonial scholars were deeply influenced by neo-Marxism, but they went beyond traditional Marxist emphasis on economic foundationalism to emphasize cultural aspects of domination with E. P. Thompson, in particular, acting as an inspiration for postcolonial scholars, such as Edward Said, Homi Bhaba, Dipesh Chakrabarty, Gyan Prakash, Gayatri Chakravorty Spivak and many others. In their writings, neo-Marxism combined with poststructuralist thinking to set the tone for postcolonialism's analysis of discursive constructions of colonial power.

Rochona Majumdar's *Writing Postcolonial History* explores the influence of postcolonial theory on a wide variety of historical writing ranging from medieval to contemporary history and from local to global history. It contextualizes the emergence of postcolonial writing in the aftermath of decolonization and provides a lucid and multi-faceted exploration of the many inflections postcolonialism took over the past three decades. Alert to the many differences within postcolonialism, Majumdar nevertheless manages to find common themes and threads that weave themselves through many different works, which would be unthinkable without postcolonial theory. She traces the manifold tensions between scholarship and politics that have played such an important role in postcolonial historical writing, and she also discusses the idiosyncrasies that characterize these writings. She demonstrates how postcolonial history, by avoiding stark contradictions between colonizers and colonized, has sought to give renewed agency to colonial subjects, while at the same time tracing the impact of the metropole on the colonial subjects. Her book underlines the degree to which postcolonialism has contributed to a fundamental rethinking and rewriting of both the history of empire and the history of nation states. And it also shows how it managed to touch a number of other themes and subjects on the way, perhaps none more so than gender, which is a central concern also in Majumdar's volume. Overall, the reader of this book is presented with a wealth of concrete examples on how postcolonial theory has reconfigured the field of history-writing over the last three decades.

Stefan Berger, Heiko Feldner and Kevin Passmore
Manchester and Cardiff, June 2010

Writing Postcolonial History

Also in the *Writing History* series

Published:

Writing History: Theory and Practice, 2nd edition
Edited by Stefan Berger, Heiko Feldner and Kevin Passmore

Writing Gender History, 2nd edition
Laura Lee Downs

Writing Contemporary History
Edited by Robert Gildea and Anne Simonin

Writing Medieval History
Nancy Partner

Writing Early Modern History
Garthine Walker

Forthcoming:

Writing the Holocaust
Edited by Jean-Marc Dreyfus and Daniel Langton

Writing the History of Memory
Edited by Stefan Berger and Bill Niven

Writing Postcolonial History

Rochona Majumdar

BLOOMSBURY ACADEMIC

First Published in India 2017
First published in 20 I 0 by Bloomsbury Academic

Bloomsbury Academic
An imprint of Bloomsbury Publishing Plc
Bloomsbury is a registered trade mark of Bloomsbury Publishing Plc

This edition published with permission from Bloomsbury Publishing Plc
50, Bedford Square, London, WC1B3DP

CIP records for this book are available from the British Library and the Library of Congress.

ISBN: 978-93-86643-22-3
10 9 8 7 6 5 4 3 2 1
For sale in the Indian subcontinent only

Bloomsbury Publishing India Pvt. Ltd
Second Floor, Building No. 4
DDA Complex LSC, Pocket C – 6 & 7
Vasant Kunj, New Delhi 110070
www.bloomsbury.com

Exclusively Distributed in India by:
Manohar Publishers & Distributors
4753/23, Ansari Road
Darya Ganj, New Delhi 110002
Tel.: 23284848, 23289100
Email: sales@manoharbooks.com, manoharbooks@gmail.com

Printed and bound in India

www.bloomsburyacademic.com

To Boria Majumdar

Preface

Rudyard Kipling's poem 'The White Man's Burden' eloquently sums up the ideas that underlay the 'civilizing mission' that many nineteenth-century Europeans regarded as their providential destiny. It is impossible to read his (in)famous poem today without seeing it also as an ideological justification for British domination of peoples in far-flung colonies.

> Take up the White Man's burden –
> Send forth the best ye breed –
> Go, bind your sons to exile
> To serve your captives' need;
> To wait, in heavy harness,
> On fluttered folk and wild –
> Your new-caught sullen peoples,
> Half devil and half child.[1]

Most readers today will agree that what to Kipling's age seemed high idealism and moral responsibility towards purportedly backward groups veiled a bundle of European prejudices. In hindsight, it is clear that the imperial convictions that resonated from Kipling's lines were undergirded by unquestioned confidence about white supremacy over non-white peoples. Over a hundred years have elapsed since the publication of 'The White Man's Burden'. Well past the age of imperialism, the world is very different now. Indeed, one of the major challenges democratic countries face in our contemporary age of globalization is the reverse of what Kipling suggested: how to treat the diverse cultures of different human groups on a plane of equality?

Mobility is a perennial factor in human history. But modern times have seen a real acceleration in the movement of humans across geographies. The growth and movements of human populations, already visible from the early twentieth century, but accelerated in the decades following the end of the Second World War and the era of decolonization, have radically altered the composition of erstwhile 'white' countries. The latter have had to acknowledge and grapple with the increased presence of many races in their midst. A variety of factors have contributed to the diverse composition of modern democracies and to the array of human rights movements that comprise the political arena in the ex-colonial and metropolitan countries alike. The decades following the era of decolonization witnessed the spread of feminism, the rise of gay rights and black power movements. More recently the world has been rocked by the impact of a series of events whose aftermath is still being worked out in particular national contexts as well as collectively by global bodies. A list of such events, by no means exhaustive, would include the fall of the Berlin Wall, the end of communism in the former Soviet Union, the end of apartheid in South Africa, the growth of radical Islamism and the challenges faced by environmentalism. Add to these the struggles of indigenous peoples and other minorities in countries across the world, and it will be clear why questions of equality and recognition feature as one of the biggest challenges of our times. These social movements for political and other rights vary widely according to national context. Taken together, however, they draw attention to the fact that while colonial rule may have come to a formal end in all parts of the globe, we still live in a world that is being shaped by demands from formerly marginalized and oppressed groups, demands that received their early articulation during nationalist movements of the late nineteenth and early twentieth centuries.

The affective freight of certain moments in global politics testifies to the ways in which colonial pasts haunt the global present. Thus the 2008 presidential victory of Barack Obama, the African-American nominee of the Democratic Party, signalled, at least symbolically, the overcoming of centuries-old discrimination suffered by African-Americans since the time of Atlantic slavery. Similarly iconic and emotional events include the public 'apology' proffered by Prime Minister Kevin Rudd on 13 February 2008 to the Aboriginal people for the wrongs they suffered during the white settlement of Australia, and the Truth and Reconciliation Commission in South Africa, which heralded the birth of a democratic polity and the end of the debilitating apartheid period. If these events bring a ray of hope, there are many others that demonstrate that we are a long way from establishing social orders that guarantee equal rights and respect for all premised upon mutual recognition of differences.

The fierce controversy over cartoons of the Prophet Mohammad in Denmark and the furore caused by the decision to ban religious symbols from the clothing of French school children as a mark of secularism highlight the importance of negotiating questions of religious identities in multiracial democracies. Similarly, race riots in different parts of England, Australia and France and the rapid growth of asylum centres and refugee camps on borders of wealthy nations draw attention to the fact that questions of race, religion, gender, migration and nationality are far from resolved. Conflicts on these issues first arose in different parts of the world during the eighteenth and nineteenth centuries in the contexts of slavery and colonial rule. But the end of formal empires did not mean a corresponding resolution of these problems. If anything, they have only been intensified in the contemporary era of globalization.

Literary and other artistic production, already visible around the years of decolonization, but growing steadily since the 1980s, registers humanistic responses to these issues. Noteworthy in this context are novels by the India-born Salman Rushdie, Sri Lankan author Michael Ondaatje, Bangladeshi–British writer Monica Ali and the Turkish–German writer Zafer Senocak. Then, there are films such as *My Son the Fanatic* (1997), *Monsoon Wedding* (2001), *Rabbit-Proof Fence* (2002) and *Bend It Like Beckham* (2002), to just name at random a few from a growing body of work. Less well-known than these examples is the fact that academic disciplines as taught and researched in universities have also been affected by these developments in ways that have sometimes challenged the fundamental tenets of these disciplines. Scholarly practice in disciplines such as history, literary studies, political science, anthropology and sociology has been forced to take stock of their fundamental categories and examine if they were somehow implicated in the inequalities of racial and/or colonial domination. In the last few decades, some of the most innovative and exciting research in these disciplines has been done by scholars who have worked on the frontiers of such questions.

Writing Postcolonial History is an effort to map the ways in which the academic historians have dealt with the intellectual aftermath of decolonization. It discusses how a new field – postcolonial history – has emerged within the discipline of history. We should not assume, of course, that the large number of works now collected under the rubric 'postcolonial histories' presents anything like a homogeneous or a uniform perspective. But despite their differences it is possible to outline some common themes and perspectives that make these works belong in a new and separate subdiscipline within history. It would be useful to delineate some general characteristics of historical works written from postcolonial standpoints, and the forthcoming chapters will offer more detailed analyses of these issues. Here, I simply want to introduce readers to some broad features of postcolonial historiography.

One of the main differences between older histories of colonial rule and what can be called 'postcolonial histories' can be elaborated as follows. Histories written during the colonial period and in the early years of decolonization often posited a sharp divide between the colonizer and the colonized. In most works of nationalist and imperialist history, the metropole and colony represented forces locked in a life-and-death struggle for domination and subordination. The story of colonial rule was thus told as a zero-sum game. Whatever the colonist gained was the colonized person's loss, and vice versa. Postcolonial historians remain interested in histories of how power was deployed in colonial situations. But in a departure from earlier modes of history-writing, they avoid creating a Manichean binary between the colonizer and the colonized. They do not deny the grosser realities of colonial rule, but they study empires – metropole and colony in tandem – as sites of entanglement and encounters that radically changed both the colonizer and colonized, often in permanent and unanticipated ways.

One by-product of this intellectual stance is that postcolonial historians are critical of the triumphalist claims of colonizers and nationalists alike. Much postcolonial history-writing thus requires a reappraisal of colonial and nationalist archives. In a marked departure from their imperialist or nationalist predecessors, postcolonial historians' analyses of empires, colonial rule and ideologies, nationalist thought and movements acknowledge the critical importance of certain European ideas. For example, in writing about the history of nationalist imagination in the colonies, the postcolonial historian recognizes the inspirational role played by ideals associated with the French, German and Scottish Enlightenments. In analysing an event such as the Haitian revolution of the late eighteenth century, to take just one example, historians demonstrate how certain European ideas of equality and liberty were put into practice by blacks in this island colony as they rose up to challenge French domination and slavery.

The roles of certain figures from the ex-colonies are similarly recuperated in much postcolonial historiography in order to demonstrate certain universalist critiques of European domination. The writings of such anti-colonial individuals as the Indian leader M. K. Gandhi (1869–1948) or the Martinique-born revolutionary intellectual Frantz Fanon (1925–61) are good cases in point. Two contrasting figures – Gandhi, one of the most eloquent and powerful votaries of non-violent resistance, and Fanon, an equally forceful proponent of redemptive violence – are invoked together in some of this literature for their attempt to imagine a social order that totally rejected the lure of the colonial civilizing mission. Gandhi cautioned as early as 1909 that Indian nationalism should not simply become an 'English rule without the Englishman', signalling the need for a thoroughgoing critique of 'modern civilization'. The latter, he declared, was 'a civilization only in name' under which 'the nations of Europe are becoming degraded and ruined day by day'.[2] Gandhi, like many other *fin-de-siècle* figures, mounted a critique of European civilization – in his case refracted through the British government in India. 'To do otherwise', he wrote, would make him 'a traitor to truth, to India, and to the Empire to which I owe allegiance'.[3] Yet at the same time Gandhi would describe himself as a proud subject of the British Empire at least until the Great War. How do we reconcile an anti-colonial thinker of Gandhi's stature with this pledge of allegiance to the British Empire? Gandhi's seemingly paradoxical stances resonate with Frantz Fanon's call in *Black Skin, White Masks* for the creation of a world in which 'There is no Negro mission; there is no white burden'.[4] Postcolonial historians revisit the works of thinkers like Gandhi, Fanon and many others to elaborate a vision of society that would not simply replace Western domination with Asian or African counter-domination. The aim rather is to explore what was shared between the colonizer and the colonized in spite of the harsh and cruel power relations that separated them. Postcolonial history-writing is thus not fuelled by a spirit of anti-colonial revenge.

Postcolonial historians often mark a distance from the excesses of nationalism, both of the imperial and anti-imperial kind. Their writings help to call into question the racist backlash in the West that often accompanied the loss of empires. Likewise, they try to expose the ways in which nationalist histories in the erstwhile colonies tend to gloss over instances of disunity or fractures in the nation. The separate and overlapping struggles of women, low castes, tribals and other minorities in new nations act as a reminder that even the sovereign states that were established after decolonization have a long way to go before they become truly representative of all the peoples or nations that make up their social body. Postcolonial historians therefore often write of the inassimilable 'fragments' that constitute a nation – writing, as it were 'in defense of the fragment', as the historian Gyanendra Pandey once put it.[5] In a large measure, the impetus for this mode of history-writing, indeed for the rise of postcolonial studies, came from the urge to make both the ex-metropole and ex-colony more democratic. As more and more ex-colonized peoples migrated to the former metropolitan countries, it was important to ensure that future generations would not experience the slights and challenges that were characteristic of colonial pasts.

Finally, a word about the general impact of postcolonial history. The nation states of Australia, Canada or New Zealand did not go through a formal decolonization movement. Nonetheless, agitations for civil rights in the United States or rights movements by indigenous peoples of North America, Australia, New Zealand and South Africa derived much inspiration from ideas about decolonization and sovereignty that shook the colonial worlds of the 1940s and 1950s. The imprint of these social movements is clearly visible in historical works of these countries. There have been efforts, since the beginning of the 1970s, by historians in Australia and New Zealand, to decolonize and deracialize their national histories.[6] This was done – as is usual in postcolonial histories – by reappraising the archives of European settlement and by listening to hitherto silenced indigenous voices in order to craft historical narratives that might forge new moral foundations for the nation. In Australia, historians seriously interrogated the settler colonial archive to demonstrate the ways in which the imperial government violated English common law and adopted the infamous doctrine of *terra-nullius*. In New Zealand, historians demonstrated the gaps between Maori and Pakeha renderings of the well-known Treaty of Waitangi (1840) to show that the origins of that state lay in a contract between settlers and indigenous people, a contract that was wilfully violated by the former. The point of these histories was to chart out paths to decolonize history-writing by shedding light on the past wrongs of the settler state towards indigenous people. In so doing historical and historiographical debates became entangled with indigenous peoples' struggles for rights and recognition.

Postcolonial scholarship has also had an impact on an area of scholarship far removed from colonial studies. A number of medieval studies scholars, for example, have begun to question the very idea of periodization and nomenclature in their own fields, exploring how terms like 'feudal' and 'medieval', coined in the age of European expansion, may have helped to undergird Europe's and Europeans' self-image as more 'modern' and 'advanced' than the peoples they ruled or dominated.

In recent years, postcolonial histories of Empire have acquired ever greater significance as new imperial formations have threatened to rear their heads in different parts of the world. Feminist historians of empires such as Catherine Hall, Fiona Paisley, Antoinette Burton, Kathleen Wilson, and Mrinalini Sinha have drawn on postcolonial scholarship to write new imperial histories. On the other hand, Linda Colley and Niall Ferguson have recently written in defence of empires, taking to task postcolonial critics for overlooking the 'positive' achievements of colonial rule. The American occupation of Iraq has only aggravated these debates.[7] The debates will continue, reminding us, as said in the beginning, that while colonial rule may have ended, the issues thrown up by 'man's domination of man' will continue to exercise historians for a long time to come.

Notes

1 Rudyard Kipling, 'The White Man's Burden', was first published in *McClure's Magazine* in February 1899 and reprinted in *Collected Poems of Rudyard Kipling* (London: Wordsworth Editions, 1994), pp. 334–5.

2 M. K. Gandhi, *Hind Swaraj and Other Writings* (ed. Anthony J. Parel) (Cambridge: Cambridge University Press, 2009), p. 32.

3 Gandhi, *Hind Swaraj and Other Writings*, p. 7.

4 Frantz Fanon, *Black Skin White Masks* (New York, NY: Grove Press, 1967), p. 228.

5 Gyanendra Pandey, 'In Defense of the Fragment: Writing about Hindu–Muslim Riots in India Today', *Representations* 37 (Winter, 1992), Special Issue: Imperial Fantasies and Postcolonial Histories, pp. 27–55.

6 For an overview of this historiography, see Bain Attwood, 'Settler Histories and Indigenous Pasts: New Zealand and Australia', in Axel Schneider and Daniel Woolf (eds), *The Oxford History of Historical Writing*, vol. 5 (London: Oxford University Press, forthcoming).

7 For a succinct and critical review of postcolonial approaches to Empire, see Suvir Kaul, 'How to Write Postcolonial Histories of Empire?' in Daniel Carey and Lynn Festa (eds), *Postcolonial Enlightenment: Eighteenth Century Enlightenment and Postcolonial Theory* (New York, NY: Oxford University Press, 2009), pp. 305–27. Also see Linda Colley, 'Empire as a Way of Life', *The Nation* (31 July 2006), p. 7; Niall Ferguson, *Empire: The Rise and Demise of the British World Order and the Lessons for Global Power* (London: Basic Books, 2002).

Acknowledgments

I want to thank the Franke Institute for the Humanities, University of Chicago, for providing me with a home during the time most of the writing of this book happened. To the series editors of *Writing History*, especially to Stefan Berger, my gratitude for all the support and feedback during the writing process. To colleagues in the conceptual history group, in particular Bo Strath, Margrit Pernau, Dominic Sachsenmeier, Ilham Makdisi, Hagen Schulz-Forberg, Paula Pannu, and Mohinder Singh I remain grateful for rich conversations on the overlaps between postcolonial, comparative, connected, and global historiographies. Emily Salz, my editor at Bloomsbury, gave me input in the final stages, which was crucial in finishing this book. My colleagues in the Department of South Asian Languages and Civilizations were always encouraging of my efforts. Bain Attwood, Orit Bashkin, James Chandler, Jennifer Cole, Kathleen Davis, Debjani Ganguly and Sangita Gopal have provided invaluable feedback at various stages of writing. Jennifer Cole and Lisa Wedeen were my support system during those nine months when much of the work of writing was done. Miranda Johnson read each chapter, sometimes more than once, for which she has my lifelong gratitude. Sravan Kannan and Gerard Siarny have helped with their computer wizardry. Roopa Majumdar, Boria Majumdar and Sharmistha Gooptu – my family in Kolkata, thanks as always. Finally, to Dipesh Chakrabarty, my most treasured interlocutor and comrade, thanks for stoking my interest in the twists and turns of postcolonial historiography.

Contents

1

Postcolonialism, decolonization and globalization

What is the postcolonial?

With postcolonial theory firmly established as a critical discourse within the Anglophone academy over the last three decades and academics from other parts of the world taking a serious interest in the field, it has become increasingly common for historians, anthropologists, sociologists and urban geographers to identify their scholarly stance as 'postcolonial'. These gestures as well as the publication of interdisciplinary scholarly journals like *Postcolonial Studies* and *Interventions* have resulted in widening the field far beyond literature departments where postcolonial studies first began. Despite the phenomenal growth in scholarly works classified under the rubric of postcolonial/postcolonial studies/ postcolonial theory, there are interesting differences among scholars about the meaning(s) inhering in the expression 'postcolonial'.

Leela Gandhi's 1998 book *Postcolonial Theory: A Critical Introduction* offers a succinct summary of scholarly differences over naming this field of study. 'Whereas some critics invoke the hyphenated form "post-colonialism" as a decisive temporal marker of the decolonizing process', there were others who queried 'the implied chronological separation between colonialism and its aftermath on the grounds that the postcolonial condition is inaugurated with the onset rather than the end of colonial occupation'.[1] Scholars of the latter dispensation preferred the unbroken term 'postcolonialism' as a more accurate approximation of conditions that ensued with colonial rule. These observations establish that one of the points of difference among scholars has to do with periodization: whether the postcolonial condition began with the onset of colonialism, or whether it commenced with the end of colonial rule following struggles for decolonization. Gandhi herself appears to favour a capacious definition of the postcolonial by dating it to the 'aftermath of colonial occupation'.[2]

In a different vein, the noted literary theorist Robert Young argues that while postcolonial ideas may have varied genealogies, the field is perhaps best defined as anti-colonial thinking that issued out of the formal end of colonial rule.[3] Significantly, however, Young made a distinction between anti-colonial ideas of the periphery and those developed at the heart of former metropolitan societies. The label 'postcolonial' is, in his opinion, more apposite to the latter. Postcolonial writings, he notes, argue for the equality of the 'cultures of decolonized nations' by taking 'the struggle into the heartland of the former colonial powers'. In Young's reckoning postcolonial thought emerged when 'the political and cultural experience of the marginalized periphery developed into a more general theoretical position that could be set against western political, intellectual, and academic hegemony and its protocols of objective knowledge'.[4] Despite their differences over the periodization of postcolonial theory, both Gandhi's and Young's remarks imply that the primary constituency of postcolonial studies is the Western academy.

Indeed, some of the most strident charges against postcolonial theory have come from scholars who have questioned its politics of location. As Ania Loomba remarked, echoing Ella Shohat, 'we might ask not only when does postcolonial begin, but where is postcoloniality to be found?'[5] She points to the differences in the historical experiences of 'minority peoples' living in the West from those of the global South, despite the fact that they may share cultural roots and a history of colonial exploitation. They might even be united in 'an opposition to the legacy of colonial domination'. Nonetheless, 'their histories and present concerns cannot simply be merged'.[6] Loomba's remarks are salutary in all projects of postcolonial history-writing, which, as we shall see in the forthcoming chapters, have been especially sensitive to these questions of historical difference.

But where Loomba reminds postcolonial scholarship to be cognizant of the specificity of place, scholars like Arif Dirlik and Aijaz Ahmad regard postcolonial theory as emanating from a particular and spatially specific phenomenon: the result of the ascendancy of a group of Third World intellectuals in the Western academy. Rebutting these charges, Padmini Mongia noted the risk inherent in these positions of a 'dangerous essentializing that suggests that identity – understood in terms of race and national belonging – offers a transparent access to the kind of critical work that is produced. The effect of such a perspective is that binary distinctions between the "West" and the "rest" are kept firmly in place.'[7] Furthermore, Ahmad's or Dirlik's views ignore the contributions of a large number of 'First World theorists' whose scholarly stance is decidedly postcolonial. It also discounts the fact that postcolonial theory 'enables non-Western critics located in the West to present their cultural inheritance as knowledge', thereby stretching the disciplinary boundaries of the humanities and (some) social sciences in the West. Last, it misses a salient feature about the postcolonial outlook: the fact that it is not motivated by a spirit of revenge towards the colonial.[8] Postcolonial studies, in Leela Gandhi's words,

> does not seek to marginalize the West. ... Its manifesto if any is this: that postcolonialism diversify its mode of address and learn to speak more adequately to the world which it speaks for. And, in turn, that it acquire the capacity to facilitate a democratic colloquium between antagonistic inheritors of the colonial aftermath.[9]

Implied in these statements is a will to go beyond certain binaries that characterized the colonial situation and the world that emerged in its wake, namely colonizer/colonized; black/white; metropolitan/periphery, in the service of a more democratic future for all those who shared the colonial past, albeit differently.

The importance of location to postcolonial theorizing is probably best illustrated by the writings of Homi Bhabha.[10] His works complicate the tidy separation between the metropole and colony. Bhabha's writings challenge notions of Englishness that bypass the question of British colonialism by claiming that it happened in faraway lands with little or no impact on metropolitan lives. He emphasizes the constitutive role of ambivalence in the colonial encounter, best captured in his use of expressions such as 'mimicry' ('almost the same but not quite'), 'hybridity' (the idea that cultures and peoples are continually constituted by practices and acts of 'translation' rather than existing as authentic, essentialized totalities). His critique of anti-colonial criticism and nationalism as well of colonial discourse questions the characterization of colonialism as a stand-off between diametrically opposed racial antagonists. Instead, his reading of the colonial archive renders problematic the idea of boundaries as hermetically sealed lines of separation between unequal powers. Colonial situations, Bhabha would argue, produced forms of hybridity or mimicry – conditions of identity predicated on the element of the 'difference within' – something that necessarily escaped the Manichean logic of the colonial encounter. Bhabha's analyses not only offer revisionary accounts of colonialism. They are equally driven by a political urge to make the West (mainly the English-speaking West in his case) more democratic, by recognizing the formative role of cultural minorities and ex-colonized peoples who now constitute a visible section of these countries' populations in the creation of a modern British (or other national) identity. Similar impulses animate recent accounts of cosmopolitanism that seek new genealogies for cosmopolitical thinking by urging that these histories be sought not only in the pasts of Western Europe.[11] For example, Sheldon Pollock's work on the Sanskrit cosmopolis, whose circulatory networks covered vast swathes of the world, from Central Asia to the South China sea, charts new ways of thinking about linguistic cosmopolitanism – 'as literary communication that travels far, indeed without obstruction from any boundaries ... and, more important, that thinks of itself as unbounded, unobstructed, unlocated'.[12] Postcolonialism, as a body of ideas, is closely affiliated to these parallel bodies of works.

While there thus remain some differences among scholars about their understanding of postcolonialism, these differences cannot be resolved once and for all. To sum up: The meaning of the term postcolonial is not the same in the hands of all authors. As we noted, many critics and postcolonial thinkers themselves make a distinction between anti-colonial and postcolonial thought. Likewise, many articulate their postcolonial stance through a critique of binaries, which they regard as a characteristic of colonial and anti-colonial thinking. Postcolonialism also includes criticisms of nationalism and an interest in the negotiation of cultural differences through a commitment to cosmopolitanism. Finally, postcolonial works are framed around an implicit periodization: colonial rule leading to anti-colonial nationalism, which in turn climaxes in decolonization struggles leading to the creation of independent nation states. In this schema postcolonial theory is born in the formally decolonized world. Dissatisfaction with nationalism and the urge to make the ex-metropole more democratic and anti-racist are among the most prominent motivations for postcolonial theorizing, even though, some may argue, its relevance today might be somewhat overshadowed by theories of globalization.

Postcolonial history and the politics of decolonization

While remaining indebted to this body of ideas, this chapter presents a more historical approach to the question of postcolonialism by demonstrating its links to certain elements in anti-colonial thought and the cultural politics of decolonization. This is not in any way to deny the distinct political geographies of anti- and postcolonial criticism. The fundamental premise of anti-colonialism was the call for political and intellectual decolonization from the West. Postcolonial writing and criticism, on the other hand, was born in the West (mainly in the English-speaking West at the beginning) during the 1980s and 1990s. There are clear differences between postcolonial thinkers – who are generally critical of decolonizing nationalisms and modernization narratives – and the early generation of nationalists who won power from their imperial masters in the 1950s and 1960s. Nonetheless, there still remain many elements in anti-colonial thinking that reverberate through postcolonial concerns with questions of cultural difference, cosmopolitanism, pluralism, etc. In what follows, postcolonialism will be demonstrated as a broad arc that begins in the period of decolonization and stretches to the era of globalization. The burden of the explication is to also demonstrate that postcolonial thinking now has renewed significance in understanding the complexities thrown up by the contemporary global condition.

In a recent article based on a lecture delivered at a symposium organized to mark the twentieth anniversary of the fall of the Berlin Wall, the historian Dipesh Chakrabarty speculated, quite astutely, that global politics in the next thirty years or so will experience much turbulence. He drew attention to the rising populations of countries like India and China and the likely acceleration of a scramble for resources that this would lead to. There will probably be a rise in the number of failed states, more political, economic and climate refugees, and a rise in the migration and movements of people both legally and through illegal means. Anticipating these changes, he called upon scholarly communities in different parts of the world to shoulder the responsibility of cross-cultural understanding. In his words, the future of global politics requires that 'we the middle and professional classes everywhere embody a degree of cultural plurality, so that distinctions between cultural borders are somewhat blurred and every nation acknowledges the diversity that constitutes it'.[13] Chakrabarty echoed the call of French political theorist Etienne Balibar, issued in the context of debates about a 'fortress Europe', for a global recognition of our postcolonial condition.[14] In Balibar's understanding, the postcolonial condition is created by the fact that we live in a formally decolonized world where the idea of (formal) empire has little political or intellectual purchase on our imagination. Further, our times are postcolonial also because we live in close proximity to peoples who have either directly or through their ancestors experienced the might of colonial domination.

Any narrative about postcolonial history must of necessity begin with a discussion of the legacy of colonial experience and anti-colonial thought. It is incumbent upon us, therefore, to consider in some detail the cultural politics of decolonization of the 1950s and 1960s.[15] This will help in clarifying why a postcolonial outlook remains a valuable heuristic for understanding our global condition. It will also demonstrate that the relevance of such modes of history-writing not only for the formerly colonized parts of the world but also for an understanding of the intellectual and cultural histories of Europe and the Enlightenment. As a prelude to the more specific discussions of postcolonial historiography presented in each chapter, these general issues are addressed here in some detail.

In an essay entitled 'An Anti-colonial History of the Postcolonial Turn', Chakrabarty argued that postcolonial theory and criticism are more deeply rooted in the debates over decolonization than are usually recognized. There is clear evidence that anti-colonial thinkers, 'on certain registers of thinking', were as interested in questions about hybridity and the entanglement of cultures as are postcolonial critics today.[16] In other words, anti-colonial thought was more complex than is presumed by those who see it as simply structured by ideas about the colonizer–colonized binary. It is important that we explore this dimension of anti-colonial thought in order to establish its continuity with the postcolonial.

Chakrabarty revisits an iconic moment in the history of decolonization, the Bandung conference of 1955 – a gathering of newly independent nations attempting to sustain a sense of Asian–African solidarity in a world divided by the Cold War. Interestingly, for a gathering whose *raison d'être* was a strident opposition to imperialism, the participants had no operative definition of the latter expression. Loosely defined as opposed to 'colonialism in all its manifestations', it was a vague anti-imperial ethic that held together a group of leaders who were otherwise deeply divided among themselves on political, cultural and ideological issues. From the Indian Prime Minister Nehru to the Philipino representative Romulos, the message was clear that the age of empire was decidedly past. This was testified to by a pictorial album produced soon after the conference in the Netherlands on the theme of nationalism and colonialism in Africa and Asia in which the Bandung meeting was described as a moment that epitomized 'the end of Western supremacy'.[17]

Chakrabarty's aim in revisiting the historic occasion of the Bandung meeting is to draw out from the speeches, letters and debates surrounding that congregation some of the complexities that attended the politics of decolonization by the new nations of Asia and Africa. Two principal motifs dominated this discourse. He names one of them the 'pedagogical' and the other the 'dialogic'. Both orientations were embedded in the colonial encounter and were formative of anti-colonial thought. Their impact on postcolonial theory and criticism will not be hard to seek. For our purposes, it is critical to note that while the pedagogical mode of politics lost its dominance world-wide sometime around the 1970s as a result of a global conjuncture of events, the dialogic one remains relevant to our times and continues to inform postcolonial history-writing.

The pedagogical and the dialogic: Postcolonial politics and its pasts

The pedagogical mode of politics recalls the histories of modernization in the ex-colonies. It is a well-known fact of colonial histories that many a nationalist, driven by their belief that colonial rule arrested economic and technological development in the colony, wholeheartedly embraced the rhetoric and practice of modernization after decolonization in order to 'catch up' with the West. For example, the first Indian prime minister, Jawaharlal Nehru, declared in the 1950s, a few years after India's independence, 'What Europe did in a hundred or a hundred and fifty years, we must do in ten or fifteen years.' A similar, breathless rush to modernize is echoed in the title of the 1971 biography of the Tanzanian leader Julius Nyerere, *We Must Run While They Walk*.[18] The desire to catch up with the West – Europe and America – produced a split in the nationalist politics of the colony. On the one hand, nationalist politicians refused resolutely to accept the colonial judgment of the native as backward. Such a stance led leaders like M. K. Gandhi to assert that even the illiterate Indian peasant was capable of self-rule by virtue of belonging to cultures with a rich civilizational history. Nationalists proclaimed the illiterate peasant-subaltern as national citizen, thereby rejecting the liberal recommendation of a gradual path towards citizenship and sovereignty through literacy and development. Unlike in the history of the franchise in Great Britain, France and other Western countries, where the right to vote initially depended on property qualifications, gender and class, and gradually became universal, every adult Indian was treated as an equal legal subject from the moment of Independence and granted suffrage. The birth of the postcolonial nation embodied one of the basic premises of anti-colonial thought, which also carried over into postcolonial criticism. This was a rejection of stadial thinking that regarded peasants, tribals and other indigenous groups in the colony as backward when measured by the standards of classical liberal theory.

Yet, once national sovereignty was established and they were faced with the question of governance, leaders like Nehru, Nasser or Sukarno could only revert to a model of rule that was also in some measure a colonial inheritance. They now became 'national' teachers committed to training their people proper citizenly conduct. Nyerere was known in his country by the name 'Mwalimu', a Swahili word for teacher. Examples of these national pedagogues, tutoring people in the protocols of citizenship, are abundant. There are innumerable vignettes ranging from leaders giving instructions on topics as seemingly trivial as singing the national anthem to larger issues such as modern education (an education that emphasized the applied sciences and technology). In all the ex-colonies, the main anxiety after independence was to portray the new nation state as progressive before an international comity of nations. Pedagogical politics was based on 'the idea that nation was more about development than diversity'. Indeed, 'leaders often assumed that development was the answer to the question of diversity'.[19]

However, this model of pedagogical politics lost much of its previous legitimacy from the late 1960s into the early 1980s. It is important to give readers a sense of the context that led to its decline since it had an impact on academic thinking and prepared the intellectual backdrop for the emergence of fields such as postcolonial studies. Since this context is referred to in more detail in later chapters, a thumbnail sketch here will explain the argument.

The 1960s witnessed an upsurge of popular discontent in many of the newly liberated nation states. Several countries in Asia, Africa and the Middle East witnessed popular protest movements fuelled by a general feeling of betrayal that people felt towards the new governments upon their failure to deliver on the promises made at the time of independence. Take, for example, the pledge to the nation that animated Jawaharlal Nehru's inaugural address, remembered as the 'Tryst with Destiny' speech. It would not be a mistake to say that Nehru's words – 'Long years ago we made a tryst with destiny, and now the time comes when we shall redeem our pledge, not wholly or in full measure, but very substantially ...' – had once stirred the soul of the newly freed Indian nation.[20] But his promise to break free of the shackles of history to a path of unbounded progress soon met formidable challenges.

By the year of Nehru's death in 1964, the nationalist pledge was in shambles. India faced severe food shortages, border conflicts with Pakistan, a lost war with China and popular protest movements in different parts of the country. By and large the same narrative held for many of the other new nations. Besides, the generation of these teacherly leaders passed away between the 1960s and early 1980s. Nasser died in 1970, Sukarno in 1970 (but was out of power by 1965); Mao's authority was under challenge by the mid-1960s, spurring him to launch the Cultural Revolution; Nyerere, the youngest of these leaders and belonging to a country that became independent later, stayed on in power till 1985 but his *ujaama* socialism was in crisis by the late 1970s. Without these charismatic leaders the brand of pedagogical politics they practised, and which depended to a large extent on the strength of their personalities, lost legitimacy, leaving in its wake a tide of popular discontent in many of the young postcolonial nations.

Protest movements within the new nation states drew inspiration from, and in turn inspired, popular dissent in the West. Recalling his time at the University of Leeds, where he was witness to many of these popular protests, the African writer Ngugi wa Thiong'o writes,

> The political struggles to move the centre, the vast decolonization process changing the political map of the post-war world, had also a radicalizing effect in the West particularly among the young and this was best symbolized by the support the Vietnamese struggle was enjoying among the youth. This radical tradition had in turn an impact on the African students at Leeds making them look even more critically at the content rather than the form of the decolonization process, taking their cue from Fanon's critique in the rightly celebrated chapter in *The Wretched of the Earth* entitled 'the Pitfalls of National Consciousness'.[21]

The Vietnam War produced a huge upsurge of anti-state sentiment in the United States of America and gave a fillip to student and peace movements in the late 1960s. Anti-war, anti-capitalist and anti-patriarchal forces came together to incarnate May 1968 in Paris as one of the most iconic moments of popular mobilization in the twentieth century. If the nation state was in crisis in the ex-colony by the late 1960s, so too did the former metropolitan countries become sites of post-imperial upheaval around this time. The critical and vocal presence of ex-colonial, professional immigrants – teachers, students, scientists, doctors, lawyers – in the West added fuel to the post-imperial atmosphere.

The post-imperial milieu also saw mobilization by indigenous peoples, women, people of colour and gay rights activists. For example, indigenous groups and minorities in the United States, Canada, Australia and New Zealand – the so-called 'fourth republic' – grew vocal in their demands for rights and compensation from their respective states. Second-wave feminism asserted rights upon women's sexual being and challenged stereotypical gender roles. Anti-colonial thinkers were rediscovered anew in these turbulent times: Gandhi by Martin Luther King Jr in the United States and Frantz Fanon by indigenous activists in Australia. Left-leaning cultural endeavours in Thacherite Britain offer one of the most interesting instances of intellectual synergy taking place in this post-imperial milieu. During the 1980s, intellectuals like Homi Bhabha from India and filmmaker and artist Isaac Julien from the Caribbean came together with the renowned Jamaican-born cultural studies scholar Stuart Hall, their senior by quite a few years, to work together in the artistic ventures of the Sankofa film and video workshop, funded by the Ethnic Minority Arts Committee of the Greater London Council on various projects pertaining to the cultural politics of the ex-colonial diaspora. These scholars were also committed to rereading Frantz Fanon, not so much as a Marxist thinker but more for his ideas 'on the significance of intellectual work, the politics of location, everyday traumas of social inequality, minorities and their experience of the contemporary metropolis …'.[22] The immediate context that brought together these intellectuals was a shared struggle against British racism.[23] But the racism they fought was 'itself of post-imperial origins: it was born of cultural adjustments necessitated by the loss of empire and rise in migration of colored peoples'.[24]

Last but by no means least, the upheaval in the political sphere did not leave undisturbed the sanctum of the University. The challenge to the legitimacy of imperialism and colonialism produced a degree of disaffection among left-leaning intellectuals about the efficacy of Marxist theories in understanding global change. The rise of poststructuralist theory signalled one such mode of critique of foundationalist thinking. Scholars in the humanities undertook a critical scrutiny of their departments and teaching curricula. Popular mobilization in rural heartlands, beginning with the Cultural Revolution in 1966 and climaxing with the Vietnam War, brought to the fore the role of the peasant as an agent of revolutionary social change, a theme that inspired academic efforts such as the *Journal of Peasant Studies* and later on *Subaltern Studies*.

Postcolonial studies emerged in the academy during this critical conjuncture of global events. Seeing its emergence against the larger context, it should come as no surprise that the field is 'marked by a dialectic between Marxism on the one hand, and poststructuralism/postmodernism, on the other'.[25] In light of the history outlined above, it is also not hard to fathom why the field is rife with 'debates between the competing claims of nationalism and internationalism, strategic essentialism and hybridity, solidarity and dispersal, the politics of structure/totality and the politics of the fragment'.[26] Postcolonial historians, while sympathetic to the works done by the British Marxist 'histories from below', were critical of the Marxist teleology of development that marked the works of historians like Eric Hobsbawm or E. P. Thompson. Likewise, debates about what constitutes high and low culture led to a renewed attention to literary texts. Which texts could be said to represent the nation state when the latter was itself fragmentary and nationalism an object of critique? Postcolonial scholars urged a serious questioning of the canon in literature departments. In the field of history, the received litanies about a unified nationalism came to be revised as people began to think of identities as interstitial or 'in between', and of mainstream nationalism as unrepresentative of the peoples that constituted the nation. These moves shared some overlaps with parallel developments towards writing the history of everyday life, such as *Alltagsgeschichte* in Germany and *microstoria* in Italy. What distinguished postcolonial historiography from these bodies of scholarship, in addition to its attention to questions of colonialism was its sympathy with certain ideas gleaned from poststructuralist philosophy, namely a critique of the notion of an unified subjectivity and teleological thinking.

In sum, the birth of postcolonial theory and criticism coincided with the death of the pedagogical mode associated with the politics of decolonization. In Chakrabarty's words,

> [T]he global space for white man's sense of supremacy and the pedagogical spirit of anti-colonial modernization died about the same time, the time from when scholars date the beginnings of the contemporary forms of globalization: the late 1970s. If decolonization was thus generally predicated on a world-wide urge on the part of the formerly colonized countries to catch up with Europe (or more broadly the West), one could say that this was a discourse that saw an imaginary Europe as the most important agentive force in the world. Decolonization thus may be thought of as the last phase in the history of what Martin Heidegger once called 'the Europeanization' of the earth.[27]

A spirit of engaged critique of this imaginary Europe marked postcolonial theory from its inception. The significance of this engagement will be revisited at the conclusion of this chapter.

Now let us turn to the 'dialogic' side to decolonization debates, which Chakrabarty claims were not resolved during anti-colonial movements. Indeed they are germane to an understanding of postcolonial studies in the contemporary era of globalization. The expression 'dialogic', which literally means to share a dialogue, highlights the commitment that many anti-colonial leaders had to communicating across cultural differences. Postcolonial theory has inherited this commitment from anti-colonial thought. How do we foster a 'global conversation of humanity' without dividing the human race into a hierarchical grid of civilizations? In other words, how do we imagine cross-cultural dialogue without the baggage of imperialism?

This is not to suggest that there was consensus among intellectuals in the era of decolonization about how to conduct communication and dialogue across difference. Quite the contrary. Let us take one example, which still animates discussions on global English. In 1955, Richard Wright, the well-known African-American author, on visiting the Bandung conference marvelled at the English language being 'twisted' and given new sounds and meanings as it came to be the *lingua franca* for thousands of ex-colonized peoples in the tropics who were not native speakers of the language. Opposed to Wright's position, there were figures like Ngugi wa Thiong'o for whom the 'literary gymnastics' involved in enriching English or French with African words was a form of neo-colonialism – so much so that Ngugi eventually vowed to stop writing in English in favour of his native Gikuyu and Kiswahili. This decision, a product of Ngugi's self-interrogation about 'the issue of appropriate language for African literature', first posed itself as a problem to him during his days in Leeds during the 1960s. In his own words, 'It was once again the question of moving the centre: from European languages to all the other languages all over Africa and the world' – a move towards 'a pluralism of languages as legitimate vehicles of the human imagination'.[28]

But the unfinished nature of these debates is what makes the era of decolonization meaningful to postcolonial scholars. For, 'it leaves us with a body of ideas that speaks to the concept of cosmopolitanism without seeking overall mastery over the untameable diversity of human culture'.[29] It is this aspect of anti-colonial heritage that reverberates through one of the principal debates on globalization in our times.

Is globalization a force that flattens out all differences? Does the spread of capitalism globally produce sameness, which is also a form of subjugation to the forces of economic liberalization? Or are there possibilities of being global while at the same time retaining a sense of difference? I submit that both these positions are constitutive of processes of globalization. It is in this commitment to moving between the local and the global, or in the search of a deep sense of locality within the global space, rather than in any decisive resolution of how to fulfil these commitments, that anti- and postcolonial thinkers overlap.

Take the case of Léopold Sédar Senghor, a major poet and theorist of the Negritude movement, who also served as the first president of Senegal. Senghor, while being an active proponent of 'assimilation' to French culture, simultaneously maintained that the real aim of colonization should be 'a moral and intellectual cross fertilization, a spiritual graft'. His cosmopolitanism found expression in his call for the development of an 'African humanities', which would seek human truths in the same way that a humanities education in Greek, Latin or romance languages did. His comments on the human condition best clarify Senghor's stand on thinking about man, not simply as an abstraction but as always already a situated human being. This was a far cry from the developmentalist discourse of many anti-colonial modernizers we have discussed above. Senghor wrote,

> Man is not without a homeland. … He is not man without color or history or country or civilization. He is West African man, our neighbor, precisely determined by his time and his place: the Malian, the Mauritian, the Ivory-Coaster; the Wolof, the Tuareg, the Hausa, the Fon, the Mossi, a man of flesh and bone and blood, who feeds on milk and millet and rice and yam, a man humiliated for centuries less perhaps in his hunger and nakedness than in his color and civilization, in his dignity as incarnate man.[30]

The idea of globality that Senghor outlined was one that accommodated both the universal and particular. Difference was not an impediment to cross-cultural dialogue. Neither did cosmopolitanism imply an erasure of difference. It was this investment in 'the incarnate man' – replete in his universal humanity and his particular cultural and historical location – that postcolonial thought inherited from decolonization discourse. Acknowledging difference while also espousing certain universal ethical values was a challenge with which leaders of decolonization movements constantly grappled. But the issue was not resolved with the formal end of colonial empires. It persists to this day. Yet, it is also what makes postcolonial criticism a useful tool in thinking about questions of migration and cultural diversity today, not just in the global South but also in the ex-colonial metropole.

Uses of postcolonial analysis in globalized Europe

To see how this is so we return to an observation by the political theorist Etienne Balibar who recently remarked:

> what has truly unified the planet is not just colonial expansion, but the revolts, the liberation struggles that put into question the notion of 'different natures' that separate peoples of the 'metropoli' from those of the colonies,

> producing a dialectic between these two demographic groups that results in a reversal of roles, a 'particularizing' of the old metropolis and a 'universalization' of the former colonies.[31]

By 'universalization' of former colonies, Balibar alludes to the large and visible presence in contemporary Europe of groups from the ex-colonies (Turks in Germany, Algerians and Maltese in France, Indonesians in the Netherlands, Indians, Pakistanis and Bangladeshis in England, to name but a few examples) as well as to the influx of peoples from the former Eastern European bloc after the fall of formal communism and the wars in the Balkans. These waves of migration of people belonging to diverse cultures, with different family and religious values in post-Maastricht Europe, have renewed questions about the relationship between universal rights and the politics of multiculturalism.

In his 2004 book *We, The People of Europe?* Balibar analyses the notion of what may be called a postcolonial Europe by expounding on the notion of 'borders'. During the colonial ventures of the nineteenth and twentieth centuries, Europe distinguished itself physically and culturally from the rest of the world by drawing political borders. This was an attempt to 'appoint itself the center of the world' as well as a strategy to 'divide up the earth' into nation states modelled after the European pattern.[32] Colonialism, writes Balibar, 'was at once a way to organize the world's exploitation and to export the "border form" to the periphery, in an attempt to transform the whole universe into an extension of Europe'.[33] The process continued into decolonization and formed the basis for the erection of a new international order. Yet, 'in a certain sense it was never completely achieved'[34] for the new nation states were not homogeneous, sovereign states but agglomerates of diverse populations – Israel, India, West and East Pakistan (which later became Bangladesh) being a few cases in point. The heterogeneity of population is a feature of states within Europe as well.

The global history of imperialism left in its wake border conflicts all over the world, from which even Europe was not exempt. The demographic and cultural diversity of European populations many of whom are 'postcolonial' – a result of immigration, repatriation of displaced peoples and colonial returnees – reflects a projection of 'global diversity' within Europe. The presence of diversity within the nation state produces tensions and challenges about these nation states' identity. Matters have been exacerbated further with the end of the Cold War and the creation of a new European Union that purports to be a supranational as well as postnational community. The interrogation mark in the title of Balibar's book reflects his insistent question of who, by what principles, will qualify as a citizen of the new Europe. The latter is understood as a supranational and postnational community in which nation states will remain, but their limit and sovereignty will no doubt be calibrated if the European Union is to be a truly democratic polity.

Reality on the ground, however, fills Balibar with a sense of foreboding about a democratic future. The Maastricht Treaty of 1993, which made the EU a reality, ruled that European citizenship, 'implying the right to vote in local elections in the country of residence and the right of petition or appeals before European tribunals', would be available only to nationals. This, he argues, 'creates a new discrimination that did not exist within each national space' as it effectively leaves outside of the ambit of citizenship all nationals of 'third' countries.[35]

The present and future of the European Union raises anew questions about universal ideas of citizenship and its attendant rights. The uneven regression of the welfare state, migration from ex-colonized countries, Eastern and Southern Europe, the deindustrialization that accompanies economic globalization, rising unemployment and the fear of a global Islamic terrorism, have all contributed to the rise of racist and xenophobic politics and policies in many European nation states, making the question of membership to the European Union a vexed one. Policing of borders has intensified along with the expansion of zones of 'nonrights' in the suburbs of many great European cities. The refusal to 'regularize' more than fifty per cent of 'clandestine' immigrants in France in 1997–8, the closure of the Sangette collection area for refugees, unjust police behavior and the demographics of a place like Bobigny, a town south of Frankfurt, rulings against minarets in Switzerland (not a formal EU member, but participating in virtually every EU activity and a member of the Schengen agreement), race riots in Britain, anti-Islamic rhetoric in Denmark, the battle over headscarves in France and Catholic crosses in the Bavarian region of Germany all bear witness to racial and religious tensions within the boundaries of many European countries.

This context makes clear why the quintessential postcolonial question, one harking back to the days of decolonization, about how we reconcile ideas concerning the universal rights of man with cross-cultural diversity, looms large in these global times. Gayatri Spivak argued that the 'universal' political subject of modernity (whose institutional figure is the citizen) is always geopolitically differentiated. The plight of millions of nationals from 'third countries', writes Balibar, 'installed for one or several generations on the soil of various European countries, and who as a whole have become indispensable to European wellbeing, culture, and civility',[36] the plight of displaced peoples from former colonies in the ex-metropole and the interference of the ex-metropole in the politics and economies of the ex-colonies, signals 'the extreme ambivalence of (Europe's) relationship with the colonial past'. This in turn, argues Balibar, makes Europe 'the postcolonial locus par excellence where the political realities of recognizing this reality will be decided'.[37]

The different modes by which European residents from 'other' countries are designated in the context of different European states – ethnic minorities,

'The encampment'[38] in Europe and around the Mediterranean Sea (2009)

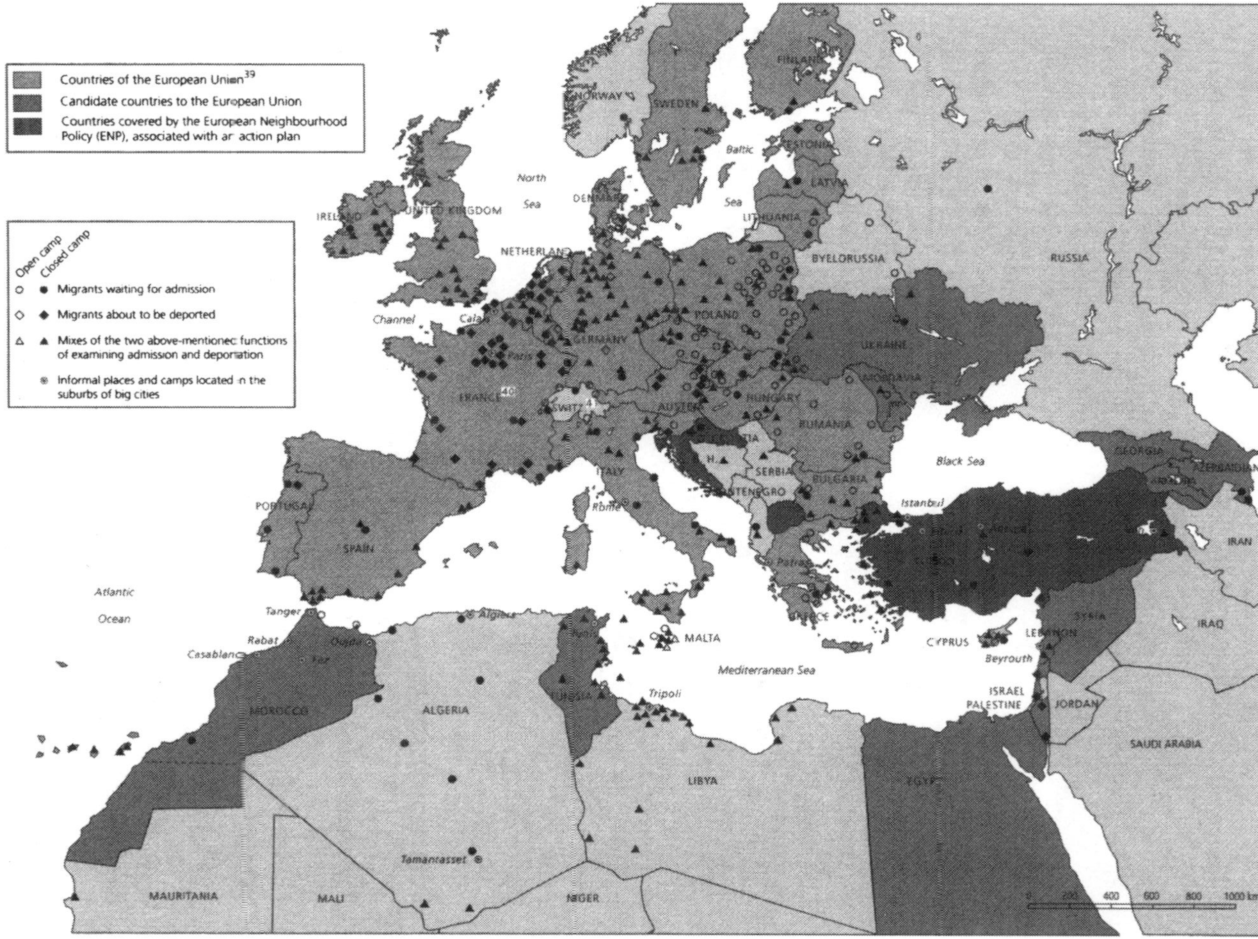

Source: I thank Olivier Clochard and Migreurop for allowing me permission to reprint this map.[42]

immigrés, extracommunatari, Ausländer – shows that as the European Union is in the making, so also is the identity of the outsider, the 'less than white (*sous blanc*), ... neither white, nor secular, nor Christian'.[43] In Balibar's analysis Europe today finds itself in a critical conjuncture. On the one hand, in the post-9/11 world there are political calls issued to Europe to stand together with the USA in the global war against terror. On the other, as a 'European' intellectual Balibar also feels a concern about the loss of political identity if Europe proves 'unable to act as a pole of resistance against American unilateralism'.[44] Not only that. As the European Union consolidates the question remains of how certain 'fundamental anthropological differences' (those of sexuality, culture and religion) are respected in tandem with the universal rights of citizenship. Balibar warns that failure to open up European citizenship to 'the diverse components of the "European people" on some basis other than the simple inheritance of nationality in a country that is the member of the European Union' will lead to an era of a 'European apartheid'. The challenge facing Europe is to seek a fulfilment of its destiny as the bearer of universal values by taking lessons from postcolonial developments both within its borders as well as in other parts of the ex-colonized world. It is as if Europe now faces the test that was issued to the Third World by Frantz Fanon in the conclusion of his famous indictment of European colonialism, *The Wretched of the Earth*. Fanon wrote, 'All the elements of a solution to the great problems of humanity have, at different times, existed in European thought. But the action of European men has not carried out the mission which fell to them ...'[45] The crossroads at which postcolonial Europe finds itself will determine if the Enlightenment promise of the ultimate perfectibility of man will be realized at the level of a universal humanity.

Postcolonialism and the Enlightenment

The above analysis makes it clear that postcolonial histories cannot be imagined without an active but critical dialogue with certain ideas associated with the European Enlightenment of the eighteenth century. Likewise, the critique of European colonial ventures during the nineteenth century is equally constitutive of postcolonial historiography's critical core. This troubled relationship with 'Europe' – where European Enlightenment thought remains an important legacy while European colonial adventurism is a painful reminder of subordination – has inaugurated a dialogue between scholars of the eighteenth-century European Enlightenment and postcolonial studies.

A charge levelled often at postcolonial scholars by those studying the European Enlightenment, as well as by other historians and theorists, is one of homogenizing a rich and often contentious constellation of ideas into a seamless body of thought. Daniel Carey and Lynn Festa, in their recently co-edited volume, *Postcolonial Enlightenment*, catalogue a list of problems shared by practitioners of both fields:

> Both 'postcolonial' and 'Enlightenment' are often construed as historical or temporal breaking points that mark and open up a political and epistemic shift; both are identified with cultural and intellectual stances that create and are created by those transformations. Both postcolonial studies and Enlightenment studies are simultaneously positive programs and modes of oppositional critique, defining themselves in relation to ideologies and political regimes that they resist.[46]

It goes without saying that any expression that contains within it such a wide cluster of possibilities can hardly be construed as homogeneous. Just as there are distinctions in the ideas of the Scottish Enlightenment compared to the French or German ones, so also the texts of postcolonial studies emerging out of particular colonial histories of India, Australia and Latin America are bound to vary.

For Festa and Carey postcolonial scholars have often displayed an attitude of obliviousness to these differences, tending to regard the Enlightenment as a 'unified construct', which in turn has produced an image of the 'West' driven solely by its colonialist motives. The Enlightenment, they argue, following scholars like Jonathan Israel and Judith Shklar, is better understood as a 'state of intellectual tension rather than a sequence of similar propositions'.[47] They cite J. G. A. Pocock, who argued that treating 'The Enlightenment' as a unity leads to the error of bundling a variety of histories and intellectual ideas as culminating in '"The Enlightenment project", a construct invented by both left and right in order that they may denounce it'.[48] But it is not simply that the Enlightenment serves as a straw man for postcolonial theorists, a product of (either) ignorant or deliberate misreading. Carey and Festa are equally critical of studies of the Enlightenment that 'fall into a circular logic, either creating a restrictive set of characteristics and only considering those eighteenth century philosophers who exemplify them, or selecting a list of philosophers and defining Enlightenment from there'.[49] The essays in *Postcolonial Enlightenment* demonstrate the yields of a postcolonial stance in 'bringing out the centrality of empire to eighteenth century studies'.[50] Taken together, they urge postcolonial writers to consider the histories by which 'the concept of Enlightenment becomes the means of constituting a pan-European entity, creating the monolith of the "West"'.[51] In addition, the essays in the collection push for closer attention to the differences within Enlightenment thinking to establish that the nineteenth-century career of European imperialism was not a 'seamless continuation' of eighteenth-century philosophy.

Postcolonial histories

The discipline of history is by definition more attentive to the specificities of space and time. As we shall see in the forthcoming pages, postcolonial historians have over the years addressed many of the charges levelled against postcolonial theory in their works. This point can be illustrated in a brief reference to Latin American postcolonial history. As part of their disciplinary practice, historians are particularly mindful of disparate chronologies, questions of power and the specificity of places – in other words, to questions of difference. Attention to these specificities is often elided in postcolonial theory. A critique voiced by scholars of Latin America is that theorists of postcolonialism often base their reasoning on the chronology of the anti-colonial nationalist movements of the twentieth century while ignoring the different timelines of Latin American nationalisms.

An early critique of modernization theory that came out of Latin American studies was dependency theory. Postcolonial history's (as well as that of 'world-systems' theory as developed by Immanuel Wallerstein *et al.*) critique of historicism, stadial thinking and transition narratives from feudal to the modern, as well as its commitment to study centre and periphery within the same conceptual frame, shares certain overlaps with dependency theory.[52] The central premise of dependency theory was that rampant capitalist modernization produced uneven development between the centre and periphery by bringing them into the simultaneity of the same currents of exchange. Underdevelopment, according this view, articulated most clearly by scholars like Paul Sweezy, Samir Amin, and Andre Gunder Frank, was caused by the simultaneous and connected development of rich centres and their dependent peripheries, and it could only be tackled by the removal of such polarizing dynamics.[53] The world-wide influence of dependency theory declined in the 1970s. But, as observed by Fernando Coronil, 'despite its shortcomings, … the dependency school represents one of Latin America's most significant contributions to postcolonial thought within this period, auguring the postcolonial critique of historicism, and providing conceptual tools for a much needed postcolonial critique of contemporary imperialism'.[54]

Even more important for our purposes, however, are works by historians or historically inclined literary scholars like Jose Rabasa and Walter Mignolo and historical anthropologists such as Fernando Coronil. Their works are indispensable to postcolonial historians of Latin America in raising questions about the possible linkages and differences between modern, northern European colonialism and the colonization of the Americas by Spain and Portugal in the early modern period. This larger frame, argues Coronil, 'modifies prevailing understandings of modern history' by expanding its geographical and temporal scope.[55] Latin

American history forces us to reconsider the standard genealogy of the modern period. According to Coronil,

> Capitalism and modernity so often assumed both in mainstream and in postcolonial studies to be a European process marked by the Enlightenment, the dawning of industrialization, and the forging of nations in the eighteenth century, can be seen instead as a global process involving the expansion of Christendom, the formation of a global market, and the creation of transcontinental empires since the sixteenth century.[56]

The dialogue between Latin American history and postcolonial studies offers critical insight into contemporary global history. The fact that Latin American colonial empires ended before the rise and fall of British, French, Dutch and other European colonialisms allows for a differentiated understanding of colonialism as a political–economic process. Coronil, for example, uses these disparate chronologies to distinguish between 'global' and 'national'/'colonial' imperialism. Such a periodization gives postcolonial historiography the lens with which to scrutinize and distinguish between early modern and nineteenth-century empires, and also analyse neo-colonial practices in the modern world.[57] Latin American history, like medieval studies (discussed in Chapter 3), offers postcolonial historians the opportunity (or challenge) to expand and review both the geographical and temporal scope of their projects.

However, postcolonial theory, as is well known, emerged in the second half of the twentieth century only in the wake of the second wave of anti-colonial independence movements in Asia, Africa, the Pacific and the Caribbean – if we consider the independence movements of Latin America in the nineteenth century to be the 'first wave'. There is no doubt, as Latin American specialists have pointed out, that forgetting of the first wave is a serious shortcoming of this body of theory. Any project that attempts to revise seriously the claims of postcolonial theory will have to engage with the ideas contained in the works of Latin American critics, thinkers and historians such as Enrico Dussel, Anibal Quijano, Walter Mignolo, Fernando Coronil, Jose Rabasa, Florencia Mallon, Barbara Weinstein and others.[58] But we also have to note that it was the era of decolonization of the late twentieth century that created the condition for the rise of postcolonial theory. This necessarily entailed a critique of postcolonial nationalisms. Latin American nations, on the other hand, gained their independence from colonial rule in the nineteenth century, which was also an age that witnessed a tide of nationalisms. Postcolonial theory could not have been arisen under these conditions.

The chapters that follow are not organized around 'regions' of the world. They do not instantiate postcolonial history in South Asia, Latin America, Ireland, the

Middle East etc. The intention, instead, is to discuss the historiographical issues and debates that mark the field of history that may be broadly described as 'postcolonial histories'. I call on diverse regional instances as they seem apposite in particular contexts of my discussion. Each of the following chapters demonstrates through a close analysis of historical works, written out of different regional contexts and covering a variety of time periods that postcolonial historiography produces a nuanced understanding of concepts such as Empire, indigeneity, nationalism and diversity.

Notes

1 Leela Gandhi, *Postcolonial Theory: A Critical Introduction* (NSW: Allen & Unwin, 1998), p. 3.
2 Gandhi, *Postcolonial Theory*, p. 4.
3 Robert Young, *Postcolonialism: An Historical Introduction* (Cambridge: Blackwell, 2001), p. 57.
4 Young, *Postcolonialism*, p. 65.
5 Ania Loomba, *Colonialism/Postcolonialism* (London: Routledge, 1998), p. 14.
6 Loomba, *Colonialism/Postcolonialism*.
7 Padmini Mongia, *Contemporary Postcolonial Theory: A Reader* (London: Arnold, 1996).
8 Gandhi, *Postcolonial Theory*, p. ix.
9 Gandhi, *Postcolonial Theory*, pp. ix–x.
10 Homi K. Bhabha, *The Location of Culture* (London and New York, NY: Routledge, 1994).
11 Carol Breckenridge, Sheldon Pollock, Homi Bhabha and Dipesh Chakrabarty (eds), *Cosmopolitanism* (Durham, NC: Duke University Press, 2002).
12 Sheldon Pollock, 'Cosmopolitan and Vernacular in History', in Carol Breckenridge, Sheldon Pollock, Homi Bhabha and Dipesh Chakrabarty (eds), *Cosmopolitanism* (Durham, NC: Duke University Press, 2002), p. 22.
13 Dipesh Chakrabarty, 'Europe in the World: Twenty Years after 1989', *Economic and Political Weekly* XLIV(45) (7 November 2009), p. 25.
14 See Etienne Balibar, 'Europe: An "Unimagined" Frontier of Democracy', *Diacritics* 33(3/4) (Fall 2003). Available at http://www.jstor.org/stable/3805803 [accessed on 30 August 2010].
15 While many Latin American nations achieved freedom from European colonial rule in the nineteenth century, their independence did not lead to a discussion of decolonization in the period, which also witnessed the global rise of the British, French and Dutch empires. Thus, this discussion of decolonization necessarily focuses on the history of the twentieth century.
16 Dipesh Chakrabarty, 'An Anti-colonial History of the Postcolonial Turn: An Essay in Memory of Greg Dening', *Melbourne Historical Journal* 37 (2009), p. 3.
17 For more details on Bandung that illustrate the validity of this viewpoint, see Jamie Mackie, *Bandung 1955: Non-alignment and Afro-Asian Solidarity* (Singapore: Editions Didier Millet, 2005).
18 William Edgett Smith, *We must run while they walk: a portrait of Africa's Julius Nyerere* (New York: Random House, 1972).
19 Dipesh Chakrabarty 'Legacies of Bandung', *Economic and Political Weekly* 40(46) (12 November 2005), pp. 4812–18.
20 Nehru's speech can be found on http://www.hindustantimes.com/news/specials/parliament/tryst%20with%20destiny.pdf [accessed on 15 January 2010].
21 Ngugi wa Thiong'o, *Moving the Centre: The Struggle for Cultural Freedoms* (London: James Currey, 1993), p. 3.
22 The culmination of these engagements with Fanon was two conferences entitled 'Working with Fanon: Contemporary Politics and Cultural Reflection' and 'Mirage: Enigmas of Race,

Difference, and Desire' held at the Institute of Contemporary Arts in London in 1995, which brought together a group of scholars and intellectuals, namely Homi Bhabha, Stuart Hall, bell hooks, Francois Verges, Isaac Julien and others. For details, see Alan Reed, *The Fact of Blackness: Frantz Fanon and Visual Representation* (London: Institute of Contemporary Arts, Institute of International Visual Arts, Seattle, WA: Bay Press, 1996).

23 See Stuart Hall, 'New Ethnicities', in David Morley and Kuan-Hsing Chen (eds), *Stuart Hall: Critical Dialogues in Cultural Studies* (London and New York, NY: Routledge, 1996), pp. 441–9. In the same volume also see Isaac Julien and Mark Nash, 'Dialogues with Stuart Hall', pp. 476–83 and 'The Formation of a Diasporic Intellectual: An Interview with Stuart Hall by Kuan-Hsing Chen', pp. 484–503.

24 Chakrabarty, 'An Anti-colonial History of the Postcolonial Turn', p. 14.

25 Gandhi, *Postcolonial Theory*, pp. viii–ix. For an analysis of the context that led to the rise of cultural and postcolonial studies, also see Simon During (ed.), *The Cultural Studies Reader* (London and New York, NY: Routledge, 1999).

26 Gandhi, *Postcolonial Theory*, p. ix.

27 Chakrabarty, 'Legacies of Bandung', p. 4815.

28 wa Thiong'o, *Moving the Centre*, p. 10.

29 Chakrabarty, 'Legacies of Bandung', p. 4816.

30 Cited in Chakrabarty, 'Legacies of Bandung', p. 4817.

31 Balibar, 'Europe'.

32 Etienne Balibar, *We, The People of Europe? Reflections on Transnational Community* (Princeton, NJ: Princeton University Press, 2004), p. 7.

33 Balibar, *We, The People of Europe?*, p. 7.

34 Balibar, *We, The People of Europe?*

35 Balibar, *We, The People of Europe?*, p. 44.

36 Balibar, *We, The People of Europe?*

37 Balibar, 'Europe'.

38 The word 'encampment' is borrowed from Barbara Harrell-Bond.

39 Iceland, Norway and Switzerland are not in the European Union, but they have integrated Treaty Schengen legislation.

40 For France, the map shows only the *zones d'attentes* (waiting zones) used regularly for detaining migrants entering the territory.

41 Migrants subject to removal orders are often detained in special sections of prisons. There are twenty-three such places in Switzerland, which cannot be all shown on this map: Appenzell, Bâle (2), Bern, Chur, Dornach, Einsiedeln, Gampelen, Glarus, Granges, Mendrisio, Olten, Saignelégier, Schaffhausen, Schüpfheim, Sissach, Solothurn, Sursee, Thônex, Widnau, Zug, Zürich (2). Migreurop do not have data for Egypt, Macedonia, Montenegro and Syria. For Byelorussia and Russia, information is incomplete.

42 European Committee for the Prevention of Torture and Inhuman or Degrading Treatment or Punishment (UNHCR http://www.unhcr.ch/): The conditions in centres for third country national (detention camps, open centres as well as transit centres and transit zones) with a particular focus on provisions and facilities for persons with special needs in the twenty-five EU member states. For Bulgaria: Red Cross, Bulgarian Helsinki Committee; Croatia: Red Cross, Croatian Law Centre; Serbia: Groupe 484, Gracanicka 10, Belgrade; Algeria: Association 'Rencontre et développement', Alger; Liban: FIDH. For Romania, Morocco and Turkey, investigations conducted by members of Migreurop.

43 Balibar, *We, The People of Europe?*, p. 44.

44 Balibar, *We, The People of Europe?*, p. 213.

45 Frantz Fanon, *The Wretched of the Earth* (New York, NY: Grove Press, 1965), p. 314.

46 Daniel Carey and Lynn Festa (eds), *Postcolonial Enlightenment: Eighteenth Century Enlightenment and Postcolonial Theory* (Oxford/New York, NY: Oxford University Press, 2009), p. 7.

47 Carey and Festa, *Postcolonial Enlightenment*.

48 Carey and Festa, *Postcolonial Enlightenment*.

49 Carey and Festa, *Postcolonial Enlightenment*, p. 6.

50 Carey and Festa, *Postcolonial Enlightenment*, p. 5.

51 Carey and Festa, *Postcolonial Enlightenment*, p. 9.

52 I discuss some of the differences between critiques of Eurocentrism that grew out of dependency and world-systems theory and postcolonial history in Chapter 2.

53 Samir Amin, *Eurocentrism* (trans. Russell Moore) (New York, NY: Monthly Review Press, 1989); Sing C. Chew and Robert A. Denemark (eds), *The Under Development of Development: Essays in Honor of Andre Gunder Frank* (Thousand Oaks, CA: Sage Publications, 1996).

54 Fernando Coronil, 'Latin American Postcolonial Studies and Global Decolonization', in Neil Lazarus (ed.), *The Cambridge Companion to Postcolonial Literary Studies* (Cambridge: Cambridge University Press, 2004), p. 223.

55 Coronil, 'Latin American Postcolonial Studies and Global Decolonization', p. 239.

56 Coronil, 'Latin American Postcolonial Studies and Global Decolonization'.

57 Explaining the global, Coronil writes, that it 'is a phase characterized by the growing abstraction and generalization of imperial modes of political and economic control'. Under global imperialism cultural difference may be characterized as 'occidentalist … involving a shift from "eurocentrism" to "globalcentrism"'. Coronil, 'Latin American Postcolonial Studies and Global Decolonization'.

58 Barbara Weinstein, 'History without a Cause? Grand Narratives, World History, and the Postcolonial Dilemma', *International Review of Social History* 50 (2005), pp. 71–93; Florencia Mallon, 'The Promise and Dilemma of Subaltern Studies', *American Historical Review* 99(5) (1994), pp. 1491–515; Walter Mignolo, *Local Histories/Global Designs: Coloniality, Subaltern Knowledges, and Border Thinking* (Princeton, NJ: Princeton University Press, 2000); Ileana Rodríguez, *The Latin American Subaltern Studies Reader* (Durham, NC: Duke University Press, 2001); Fernando Coronil, 'Can Postcoloniality be Decolonized? Imperial Banality and Postcolonial Power', *Public Culture* 5(1) (1992), pp. 89–108; Fernando Coronil, 'Beyond Occidentalism: Towards Nonimperial Geohistorical Categories', *Cultural Anthropology* 11(1) (1996), pp. 52–87.

2

Subaltern studies as postcolonial history

It is common to argue that postcolonialism, as a body of ideas, belongs principally to literature departments and cultural studies centres. It is, of course, true that the contemporary field of postcolonial studies owes much of its origins to the way Salman Rushdie's novel *Midnight's Children* (1981), and other literary works by authors inspired by his example, challenged the literary canon that dominated English literature departments in Anglo-American universities. But this focus on the literary career of postcolonial studies sometimes blocks from our view the way postcolonial thinking has shaped social science disciplines such as history and how in turn it has been shaped by developments in fields other than literary or cultural studies. This chapter demonstrates how *Subaltern Studies*, a series of publications brought out from 1982 onwards by a group of historians working on India, is one of the earliest instances of writing history in the postcolonial vein.

It would be no exaggeration to say that the writings of the *Subaltern Studies* collective have contributed very significantly towards globalizing Indian history and, through its impact on Latin American, African and Asian histories, helped to establish the field of postcolonial history (or histories). However, while there has been some discussion of '*Subaltern Studies* as Postcolonial Criticism' – as Gyan Prakash's essay with that title suggests – the available literature on this topic is dispersed and fragmented. What I attempt here is to bring together this discussion by way of some critical reflections on the question of why *Subaltern Studies* historical scholarship could be seen as a pioneering as well as typical instance of postcolonial historiography.[1]

Subaltern studies: A background

The historian David Ludden traces the beginnings of the 'impressive career' of the *Subaltern Studies* collective to the end of the 1970s, when 'conversations on subaltern themes among a small group of English and Indian historians led to the proposal to launch a new journal in India'.[2] The eight scholars who formed the collective in the early years were either graduate students or young professors at universities in the UK, Australia and India. Ranajit Guha, the editor of the series until 1989, provided the historical and political–theoretical background to the 'conversations' to which Ludden alluded when he wrote that by the 1970s some scholars of his generation (those born and educated in the years before the independence of India from British rule in 1947) found a shared bond with younger historians (Guha later described them as the generation of the 'midnight's children' after Salman Rushdie's book) in their collective disappointment with the failure of the postcolonial Indian state to live up to the promises it held out both prior to and after Independence. India had by the mid-1960s fought border wars with China and Pakistan, experienced an acute food and refugee crisis in 1970–1 consequent on the Bangladesh war, witnessed numerous insurgencies within the country and had gone through a period of 'national emergency' during the prime ministership of Indira Gandhi that involved a brutal suppression of civil rights in 1975–7. The 1960s had also seen a Maoist insurgency in the country that was brutally suppressed by the early 1970s. In his conception of *Subaltern Studies*, Guha was able to capture the political mood of younger historians on the left, who had grown up through these years. The questions that motivated the group are best summarized in Guha's own words and clearly exemplify the postcolonial tone of their inquiry:

1 What was there in our colonial past and our engagement with nationalism to land us in our current predicament – that is, the aggravating and seemingly insoluble difficulties of the nation state?
2 How are the unbearable difficulties of our current condition compatible with and explained by what happened during colonial rule and our predecessor's engagement with the politics and culture of that period?[3]

Note the striking parallel between Balibar's characterization (cited in the last chapter) of the relationship between the past of European colonization and its present, and Guha's conceptualization of the *Subaltern Studies* project as an attempt to see the problems besetting postcolonial India as a legacy of her colonial past.

It may justifiably seem as if the early themes taken up by *Subaltern Studies* historians – peasant movements, tribal revolts, working-class histories – were much the same as those taken up by several others in different parts of the world around that time. The late 1970s and early 1980s witnessed global academic interest in works such as E. P. Thompson's *The Making of the English Working Class* (1963), Eric Hobsbawm's *Primitive Rebels* (1959) and Christopher Hill's works on radical politics during the English revolution.[4] Despite thematic overlaps with other studies focusing on the oppressed, what was novel to the *Subaltern Studies* approach was, as Ludden put it, 'its striving to rewrite the nation outside the state-centered national discourse that replicates colonial power/knowledge in a world of globalization'.[5] In other words, it was precisely its postcolonial thrust that marked the *Subaltern Studies* intervention as distinct from existing works on marginal social groups. From its earliest phase *Subaltern Studies* historians made a serious effort to situate their critical stance on nationalism, liberalism and democracy within larger critiques of Eurocentric conceptions of modernity. This, however, did not mean a simple, 'nativist' rejection of European modernity. Rather, these historians theorized the modern condition by showing (a) the contradiction inherent in anti-colonial nationalisms outside Europe since as ideas they drew on the European traditions while as politics they were committed to overthrowing European domination, and (b) how certain ideas whose origins lay in the European Enlightenment were transformed and translated by peoples in different parts of the non-Western world.

Given the span of the project, it is but natural that the central focus of *Subaltern Studies* has undergone significant shifts over the last twenty-five years and more. While the group started out with the stated goal of correcting the elitist biases of the subject called 'Indian' or 'South Asian' history, they subsequently went on to theorize more broadly about the nature of nationalism and modernity under colonial conditions. The *Subaltern Studies* group did not initially think of themselves as working in the area of postcolonial criticism, but their work resonated with intellectual concerns generated by Edward Said's *Orientalism*. Thus, it was not surprising that Said should formally introduce a selection of essays from the series to 'the Western reader' in 1988, calling it a 'self-conscious part of the vast post-colonial cultural and critical effort'.[6] The collective also received friendly criticism from feminists and poststructuralists who remarked on the absence of gender as a category of analysis from *Subaltern Studies* and about the conception of 'the subaltern subject' that seemed ignorant of critiques of the very idea of subjecthood launched (in English) in the 1980s by the popularization of French thinkers such as Foucault, Derrida, Lacan and others. Most notably, Gayatri Spivak's intervention, together with the rise of new cultural history and the linguistic turn in historical studies, led to significant impacts on and shifts in the output of *Subaltern Studies*. The collective gradually came to be identified as having pioneered the field of postcolonial history, even when the series did not explicitly theorize itself as such.

The remainder of this chapter will map three phases in the *Subaltern Studies* corpus. The division is broadly chronological but also corresponds to a shift in thematic focus. This is not to suggest that the problems dealt with during each phase were discrete and unrelated to one another. The periodization proposed is a retrospective act and is indicative of how, with hindsight, one may view the collective's responses to both outside influences and criticisms and to political introspection within the group.

Phase one

The subaltern as political subject

Central to the project of articulating the political imagination of the 1960s and 1970s and to tracing the roots of India's postcolonial crisis back to the period of British colonial rule was a restitution of the 'subaltern' to his deserved place in Indian history. The category of subaltern was taken from the Italian Marxist Antonio Gramsci whose *Prison Notebooks* were in wide circulation in the English-speaking world by 1982, the year in which the first volume of *Subaltern Studies* was published. The *Prison Notebooks* first appeared in English in 1971, but it was Raymond Williams's 1977 book *Marxism and Literature* and critical commentary in journals such as *The New Left Review* that stimulated the discussion of Gramscian ideas in the Anglo-American academy. We will analyse the conceptual significance of the category subaltern soon. For now, suffice it to say that Guha used it to refer to people of inferior rank, thereby drawing attention to questions of disempowerment and hierarchy rather than to a sociological and stratifying concept of class. Guha and his colleagues also drew inspiration from Mao Zedong, particularly his 1927 report on the peasant movement in the Hunan district of China. But, as recently observed by Dipesh Chakrabarty a founding member of the collective, their use of Mao or Gramsci should be set in the context of leftist politics in the 1970s. 'Both Gramsci and Mao were celebrated as a way out of Stalinist or Soviet Marxism after Czechoslovakia of 1968.'[7]

In a founding and programmatic statement entitled 'On Some Aspects of the Historiography of Colonial India', Ranajit Guha argued that Indian history-writing had until then (1982) been dominated by 'elitism' – both of the 'colonialist' and of the 'bourgeois-nationalist' type. Both originated, he argued, 'as the ideological product of British rule in India but have survived the transfer of power and been assimilated to neo-colonialist and neo-nationalist forms of discourse in Britain and India respectively'.[8]

The histories written by colonial scholars and administrators, following the traditions of imperial history-writing, depicted British rule in India as beneficial to the subcontinent. These views were opposed by nationalist-minded historians, who argued that, contrary to the assertions by colonialist/imperialist scholars, British rule had denuded India of her economic wealth, leading to famines and a general impoverishment of the country. They alleged that the British policy of divide and rule had produced sectarian strife, culminating in the bloody partition of 1947 and the birth of the two nation states of India and Pakistan. Most debates in Indian history until the late 1970s centred on the nature of and the clash between nationalism and colonialism in India.

This historiography was useful up to a point, noted Guha, because it shed light on the workings of the colonial state with the help of a section of the Indian elite classes. It provided knowledge about class structure and the nature of high politics in colonial India. But missing entirely from these texts in his reckoning were any accounts of the 'contribution made by the people *on their own*, that is, *independently of the elite*' to the making of Indian nationalism and politics.[9] 'The poverty of this historiography', he wrote, 'is demonstrated beyond doubt by its failure to understand and assess the mass articulation of this nationalism, except negatively, as a law and order problem or positively if at all either as a response to the charisma of certain elite leaders or in the currently more fashionable terms of vertical mobilization by the manipulation of factions'.[10] The absence of the 'people' – which Guha uses synonymously with the category 'subaltern' – from history was not merely a fault in the historians' interpretive skills as scholars of nationalism. It reflected a bigger problem in the phenomenon of nationalism itself.

Combining leftist inclinations with a sharp interest in cultural issues, Guha and his colleagues turned their attention to an analysis of the subalterns whom they defined as 'the demographic difference between the total Indian population and all those ... described as the elite'.[11] Defining subaltern groups in such a manner resonates with two central preoccupations of postcolonial history-writing – a critique of the nation state as a unity that claims to represent all its constituent elements; and a characterization of groups whose practices do not conform to liberal, secular modes of being as modern. The critique is clearly expressed in the following statement by Guha:

> This (subaltern groups) was an autonomous domain, for it neither originated from elite politics nor did its existence depend on the latter. It was traditional only in so far as its roots could be traced back to pre-colonial times, but it was by no means archaic in the sense of being outmoded. Far from being destroyed or rendered virtually ineffective, as was elite politics of the traditional type by the intrusion of colonialism, it continued to operate vigorously in spite of the latter adjusting itself to the conditions prevailing under the Raj and in many respects developing entirely new strains in both form and content. As modern as indigenous politics, it was distinguished by its relatively greater depth in time as well as in structure.[12]

For Guha and his colleagues the fact of the coexistence of these two domains of politics – elite and subaltern domains, which, though not entirely sealed off from each other, often existed autonomously – signalled a key historical truth, namely, 'the failure of the Indian bourgeoisie to speak for the nation. There were vast areas in the life and consciousness of the people which were never integrated into their hegemony.'[13]

Fundamental to the writing of subaltern history was the act of taking cognizance of mobilization, on their own, by subaltern groups of peasants, workers and tribals. This implied, first, that the subaltern be reinstated as an agent where he/she had been rendered absent by existing historiography. Second, and more challenging, was to read such subaltern mobilization as modern 'political' action.

Redefining politics

Guha emphasized that a fundamental flaw in existing analyses of nationalism was that they did not address the question of the mass articulation of nationalist sentiments. Other members of the collective substantiated this critique through their studies of peasant and tribal societies in India (Amin, Hardiman, Chatterjee); of the working classes (Chakrabarty, Pandey); of sectarian conflict and communalism (Pandey); and of certain institutions like the colonial prison (Arnold). The main aim of *Subaltern Studies* historians was to represent subaltern activity on its own terms.[14]

These scholars consulted many of the same 'sources' used by nationalist or Marxist historians to reconstruct the history of colonialism and nationalism – newspaper reports, police files, government and municipal records. But the difference lay in the ways in which they approached and read the archive. Guha noted the importance of reading official documents against the grain in order to find therein traces of subaltern consciousness.[15] One of the challenges of doing subaltern history was to study groups who did not leave their own written records. Records produced by the counterinsurgency arms of the state – police, army and legal personnel – detailed events like peasant riots, looting of the landlord's coffers and other insurgencies, events that were frequently attributed by the 'rebels' to inspiration from religious leaders, as criminal activity. To the historian of *Subaltern Studies*, however, these activities represented a political churning among the masses. Guha emphasized that the historian should be self-conscious about his reading strategy so as to be able to simultaneously discern elite biases in historical documents, and also analyse the textual properties of these documents in order to get to the history of power that produced them.[16] Dipesh Chakrabarty, in his analysis of Guha's work, notes that 'the interventionist metaphor of reading resonates as the opposite of E. P. Thompson's use – in the course of his polemic with Althusser – of the passive metaphor of listening in describing the hermeneutical activity of the historian. This emphasis on reading also left *Subaltern Studies* historiography open to influences of literary and narrative theory.'[17]

It has often been alleged that the attempt to restore subaltern consciousness to its place in history is merely an 'Indian' instance of the broader movement for history-from-below pioneered by scholars like E. P. Thompson and Eric Hobsbawm. In his essay cited above, Chakrabarty refuted this charge (made powerfully by Arif Dirlik among others) and made a case for *Subaltern Studies* as postcolonial history.[18] A fundamental distinction between *Subaltern Studies* and the history-from-below approach of some British historians, noted Chakrabarty, was that the former repudiated the stadial view of popular consciousness often espoused by earlier generations of Marxist historians. Doing 'subaltern studies', he argued, entailed 'a relative separation of the history of power from any universalist histories of capital, a critique of the nation form, and an interrogation of the relation between power and knowledge (hence of the archive itself and of history as a form of knowledge)'.[19] In these three features 'lay the beginnings of a new way of theorizing the intellectual agenda of postcolonial histories'.[20] They amounted to a new understanding of political subjectivity for the oppressed and underprivileged groups of society in the colonial world in ways that also distinguished the histories written by authors of the *Subaltern Studies* collective from the history-from-below approach pioneered by the likes of Thompson and Hobsbawm. 'The critical theoretical break', Chakrabarty noted, 'came with the way in which Guha sought to redefine the category political with reference to colonial India.'[21]

In his seminal book *Elementary Aspects of Peasant Insurgency*, Guha rejected Eric Hobsbawm's characterization of banditry and rebellion in *Primitive Rebels* as 'pre-political'. Hobsbawm described the rebels as a 'pre-political people who have not yet found, or only begun to find, specific language in which to express their aspirations about the world'.[22] In Hobsbawm's analysis these acts of rebellion could not be treated as 'modern' political action since they were inspired by a belief in other-worldly, and hence non-secular, factors. *Subaltern Studies* rejected this stance and made a powerful argument for the peasant's inclusion in the modern political sphere. Such inclusion had happened, they insisted, not after the peasant had been properly schooled in the ideologies of post-Enlightenment rationalism, but by their direct action against the daily oppression they experienced at the hands of the colonial and indigenous elite. *Subaltern Studies* was critical of the ideological separation between religion and the state, between the public and private realms of life, that was built into the analytical apparatus made available by classical liberal or Marxist thought.[23]

Marxist historiography, coming out of India and the West, had been uncomfortable (or dismissive) about treating religion as anything other than an expression of false consciousness or as performing a 'safety-valve' function in the overall social system. To understand subaltern action as 'political' requires that the historian remain alert to the constant braiding and confrontation of historical logics – one of formal-legal and secular frameworks of governance and another of relationships of direct domination whose basis was often *dharmic* (religious) and non-secular – in everyday life in the colony and postcolony. The failure of the postcolonial state, and also of elite historiography, to acknowledge and comprehend the coexistence of these two distinct domains of practice symbolized for Guha (and his colleagues) that there were vast areas in the life and consciousness of the people that were never integrated into the domain of the state. This is why he went on to describe the colonial state and the national state that followed it as a 'dominance without hegemony'.[24]

This critique established *Subaltern Studies* as postcolonial history par excellence. Unlike anti-colonial accounts that treated the colonial state as illegitimate and called for its overthrow, *Subaltern Studies*' critique of elitism was an indictment of the sovereign Indian nation state whose origins they traced back to the colonial one. But the politics of history professed by the group in the early years could not replicate the anti-colonial one. Rather, their main task was to critique historiography to highlight the elitist biases of Indian politics whose roots were traced back to the colonial period.[25]

Phase two

Postcolonial nationalism

Subaltern Studies scholarship became a subject of global historical debate from the mid-1980s. It also produced a set of inspired conversations in the global south through the 1990s, one instance of which was the publication of a collection under the title *A Latin American Subaltern Studies Reader*.[26] It was also from this period that we find a subtle shift in the orientation of the project from what was a recuperation of subaltern consciousness to a critical consideration of the discursive apparatus that had helped conjure the image of a sovereign consciousness.[27] In other words, from the mid-1980s *Subaltern Studies* began a sustained and self-conscious critique of Eurocentrism, especially of certain lines of thought associated with post-Enlightenment humanism and classical liberalism. The scope of *Subaltern Studies* from the mid-1980s expanded beyond the study of economically marginalized groups in society. Cultural marginality of women and of certain caste groups became the subject matter of *Subaltern Studies*. Most radical, however, was the turn within the collective to think about the *intellectual* history of nationalism and postcolonial modernity, particularly after the publication of Partha Chatterjee's *Nationalist Thought and the Colonial World* and, following that, *The Nation and Its Fragments*. It marked a shift of *Subaltern Studies* towards welding together a history of ideas with postcolonial history.

Chatterjee's central theme developed in these two books was to analyse what, if anything, was unique to the nationalisms that arose in numerous countries of Asia and Africa in the era of decolonization around the mid-twentieth century. Theories of nationalism – conservative, liberal, Marxist – all converged, he argued, on the idea that nationalism as a phenomenon originated in Western Europe. This held true for theorists as varied as John Plamenatz, Hans Kohn, Karl Deutsch, Elie Kedourie, Ernest Gellner and Benedict Anderson. Chatterjee devoted much critical attention to the last, especially to Anderson's *Imagined Communities* (1983).

Chatterjee observed that, unlike previous theorists of nationalism, Anderson refused to define the nation 'by a set of external and abstract criteria'. He eschewed all functional determinism by asserting that the nation is 'an imagined political community'. In describing the nation as a work of the imagination, Anderson (unlike Gellner) was not suggesting that the nation was a falsity or fabrication. Rather, it was the twin forces of Protestantism and print capitalism and the remarkable changes that followed in their wake that made it possible to 'think' the nation. Anderson argued that there were three kinds of nationalisms that emerged as a result of these developments: Creole nationalism in the Americas, linguistic nationalisms of Europe and official or state-sponsored nationalism as exemplified by Russia. After their full development and fruition in Europe and America, these nationalisms came to serve as models for the rest of world. Nationalist leaders of Asia and Africa could now draw upon these models, which had developed over a more than a century and a half of human experience. In a world dominated by the idea of nation states, nationalist leaders could pick from a variety of modules rather than rely on a commonality of language or blood to create an ideological sense of nationhood. Nationalism in this framework, argued Chatterjee, became, 'a matter of a vanguard intelligentsia coming to state power by "mobilizing" popular nationalism and using the "Machiavellian" instruments of official nationalism. Like religion and kinship, nationalism is an anthropological fact, and there is nothing else to it.'[28]

Was there something to be contested in this narrative, especially when viewed from the perspective of the ex-colonized countries of Asia, Africa and Latin America? After all, there was nothing in Anderson's framework that would account for third world imaginations at work in 'the intellectual process of creation' of their nationalist movements. Without such histories, peoples from vast swathes of the world were simply reduced to being passive consumers of a model created in the 'West'.

Chatterjee's primary goal was thus to question the ideological primacy of the West in the intellectual history of nationalism. In his 1986 *Nationalist Thought and the Colonial World*, he stated the problem in the following manner: Nationalist texts/thought had to bear the twin burden of proving to the 'people' of a nation that they were capable of sovereignty, and also call into question the colonial ruler's legitimacy to rule in an alien land. 'To both, nationalism sought to demonstrate the falsity of the colonial claim that the backward peoples were culturally incapable of ruling themselves in the conditions of the modern world.' Thus, nationalism could only succeed (1) by challenging the 'alleged inferiority' of the colonized and (2) by asserting that a backward nation could modernize itself while preserving its cultural authenticity. While this was a huge achievement of nationalist thought, Chatterjee also drew attention to the fact that the founding premise of this achievement was an allegiance to universal reason, the same premise on which the colonizing mission was also based. Nationalist thought was always a discourse of power and could not be considered independently of post-Enlightenment, bourgeois-rationalist forms of knowledge.

This produced a contradiction that went to heart of this thought, namely, that even as it challenged the colonial claim to political domination, it also accepted the intellectual premises of 'modernity' on which colonial domination was based. 'Modernity' in this context describes a certain condition of a 'marriage between Reason and capital', and 'nowhere in the world has nationalism qua nationalism' challenged the legitimacy of this union.[29] The state that is born out of such nationalism bears the marks of this duality, which haunts its postcolonial career.

Using Gramsci's idea of passive revolution, Chatterjee outlined an ideological history of nationalism by taking as 'paradigmatic' the career of the colonial Indian state from the late nineteenth century until the declaration of Independence in 1947. Using the Gramscian schema, he traced the history of nationalist thought in India in three 'moments': those of departure, manoeuvre and arrival. He concluded that nationalist thought resolved the contradiction between 'metropolitan capital' and 'the people-nation' by 'absorbing the political life of the nation into the body of the state'. The absorption of nation(s) into the state is the result of the 'cultural-ideological' work of nationalism. Hereafter the state became the 'principal mobiliser, planner, guarantor, and legitimator of productive investment'.[30] Any political movement that questioned the artificial identification between the state and the people was denied legitimacy.

During the transition from the colonial to the postcolonial, or in Chatterjee's terminology at 'the moment of arrival', Reason and Capital attain the status of an 'epistemic privilege' in the life of the state under the banner of 'development'. Away from India, nationalisms in Algeria and Mexico, also serve as dramatic examples of these processes.[31]

The tenor of *Nationalist Thought and the Colonial World: A Derivative Discourse* was much more sombre than previous *Subaltern Studies* writings. By characterizing nationalism's relationship to post-Enlightenment thought as both agonistic and derivative, Chatterjee fundamentally questioned the possibility of nationalist thought in the erstwhile colonized parts of the world being genuinely emancipatory. The book's analysis of Gandhi in particular showed how the state successfully managed to absorb alternative, revolutionary thinking into its fold, thereby neutralizing its radical potential. Chatterjee argued that this tendency to subvert radical thought, or to absorb it into the apparatus of the state, is constitutive of postcolonial nation states.

Despite these compromises, however, there remained something uniquely radical about nationalist thought in the ex-colonized third world. In 1993 Chatterjee issued a far-reaching critique of the history of the postcolonial nation state and of Eurocentrism in his book, *The Nation and Its Fragments*. In the opening pages, he responded to the question he had raised in *Nationalist Thought* but had answered with some equivocation, namely, where in third world nationalisms was the work of the imagination? Still continuing his polemic with Anderson, he wrote,

> I have one central objection to Anderson's argument. If nationalisms in the rest of the world have to choose their imagined community from certain 'modular' forms already made available to them by Europe and the Americas, what do they have left to imagine? History, it would seem, has decreed that we in the postcolonial world shall only be perpetual consumers of modernity. Europe and the Americas, the only true subjects of history, have thought out on our behalf not only the script of colonial enlightenment and exploitation, but also that of our anticolonial resistance and postcolonial misery. ... I object to this argument because ... I cannot reconcile it with the evidence on anticolonial nationalism. The most powerful and creative results of the nationalist imagination in Asia and Africa are posited not on an identity but rather on a difference with the modular forms of national society propagated by the modern West.[32]

Another scholar of the collective, Gyanendra Pandey, had written about the need for historians to pay greater attention to 'fragmentary' histories in order to counter seamless narratives of the nation state. As Pandey put it, 'Part of the importance of the fragmentary point of view' is that 'it resists the drive for a shallow homogenization and struggles for other, potentially richer definitions of the "nation" and the future political community'.[33] Chatterjee used Pandey's defence of the fragment to tell a comprehensive history of anti-colonial nationalism. He charted this history by looking at specific moments and groups whose fit with the official anti-colonial nationalism was always uneasy – women, lower castes, peasants, the history of the vernacular press and so on. Analysis of these actors and movements in the colony allowed Chatterjee to come up with a theory of sovereignty that could account for the autonomy of the consciousness of the colonized *vis-à-vis* the colonizer.

In an argument that has been debated over endlessly in history classrooms of the Anglophone academy, Chatterjee claimed that 'anticolonial nationalism creates its own domain of sovereignty well before it begins its political battle with imperial power'.[34] In his schema both the history of nationalism and of the postcolonial state that followed are always marked by a binary division between the inner/outer, spiritual/material and private/public realms of life. The inner–spiritual–private domains corresponded to the realms where the colonized have successfully resisted the thrall of the colonizer and have staked their sovereignty *vis-à-vis* the West, while the outer–material–public realms included the arena of official politics and professional life where the East had succumbed to the political will and ideological power of the West. Nationalism's success at holding the colonizer at bay from the inner domain did not mean this realm remained unchanging or sequestered from change. Rather, as Chatterjee argued, 'here nationalism launches a "modern" national culture that is nevertheless not Western. If the nation is an imagined community, then this is where it is brought into being. In this, its true and essential domain, the nation is already sovereign, even when the state is in the hands of the colonial power.'[35]

Chatterjee's analysis of the nationalist separation of inner/outer or material/spiritual division raised many criticisms. It has been argued, with some justification, that these binaries mapped neatly on to a classical liberal separation between church and state, or the home and the world, and therefore remained a modular variant of the metropolitan model. Feminist critics in particular argued that the equation of women with the inner/spiritual/private realm underplayed late-nineteenth- and early-twentieth-century critiques of patriarchy and of women's increasing participation in professional and political life.

Notwithstanding these and other criticisms, Chatterjee's work is of signal importance for an understanding of the politics of postcolonial states. His argument about the 'modernity' of the fragment challenges historians to explore the discursive conditions that make it possible for theories of exceptionalism to flourish in a globalized world. It also demonstrates 'that the alleged exceptions actually inhere as forcibly suppressed elements even in the supposedly universal forms of the modern forms of power'.[36] He provides a critical vocabulary with which to think through practices that thrive in the contemporary world but are often criticized as traditional or conservative when analysed in liberal-rationalist terms.[37] Chatterjee's work made way for historians to think of 'new forms of modern community' and inspired thinking about 'new forms of the modern state'.[38]

Taken together Chatterjee's two books, Gyanendra Pandey's *The Construction of Communalism in Colonial India* and his article 'In Defense of the Fragment' mentioned above and Shahid Amin's *Event, Memory, Metaphor* (1995) are works that provided historical and epistemological grounds for questioning the efficacy of totalizing national histories in narrating the politics of subaltern lives. With them the postcolonial merged into the postnational as well.[39]

Phase three

Where does *Subaltern Studies* stand in the new millennium? The project, many would agree, is fragmented. Given the internal variations in the writings of individual contributors, it is a challenge for the historian to sift through them all to arrive at a conclusion about what *Subaltern Studies* today means as a project of writing postcolonial history. Three main trends stand out in my assessment. First, an overt philosophical and historiographical shift was marked by Ranajit Guha's book *History at the Limit of World History* (2002) where Guha proposed a critique of viewing the world based on a Hegelian idea of 'world history' by positing against it the category of 'historicality'. The latter is a way of thinking about the past in ways that elude histories written from within what Guha calls 'the statist predicament'. The second trend was exemplified by Partha Chatterjee's 2004 collection of essays entitled *The Politics of the Governed*. The reader will notice that the subaltern has been renamed in this collection as the 'governed'. This renaming is not simply an exercise in semantic jugglery. Rather it signals a serious interrogation of the political histories and theories of democracy in the contemporary world based on European political theory. Taken together, these two contributions point up different though related developments of the *Subaltern Studies* mandate of mounting a critique of Eurocentrism from a third world vantage point. Somewhat different from these was a third trend marked by Dipesh Chakrabarty's *Provincializing Europe* (2000), a book that has had a far-reaching impact on postcolonial history-writing. But a discussion of the last is reserved for the next chapter because of its unique engagement with and departure from the *Subaltern Studies* paradigm.

World history and historicality

Central to Guha's critique of the discipline of history is the distinction he draws between history and historicality. The former refers to written and recorded histories by professional historians and is deeply tied to the project of the nation state. In talking about history thus, Guha's principal interlocutor is Hegel for whom a people without a modern state, or those without the imagination of such a state, were a people devoid of history. Arguably, the idea in many ways predated

Hegel. Guha traces it back to European explorers of the fifteenth and sixteenth centuries, who as they encountered peoples without a written alphabet – on parchment, rock or paper – concluded that they were beyond the pale of civilized society endowed with historical sense. This notion received its most sophisticated elaboration in Hegel.

Guha discusses at length Hegel's ideas about the fundamental relationship between the state and history. It was only within the state form, argued Hegel, that people are able to rise above their multiple pluralities and differences to recognize what is general, common or universal. All others – and places like India and China are among them – were yet to break out of their mythic and poetic stupor to discover in their midst some principle of universal governance. Writing of India and China, Hegel remarked,

> The two nations are lacking – indeed completely lacking – in the essential self consciousness of the concept of freedom. The Chinese look on their moral rules as if they were sacred laws of nature, positive external commandments, coercive rights and duties, or rules of mutual courtesy. Freedom, through which the substantial determination of reason alone can be translated into ethical attitudes is absent. … And in the Indian doctrine of renunciation of sensuality, desires, and all earthly interests, positive ethical freedom is not the goal and the end, but rather the extinction of consciousness and the suspension of spiritual and even physical life.[40]

Freedom for Hegel 'is nothing more than a knowledge and affirmation of such universal and substantial objects as law and justice, and the production of a reality which corresponds to them – i.e. the state'. The only place where he saw the realization of the state so defined was in Europe. Europe, with its particular kind of statehood, was designated as the locus of World history, while other parts of the world, with their respective forms of prose and poetic expression – historicality for short – were left to stagnate in 'prehistory'.[41]

Let us clarify what Guha meant by historicality. Briefly, it refers to a sense of the past that captures the multiple, plural and wondrous aspects of human existence. Its mode of transmission was not through historical narratives as we understand them today but rather through myths, poems, fables and ordinary lore. In short, it refers to literary expressions of individuals, qua individuals, that existed in defiance of the rules of modern historiography that were accepted since the nineteenth-century European colonizations as the best means of representing the past the world over.[42] Going back to the spirit of his earlier manifesto on an Indian historiography for India, Guha argues that it was the success of colonialist forms of knowledge – history paramount among them – that produced a dominance of statism in the colonized world. The production of knowledge in the model of World history was so internalized by Indians from the colonial period onwards that as practising historians today we are even unable to apprehend it as a problem. Official and subsequently professional histories superseded as true knowledge all previous narratologies – the epics, *puranas*, myths – those myriad, wondrous tales replete with a sense of what Guha, after Rabindranath Tagore, calls 'historicality'.[43]

The task of the subaltern historian now, Guha seems to suggest, would be to recognize her 'statist predicament'. First of all this implies a recognition that all the categories we work with in analysing the different histories of oppression in the world in effect level out the individual figure into a general and generalizable category of the dispossessed and powerless, be it 'worker', 'peasant' or 'tribal'. Secondly, since most histories are directed towards unveiling how the powerless have been rendered thus, and to advance their struggle to secure more rights within the rubric of the nation state, they become by default a history of the state itself. Drawing inspiration from Tagore, Guha argues that the spirit of a democratic history would rescue the uniqueness of historical actors from the abstract totalities of academic/world history.

There is no doubt that many find this plea of Guha's to be a romantic one. The *guru* of subaltern historiography has been accused to aestheticizing the subaltern experience.[44] Nonetheless, I would maintain that in privileging individual life and experience there remains something fundamentally democratic in Guha's advocacy of historicality. A criticism, however, continues to linger. *History at the Limit of World History* fails to acknowledge the centrality and importance of the state in postcolonial lives. Many in India, the place that Guha engages with most closely, have actually found ways to better their condition through a struggle and engagement with statist politics. Without thinking about the role of the state, it would be impossible to understand the nature and history of democracy in postcolonial India. Postcolonial history-writing, it would appear, can ill afford to reject the statist predicament. It needs rather to engage with it in a critical spirit.

Political society

The Politics of the Governed by Partha Chatterjee sets out to do precisely this. The book consists, in Chatterjee's own words, of 'reflections on popular politics in most of the world'.[45] 'Popular politics' is defined as political practices by people (refugees, squatters, migrants, peasants, workers and various other categories who together fall within the ambit of the 'governed') that are not *bound* by institutions of law or governance but are *conditioned* by such institutions. This kind of politics shapes the relationship between governments and populations in most parts of the world. Chatterjee's formulation of 'most of the world' is interesting. He argues that the world now consists of modern capitalist democracies that are often clubbed together as the 'West'. But the West/non-West dichotomy is increasingly complicated in the postcolonial world because 'the modern West has a significant presence in many modern non-Western societies, just as, … there are large sectors of contemporary Western society that are not necessarily a part of the historical entity known as the modern West'.[46] Such a formulation of the West and non-West returns us to Balibar's description of Europe's postcolonial predicament. It also suggests that we need to parse out the meanings, practices and institutions encapsulated in these broad geographical placeholders – West/non-West – in order to have some sense of political practice in the modern world. This is the task that Chatterjee sets for himself in this book.

Chatterjee argues that in the aftermath of the era of decolonization and the emergence of mass democracies in the industrial countries of the West there arose increasingly, in the realm of governance, a distinction between citizens and populations. The distinction is elaborated as the following: 'Unlike the concept of the citizen, the concept of the population is wholly descriptive, empirical; it does not carry a normative burden. Populations are identifiable, classifiable, and describable … and are amenable to statistical techniques such as censuses and sample surveys.'[47] If the concept of citizen can be allied with ideas of sovereignty, the concept of population is one meant for government and regulation. As the twentieth century progressed, argues Chatterjee, ideas of participatory citizenship and political representation that were key to the Enlightenment notion of politics yielded place to 'the triumphant advance' of governmental intervention that promised increased welfare to more people at less cost.[48] 'Indeed one might say that the actual political history of capital has long spilled over the normative confines of liberal political theory to go out and conquer the world through governmental technologies.'[49] Chatterjee finds evidence for his claims in communitarian or republican critiques that argue that governance has implied a diminished engagement with politics. Politics, or what was carried out in its name, became over the long twentieth century more a matter of management and manipulation in many Western capitalist democracies.[50]

The distinction between citizens and the population/governed also raised certain other conceptual and historical conundrums. Citizens were by definition an unity bound by their common affiliation to a nation state. The governed, however, could never be conceived as a single indivisible entity, comprised as it was of tribes, races, classes – that is to say, multiplicities with different defining characteristics. This situation is true of ex-colonized countries too, where the aspiration of nationalists was to create a single homogeneous citizen body by liberating the country from colonialism. But following decolonization, during the developmental or modernizing phase in most of these countries, there was a continuation of colonial policies of mapping, enumerating and classifying that citizen body as 'the governed'. From this Chatterjee formulates the following problem:

> We have therefore described two sets of conceptual connections. One is a line connecting civil society to the nation state founded on popular sovereignty and granting equal rights to citizens. The other is the line connecting populations to governmental agencies pursuing multiple policies of security and welfare. The first line points to a domain of politics described in great detail in democratic political theory in the last two centuries. Does the second line point to a different domain of politics? I believe it does. To distinguish it from the classic associational forms of civil society, I am calling it *political society*.[51]

While the elite/subaltern division was meaningful in the context of anti-colonial nationalisms, its postcolonial instantiation is the civil/political society split. In a country like India the colonial state labelled much subaltern activism as criminal, insurrectionary or rebellious. But the national state that followed had to find a different political and conceptual vocabulary to deal with large parts of the population whose activities were very different from those groups defined as civil society – 'a small section of culturally equipped citizens'. Several of the actions undertaken by the vast mass of people who constitute political society often transgress the 'strict lines of legality'.[52] Many of these groups live in illegal squatter settlements, access water or electricity illegally and travel without tickets in public transport, to cite just a few of Chatterjee's examples. These practices are so ubiquitous in the life of the modern nation state in India that they cannot be ignored, nor can the government deal with these groups as civic associations following legitimate social pursuits. The shifting groups of political society are vote banks for political parties and supplement the state's flawed schemes of social welfare, albeit in non-legal ways. Given the ties of such behaviour to questions of livelihood, political maneuverability and violence Chatterjee wants to restitute such activities as 'political' – the real stuff of democratic politics as it takes place in a postcolony like India.

In a tone that is reminiscent of the critique voiced by *Subaltern Studies* in the late 1980s and 1990s, he writes somewhat wryly that, 'Our political theory today does not accept Aristotle's criteria of the ideal constitution. But our actual governmental practices are still based on the premise that not everyone can govern.' The concept of political society demonstrates that people in many parts of the world often override or set aside the abstract promise of popular sovereignty by devising new ways of meeting the challenges of livelihood. This is also an articulation of how they visualize being governed. Chatterjee concludes, in a spirit of postcolonial irreverence towards canonical political theory, writing that,

> Many of the forms of political society … would not, I suspect, meet with Aristotle's approval, because they would appear to him to allow popular leaders to take precedence over the law. But we might, I think, be able to persuade him that in this way the people are learning, and forcing their governors to learn, how they would prefer to be governed. That, the wise Greek might agree, is a good ethical justification for democracy.[53]

Conclusion

The trajectory of the *Subaltern Studies* collective over the three decades of its existence makes clear some of its lasting contributions to the project of postcolonial history-writing. First, the collective developed one of the most sustained modes of critique against the Eurocentrism that had marked much history-writing all over the world. Secondly, it located a critique of the contemporary nation state in the legacy of Eurocentrism that came to many centres of the world through the vehicle of colonialism. Finally, it provided historians with a critical vocabulary with which to rewrite the subaltern back into history as a political subject.

Our analysis so far has established that while the category of the subaltern was drawn from Antonio Gramsci, in its deployment in the works by historians of the collective it was also unmoored from its Gramscian and Maoist genealogy. Works by the collective demonstrated no faith in the party, *à la* Mao. Nor did they share Gramsci's scepticism about 'spontaneity' of subaltern action. As recently observed by Dipesh Chakrabarty,

> *Subaltern Studies* was perhaps the last – or the latest – instance of a long global history of the Left: the romantic-popular search for a non-industrial revolutionary subject that was initiated in Russia, among other places in the second half of the twentieth century. This romantic populism shaped much of Maoism in the twentieth century, and left its imprint on the antinomies and ambiguities of Antonio Gramsci's thoughts on the Party as the Modern Prince.[54]

There is much to be drawn from Chakrabarty's insight that the 'subaltern' was probably the latest instantiation of the search for a global revolutionary subject. It was preceded and succeeded in different centres of the world by names like 'peasant' (Mao), 'the wretched of the earth' (Fanon), 'the party as Subject' (Lenin/Lukacs), 'multitude' (Hardt and Negri) and 'the governed' (Chatterjee). 'Recognizing the stand-in nature' of each one of these categories, he argues, 'is the first step towards writing the histories of democracies that have emerged through the mass-politics of anti-colonial nationalism.'[55] But in order to fully apprehend the mass-subject who is at the centre of these histories, postcolonial history-writing has to consciously work 'through the limits of European thought'.[56] Only then can it begin to answer the question that preoccupied one of the leading postcolonial critics of our times, Homi Bhabha, namely, how does newness enter the world? One step in that direction would therefore be through the project of provincializing Europe.

Notes

1 The essay by Dipesh Chakrabarty (one of the founding members of the collective), 'A Small History of Subaltern Studies', in *Habitations of Modernity* explicitly theorizes on the subject of *Subaltern Studies* historiography as postcolonial history. Dipesh Chakrabarty, *Habitations of Modernity: Essays in the Wake of Subaltern Studies* (Chicago, IL: University of Chicago Press, 2002), pp. 3–19.

2 David Ludden (ed.), *Reading Subaltern Studies: Critical History, Contested Meaning, and the Globalisation of South Asia* (New Delhi: Permanent Black, 2001), p. 1.

3 Ranajit Guha (ed.), *A Subaltern Studies Reader 1986–1995* (Minneapolis, MN and London: University of Minnesota Press, 1997), p. xi.

4 Notable among them were B. B. Chowdhury, David Ludden, Steven Henningham, Hamza Alavi, Stephen Fuchs, J. C. Jha, Ghansyam Shah, Kathleen Gough and A. R. Desai. There was in addition to these works by British Marxist historians, two journals – *The Journal of Peasant Studies* (1973) and *The Peasant Studies Newsletter* (1972) – that had been launched in the decade preceding *Subaltern Studies*.

5 Ludden, *Reading Subaltern Studies*, p. 20.

6 Edward Said, 'Foreword', in Ranajit Guha and Gayatri Spivak (eds), *Selected Subaltern Studies* (New York, NY: Oxford University Press, 1988), p. ix.

7 Dipesh Chakrabarty, 'Foreword: The Names and Repetitions of Postcolonial History', in Rachel Harrison and Peter Jackson (eds), *The Ambiguous Allure of the West* (Hong Kong: University of Hong Kong Press, 2010), p. xiii.

8 Ranajit Guha, 'On Some Aspects of the Historiography of Colonial India', in Ranajit Guha and Gayatri Spivak (eds), *Selected Subaltern Studies* (New York, NY: Oxford University Press, 1988), p. 37.

9 Guha, 'On Some Aspects of the Historiography of Colonial India', p. 39.

10 Guha, 'On Some Aspects of the Historiography of Colonial India'.

11 Guha, 'On Some Aspects of the Historiography of Colonial India', p. 44.

12 Guha, 'On Some Aspects of the Historiography of Colonial India', p. 40.

13 Guha, 'On Some Aspects of the Historiography of Colonial India', pp. 41–2.

14 Some of the most remarkable instances of this project can be found in David Hardiman, 'Origins and Transformations of the Devi', in Ranajit Guha (ed.), *A Subaltern Studies Reader 1986–1995* (Minneapolis, MN: University of Minnesota Press, 1997), pp. 100–39; Gautam Bhadra, 'The Mentality of Subalternity: Kantanama and Rajdharma', in Ranajit Guha (ed.), *A Subaltern Studies Reader 1986–1995* (Minneapolis, MN: University of Minnesota Press, 1997), pp. 63–99; Shahid Amin, 'Gandhi as Mahatma', in Ranajit Guha and Gayatri Spivak (eds), *Selected Subaltern Studies* (New York, NY: Oxford University Press, 1988), pp. 288–342; Ranajit Guha, 'The Prose of Counter-insurgency', in Ranajit Guha and Gayatri Spivak (eds), *Selected Subaltern Studies* (New York, NY: Oxford University Press, 1988), pp. 45–84; and Dipesh Chakrabarty, 'Conditions of Knowledge of Working-class Conditions', in Ranajit Guha and Gayatri Spivak (eds), *Selected Subaltern Studies* (New York, NY: Oxford University Press, 1988), pp. 179–230.

15 Guha's essay 'The Prose of Counter-insurgency' and his book *Elementary Aspects of Peasant Insurgency in Colonial India* are as much about subaltern history and the subaltern subject as they are about ways of recovering such subjectivity and consciousness through a critical reading of archival records left by elite groups in colonial society.

16 Guha demonstrates this strategy in his essay 'The Prose of Counter-insurgency', pp. 45–84.

17 Dipesh Chakrabarty, *Habitations of Modernity: Essays in the Wake of Subaltern Studies* (Chicago, IL: University of Chicago Press, 2001), p. 16.

18 Arif Dirlik made this criticism in 'The Postcolonial Aura: Third World Criticism in the Age of Global Capitalism', *Critical Inquiry* 20(2) (Winter 1994), pp. 328–56.

19 Chakrabarty, *Habitations of Modernity*, p. 8.

20 Chakrabarty, *Habitations of Modernity*.

21 Chakrabarty, *Habitations of Modernity*.

22 Cited in Dipesh Chakrabarty, 'A Small History of Subaltern Studies', in Dipesh Chakrabarty (ed.), *Habitations of Modernity: Essays in the Wake of Subaltern Studies* (Chicago, IL: University of Chicago Press, 2001), p. 9.

23 David Hardiman, a member of the collective, argued in his study of the influence of the devi (goddess) in the Western Indian state of Gujarat that 'religious belief and practice often reflected an aspiration for a better life, which was not merely located in the hereafter but also very much in the here and now. This aspiration grew from daily experience representing an attempt to build a better future on an existing base.' See Hardiman, 'Origins and Transformations of the Devi', p. 106.

24 This view is developed at length in Ranajit Guha, *Dominance without Hegemony: History and Power in Colonial India* (Cambridge, MA: Harvard University Press, 1997).

25 Guha's later book *Dominance without Hegemony*, Partha Chatterjee's *The Nation and Its Fragments* and Gyan Pandey's article 'In Defense of the Fragment' further developed the postcolonial critique about the unrepresentative character of bourgeois nationalist discourse.

26 Ileana Rodríguez (ed.), *A Latin American Subaltern Studies Reader* (Durham, NC: Duke University Press, 2001).

27 Gayatri Spivak's landmark essay 'Can the Subaltern Speak?' offered one of the most powerful critiques, via an analysis of a conversation between Giles Deleuze and Michel Foucault, of the notion that historical scholarship could simply recover subaltern speak. Gayatri Chakravorty Spivak, 'Can the Subaltern Speak?', in P. Williams and L. Chrisman (eds), *Colonial Discourse and Postcolonial Theory: A Reader* (New York, NY: Columbia University Press, 1994), pp. 66–111. Also see Rosalind O'Hanlon, 'Recovering the Subject: Subaltern Studies and Histories of Resistance in Colonial South Asia', in David Ludden (ed.), *Reading Subaltern Studies* (New Delhi: Permanent Black, 2001), pp. 135–86.

28 Partha Chatterjee, *Nationalist Thought and the Colonial World: A Derivative Discourse* (London: Zed Books, 1986), p. 22.

29 Chatterjee, *Nationalist Thought and the Colonial World*, p. 168.

30 Chatterjee, *Nationalist Thought and the Colonial World*, pp. 168–9.

31 Chatterjee, *Nationalist Thought and the Colonial World*.

32 Partha Chatterjee, *The Nation and Its Fragments: Colonial and Postcolonial Histories* (Princeton, NJ: Princeton University Press, 1993), p. 5.

33 Gyanendra Pandey, 'In Defense of the Fragment: Writing about Hindu–Muslim Riots in India Today', in Ranajit Guha (ed.), *A Subaltern Studies Reader, 1986–1995* (Minneapolis, MN: University of Minnesota Press, 1997), p. 3.

34 Chatterjee, *The Nation and Its Fragments*, p. 6.

35 Chatterjee, *The Nation and Its Fragments*.

36 Chatterjee, *The Nation and Its Fragments*, p. 13.

37 For instance, it is possible to understand the politics surrounding the veil in many parts of the world, or the demand by subaltern groups for an expansion of primary school curricula to include their languages, or the invocation of piety by women's groups in parts of the Middle East as a mode of political empowerment through his heuristic model.

38 Chatterjee, *The Nation and Its Fragments*.

39 For a discussion of the changes in *Subaltern Studies* historiography in the 1990s, see Chakrabarty, *Habitations of Modernity*, pp. 16–18.

40 Ranajit Guha, *History at the Limit of World History* (New York, NY: Columbia University Press, 2002), p. 38.
41 Guha, *History at the Limit of World History*, p. 23.
42 Guha refers to the dominance of 'world history' as the narratological revolution. See Guha, *History at the Limit of World History*, pp. 5–6.
43 For Guha's discussion of Tagore, see Guha, *History at the Limit of World History*, Chapter 5, pp. 75–94, and also his translation of Tagore's essay 'Sahitye Aitihasikata' (Historicality in Literature), pp. 95–9.
44 For a discussion of some of the criticisms levelled against Guha's book as well as the Italian Academy of Advanced Studies lectures held at Columbia University in October–November 2000, on which the book is based, see Dipesh Chakrabarty, 'History and Historicality', *Postcolonial Studies* 7(1) (2004), pp. 128–9.
45 Partha Chatterjee, *The Politics of the Governed: Reflections on Popular Politics in Most of the World* (New York, NY: Columbia University Press, 2004).
46 Chatterjee, *The Politics of the Governed*, p. 3.
47 Chatterjee, *The Politics of the Governed*, p. 34.
48 In arguing thus Chatterjee is drawing upon the works of sociologists Nikolas Rose, Peter Miller and Thomas Osborne, historian Mary Poovey and philosophers Michel Foucault and Ian Hacking.
49 Chatterjee, *The Politics of the Governed*.
50 Chatterjee argues that while governmental regulation of citizen's lives has become a subject of discussion in the United States and Great Britain after the events of 11 September 2001, in fact the phenomenon predated that tragic event by several decades.
51 Chatterjee, *The Politics of the Governed*, pp. 37–8.
52 Chatterjee, *The Politics of the Governed*, p. 40.
53 Chatterjee, *The Politics of the Governed*, pp. 77–8.
54 Dipesh Chakrabarty, 'Foreword: The Names and Repetitions of Postcolonial History', p. xiv.
55 Chakrabarty, 'Foreword: The Names and Repetitions of Postcolonial History', p. xv.
56 Chakrabarty, 'Foreword: The Names and Repetitions of Postcolonial History'.

3

The idea of provincializing Europe

To 'provincialize' Europe ... was to ask a question about how thought was related to place.[1]

Dipesh Chakrabarty's 2000 book *Provincializing Europe: Postcolonial Thought and Historical Difference* (hereafter *PE*) marked a critical moment in postcolonial history-writing. While the conception of the book owed much to Chakrabarty's close association with the *Subaltern Studies* project, explored in the previous chapter, it also departed from that paradigm of historiography in marked ways. Given *PE*'s wide reception in historical studies, reaching far beyond the scope of South Asian history, this chapter will be organized as follows.[2] We begin with an analysis of the main themes of the book in order to explicate the ways in which *PE* has helped to shape the agenda of postcolonial history-writing. Following this, I will analyse in some detail the ways in which the historiographical insights presented in *PE* have been utilized by historians working in fields hitherto unrelated to postcolonial historiography. My aim is to demonstrate how the postcolonial turn has opened up for Europeanists, medievalists, historians of religions and American historians a new set of questions that end up recalibrating the discipline of history. I will close this chapter with a few remarks that situate the nature of postcolonial historiography's critique of Eurocentrism *vis-à-vis* other recent historical writings that have attempted to de-centre the place of Europe in global or world history.

PE is a challenge to Eurocentric thought that has for years – at least for the years over which the idea has prevailed (in various forms) that the non-West must develop and catch up with the West – functioned as the central organizing principle of much historical thinking and writing around the world. It does so by raising three related questions. First, do universal ideas bear an imprint of their particular, local provenance? Or, is it the case that ideas that are acknowledged as universally valid are simply abstractions that would look the same no matter where they are manifested in practice? The answer, one would conclude from Chakrabarty's peregrinations into the subject, is that 'European ideas that were universal were also, at one and the same time, drawn from very particular intellectual and historical traditions.'[3] This is not, however, to imply that the global relevance of these ideas is diminished. This leads to the second theme of the project, which is to ask how universal ideas that are not so universal to begin with get translated (and transformed) as they journey from their place of origin to other settings. What historical changes are entailed in such translations? And how do ideas travel? Finally, what historical conditions make it necessary to embark on such a project of provincializing Europe? Taking our cue from Chakrabarty, the questions stem from an impulse to generate critical awareness about certain forms of stadial thinking that have dominated the modern world following European expansion into the realms of thought and politics since the nineteenth century. Chakrabarty calls this kind of stadial or developmentalist thinking 'historicism'. Let us unpack these propositions by looking closely into the arguments of *PE*.

Before launching into a discussion of *PE*, it is important that we clarify the way in which the author uses the category 'Europe' throughout the work. Europe in this book does not have a one-to-one correspondence with the geographical region of the world called Europe. Rather it is used in the book as a 'hyperreal' term that invokes 'certain figures of imagination whose geographical referents remain somewhat indeterminate'.[4] Chakrabarty is aware of the internal heterogeneity of the European histories and regional diversity that marks the field. Despite these internal variations, the argument he gives for positing a global Europe as a category of *thought* is that 'just as the phenomenon of Orientalism does not disappear simply because some of us now have attained a critical awareness of it, similarly a certain version of "Europe," reified and celebrated in the phenomenal world of everyday relationships of power as the scene of the birth of the modern, continues to dominate the discourse of history'.[5]

History and European domination

PE begins with the argument that 'Europe' is a sovereign, central figure in the discipline of history (that is to say, the subject crafted and written by academic historians, and produced and taught in colleges and universities). This is true, argues Chakrabarty, of even those histories that are ostensibly about other regions of the world, be it India, China or Kenya. An obvious everyday example of this European domination is the fact that while most third world histories refer to the work of European historians, there is no corresponding urgency in the works of European historians to do the same. Such a statement does not stem from the third world historian's resentment of her European counterpart. It is a symptom of a larger phenomenon, namely, that much historical or other social scientific work in the modern world rests on theoretical/philosophical assumptions that have been deliberated upon and deduced by European scholars and philosophers since the Enlightenment and before. Concepts such as equality, liberty, modern justice, electoral democracy, civil society, culture, development, the public sphere, to name just a few of such categories, which are indispensable to the historian's craft everywhere in the world, received their earliest theoretical elaboration in the hands of European thinkers. The latter produced these ideas, more often than not, with no direct knowledge of the rest of the world. But this fact does not undermine their utility for non-European historians or peoples. As examples, Chakrabarty cites the importance of figures like Marx, Weber, Hegel or even Freud to much historical writing and thinking. Historians, irrespective of their location, have most likely utilized ideas propounded by these thinkers to think through their particular empirical research questions.

While many of these thinkers did not explicitly look upon other parts of the world as the loci of backwardness (although some like John Stuart Mill or John Locke did) their ideas have been the ballast for theories of development, or narratives of transition to capitalist/socialist modernity, in different historical settings. Marxist histories abound in references to historical phases described as the pre-capitalist, feudal or pre-bourgeois. The implicit or explicit assumption undergirding the use of such categories is that as societies move from the pre-capitalist to the capitalist, or from feudal to modern, they eventually converge on the global stage. Until then, however, non-Western societies must strive to follow the model set by those ahead of them in the developmental race.

The political implications of this type of stadial thought are not hard to deduce. A look at the history of colonization in the late eighteenth and nineteenth century leaves no scope for doubt that the logic of European domination of places such as India, Africa or before that the New World, were often premised on the notion that peoples in these faraway lands had no civilizations or traditions that qualified them for political autonomy in a modern world. Until they were schooled in protocols of Western politics and civility – in other words 'political modernity' – they were deemed incapable of self-rule. 'Historicism' is Chakrabarty's specific label for this particular mode of apprehending the pasts of nations and the world. As he argues, 'Historicism is what made modernity or capitalism look not simply global but rather as something that became global *over time*, by originating in one place (Europe) and then spreading outside it.'[6] The vehicle of this spread was colonialism. It was this mode of thinking, he goes on to argue, that made possible what Johannes Fabian called 'the denial of coevalness' to populations in disparate parts of the world with their European rulers. Or, in what has become an influential shorthand of the idea of *PE*, historicism is the means by which large sections of the world's populations are relegated to an imaginary 'waiting room' where they are told that they are 'not yet' ready for the rights, which are in principle considered universal. The response to the colonizer's injunction of the 'not yet' came with the nationalist's assertion of the 'now'. Most anti-colonial nationalisms asserted that the colonized were always ready for self-rule, regardless of their level of education or political consciousness measured by the yardsticks of Western, classical, liberal thought.[7]

The success of anti-colonial nationalism did not signal the death of stadial thought. As most students of non-Western histories are aware, developmentalist ideas dominate governmental practices geared towards cultivating proper citizenly behaviour among vast masses of uneducated people in the third world. Yet, with the coming of political democracy to many of these countries, the illiterate subaltern simultaneously acquires the status of a citizen through the act of casting a vote during the time of elections. This duality in the subaltern as citizen produces a tension in the 'history and nature of political modernity' in these ex-colonized nations. Comparing it to what Homi Bhabha, in a slightly different usage, had described as the tension between the 'pedagogic' and the 'performative', Chakrabarty renders the fraught complexity of the subaltern-citizen as the following:

> One is the peasant who has to be educated into the citizen and who therefore belongs to the time of historicism; the other is the peasant who, despite his or her lack of formal education, is already a citizen. ... How do we *think* the political at these moments when the peasant or the subaltern emerges in the modern sphere of politics, in his or her own right, as a member of the nationalist movement ... or as a full-fledged member of the body politic without having had to do any 'preparatory' work in order to qualify as the 'bourgeois-citizen'?[8]

The reader will remember that this question about how to think of the unlettered peasant as a modern political actor was also one of the central preoccupations of *Subaltern Studies*. While acknowledging his debt to *Subaltern Studies*, of which he was a founding member, Chakrabarty takes this analysis of the subaltern in a different direction. He takes recourse to two critical philosophical traditions in European thought, demonstrating thereby that it is not a spirit of 'postcolonial revenge' that drives this mode of history-writing, but a desire to renew the European idea of humanism by drawing attention to the ambiguities within thought itself. These inclinations of *PE* are more in line with the ideas of thinkers like Frantz Fanon who engaged deeply with European philosophy with the aim of stretching such thought to its limits by confronting it with the category of race. Chakrabarty does not so much consider race as such – for race was perhaps not as powerful a factor in British colonial rule in India as in the histories that Fanon confronted – but his point of departure is Fanon's recognition of the way European colonists usurped the category 'human' to advance their own narrow interests.

Chakrabarty uses Marx and Heidegger – representing the analytic and the hermeneutic traditions of European philosophy respectively – to think through ideas of subalternity and political modernity in the non-Western world.[9] If Marx represented a strand of thought whose main contribution was to demystify the world by demonstrating the operation of ideologies that cloud judgment, Heidegger for Chakrabarty stood for a mode of thought that paid attention to how different groups of people sought to make themselves at home in the world. Heidegger is Chakrabarty's inspiration for writing 'affective histories'.[10] The latter line of thought allows the historian an access into the multiplicity of human lifeworlds. Bringing the philosophical differences of these two foundational thinkers into a conversation around subaltern or third world pasts allows Chakrabarty to shed new light on the history of the postcolonial condition in the following manner: (1) He undertakes a close reading of Marx's category 'capital' to see how 'both history and the secular figure of the human' result from the way capitalism produces a new world order, or 'the global'.[11] In other words, the idea of equality of all human beings is a legacy of European thought, of which Marx was an exemplar. (2) He demonstrates that the figure of the abstract and equal human being so central to Marx's analysis and a legacy of Enlightenment thought also 'occludes questions of belonging and diversity', that is to say, the notion of historical difference, that are critical to the historian's enterprise.[12] (3) Finally, using Heideggerian insights he suggests a new path for the postcolonial historian to prise open the abstract figure of the universal human to reinstate alongside it particular accounts about the ways in which place shapes human belonging and produces historical difference.

Chakrabarty calls the universal logic of capitalist development as analysed by Marx, History 1. This includes, he argues, all historical developments posited by Capital as its precondition.[13] Marxist histories are full of examples of History 1. The histories of industrialization in different countries, the transition from feudalism to capitalism and the mechanization of labour are all instances of it. But there is another kind of history, which Chakrabarty calls History 2, which also comprises 'antecedents' of capital. The distinction between these antecedents of capital (History 2) and the past posited by capital itself (History 1) is that the former is not a part of capital's life process. History 2 does not contribute to 'the self-reproduction of capital'. In that sense, it is not intrinsic to Marx's logic of capital.

The significance of this distinction for Marxist historiography is considerable. A close reading of the commodity form, money and real and abstract labour allows Chakrabarty to find evidence in Marx's own writing that suggests 'that the total universe of pasts that capital encounters is larger than the sum of those elements in which are worked out the logical presuppositions of capital'.[14] The logic of capital demands that History 1 eventually destroys or subjugate all History 2s. Yet, Marx himself wrote that the limits to capital are 'constantly overcome but just as constantly posited'.[15] Chakrabarty concludes that:

> History 1 and History 2, considered together, destroy the usual topological distinction of the outside and inside that marks debates about whether or not the whole world can be properly said to have fallen under the sway of capital. Difference, in this account, is not something external to capital. Nor is it something subsumed into capital. It lives in intimate and plural relationships to capital ranging from opposition to neutrality.[16]

Chakrabarty's reading demonstrates clearly that built into the logic of capital – whose temporal moment he calls modernity – is historical difference – difference between peoples, nations, races and genders. As it spread globally, capital brought to every place 'some of the universal themes of the European Enlightenment'. This is the history of transition to the capitalist mode of production. It refers to the processes by which History 1 seeks to bring under its sway and domesticate diverse life practices into one, universal register of being human. But part of this process are also acts of 'translation', for which there are no pre-existing blueprints, whereby the universal is modified by History 2s that are as varied as the world itself. It is Chakrabarty's proposition that we make ourselves at home in the otherwise abstracting logic of capital to the degree that our different History 2s are mobilized to modify that logic in the cause of furthering the existence of particular lifeworlds that do not owe their existence, historically speaking, to capital's logic.

What does this mean for the writing of history? Consider the question of place. In the logic of History 1, place is an abstract category, ultimately exchangeable with any other. But History 2 urges the historian to be mindful of the particularities of human experiences in ways that defy such abstracting mechanisms. They draw attention to the particularity of place, regions and localities. The project of provincializing Europe, as the above discussion demonstrates, can only take place in a globalized world – a world already transformed by the spread of Capital and the universal logic of History 1. Now, it is possible that in some particular cases, capital actually furthers specific histories of being human. But the idea of History 2 allows us to find a 'position from which to speak [also] of the losses that globalization causes'.[17] By conceptualizing the history of capitalism and ideas of progress associated with the latter in this manner, the postcolonial critique embodied in *PE* holds up in clear relief the problems of Eurocentrism. But, to provincialize Europe is not to reject the categories of European ideas. It is, rather, to demonstrate the inadequacies of European thought to the task of understanding and explaining the 'plural normative horizons' specific to the lives and existence of different populations in the world.

Chakrabarty's own examples of such history-writing are drawn from late-nineteenth- and early-twentieth-century Bengal. 'In order to provide in-depth historical examination for my propositions', he explains 'I needed to look at a group of people who had been consciously influenced by the ideas of rights, citizenship, fraternity, civil society, politics, nationalism and so on.'[18] So the Bengali middle classes in *PE* are by no means representative of the postcolonial Indian nation. Rather, his point is to show both the indispensability and inadequacy of the categories/concepts of European thought listed above in understanding the history of a social group that had self-consciously seen itself as being moulded by the values drawn from European Enlightenment. For example, in his account of changes in the family system in Bengal at the turn of the twentieth century, Chakrabarty demonstrates the ways in which ideas of the nuclear family were always confronted with competing ideals of devotion of a wife towards her husband, or of children towards their parents. The modern, Bengali, 'nuclear' family thus looks quite different from its counterpart in France or England. Likewise, contemporary memories of the Bengali social practice of *adda* – long, unstructured conversations taking place in public and sometimes private spaces of the city – that may ostensibly resemble the kind of public sphere that Habermas theorized for eighteenth- and nineteenth-century Europe, are eloquently described as 'a requiem for a practice of urban modernism now overtaken by other pleasures and dangers of the city'.[19] Instead of viewing *adda* as symbolic of a lack of modern discipline, since the conversations often took place during the time of work, and as a sign of innate Bengali laziness, Chakrabarty documents it as a social practice deeply rooted in Bengalis' efforts to be at home in modernity.

PE marked a definite step forward in the critique of Eurocentrism pioneered by the likes of Edward Said in *Orientalism*. Its lasting contribution was to introduce ideas of postcoloniality to areas of history-writing hitherto quite removed from such influences. It is important to remind ourselves once more that postcolonial historiography is not symbolic of a nativist turn brought about by an outright rejection of European categories; but a patient historical documentation of the indispensability and inadequacies of these categories in the writing of history. The idea of provincializing Europe is therefore far from a crude or simple-minded project of 'bashing the Enlightenment and modernity', which the historian Frederick Cooper alleges 'have become favorite activities within colonial and postcolonial studies'.[20] The remainder of this chapter illustrates some of the ways in which the idea of provincializing Europe has been taken up and deployed by historians working in other areas.

Postcolonial history and American empire

Postcolonial history-writing involves challenging histories written from the vantage point of hegemonic centres of power. *PE* marked a step forward in this project by opening up new ways of studying the history of imperialism and colonization.

Julian Go's invocation of the ideas of *PE* in his revisionist account of American exceptionalism provides a good starting point to chart the impact of postcolonial history in new areas. Go's work analyses the history of the new American empire in the early twentieth century, when the United States became an empire by formally acquiring previously unincorporated territories. The creation of formal empire also coincided with the earliest articulation of American liberal exceptionalism. Advocates of this thesis readily acknowledged that although an imperial power, the American empire differed substantively from British, Spanish or other empires that preceded it. The claims to exceptionalism stemmed from what was seen as American benevolence in establishing a rule by consent and accommodation in its colonies in a manner unlike the (eighteenth- or nineteenth-century) empires that preceded American domination.

Through a careful analysis of the particular conditions that attended the establishment of American sovereignty on these different territories, Go shows that while US policy in the Philippines was indeed benign, the same did not hold true for Samoa and Guam. Thus the claim to liberal exceptionalism, he argues, needs to be modified according to context. In his argument, even though liberal exceptionalism took colonial form in Puerto Rico and Philippines, it did not originate in America's distinctive political values or special national character. Rather, the tutelage policy emerged from specific features of and developments in the colonies themselves. This illustrates the 'provinciality' of America's empire: if American rule appeared exceptional at all, it was not because of America's exceptional character but for the distinct characteristics of those whom empire aimed to rule.[21]

Critics of the exceptionalism thesis argued that the American empire was not benign at all because 'true' American values and 'character' were rendered corrupt by imperialism. Through a novel application of the idea of provincializing Europe, Go challenges both the proponents and opponents of the exceptionalism thesis. He writes,

> provincializing Europe does not mean wishing traditional European narratives away but rather disclosing how these narratives and 'Europe'

> itself have always been shaped and reshaped in relation to peripheralized spaces and peoples. 'Europe' was never a privileged center that was then extended to the imperial provinces, its very identity and narratives were constituted ... through complex interactions with and in empire's provinces.[22]

Extending the same analogy to American empire, he holds up the blind spots of the liberal exceptionalism thesis. America's professed exceptionalism was not a product of some innate American virtues, but rather the result of interaction between imperial policy and the 'provincial spaces' of empire.

De-centring Europe

The idea of provincializing Europe has also been particularly influential in the writing of revisionist, postcolonial histories of countries considered marginal to Europe, such as Turkey or what in some diplomatic circles is cynically referred to as PIGS (Europe's 'south', consisting of Portugal, Italy, Greece and Spain). Much of this work is a postcolonial, intellectual/literary history that interrogates Eurocentrism through revisionist readings of European literary and philosophical traditions from the vantage point of Europe's borders or margins.

Postcolonial literary history

Roberto Dainotto offers an excellent example of a postcolonial literary history in his article 'The Discreet Charm of the Arabist Theory'. Responding to a call by another postcolonial historian, Gyan Prakash, who noted that it was important for Europeanists to start using the frameworks of postcolonial and subaltern studies, and to Chakrabarty's idea of provincializing Europe, Dainotto provides a 'border gnoseology' in order to 'articulate *from within* Europe ... a critical reflection on knowledge production from ... the interior borders of the modern/colonial world system'.[23] Dainotto argues that the 'Europe' – the hypostatized Europe – that Chakrabarty provincializes in his book was one whose roots go back to the eighteenth century. It was, he notes, a distinctly 'French' or Franco-centred Europe whose conceptualization was being challenged from the eastern and southern margins of the continent. The French Enlightenment made 'reason' the basis of 'modernity'. In so doing French philosophers and encyclopaedists had to render eighteenth-century France the true heir to classical Greece and Rome. At the same time in works like *The Spirit of the Laws* a new world map was drawn that charted a novel spatial history of modernity. All those parts of the world – Asia, Africa, America – where reason did not hold sway and where the rule of law had not been elaborated upon in the manner of post-Frankish France became sites of the 'primitive'. The same hierarchy between modern and barbaric was also projected in denominating certain parts of Europe – Italy and Spain foremost among them – the primitives *within* Europe. Literature played an important role in this characterization of southern Europe as a backward zone within Europe and in holding up France as the true heir of classical civilizations. Petrarch's taste for embellishment and the Spanish baroque were juxtaposed to the French *belle lettres* and (much more) to French thought, reason and the rule of law. These latter qualities made France the centre of Europe's modernity.

Turning his attention to the works of Juan Andres, in particular his *Origin and Progress of All Literature*, Dainotto makes three important moves in order to complicate the notion of historicism, a category central to the project of provincializing Europe. First, he argues that the French Enlightenment had produced 'monologic' histories – that is to say, histories with one telos, from savage to civilized, with one direction of progress 'pointing invariably towards France'. A true historicism 'was a concept of relativism' radically opposed to such a linear notion of progress. It recognized that 'each place has a history of its own – and has to be judged on the basis of this local history, not from the perspective of a putative end of history located in a western and northern modernity'.[24] Progress in this schema was not a teleology of continuous perfectibility but a 'chronological passage of cultural hegemony from one decaying nation to a rising one'.[25] To demonstrate the working of such a historicism Dainotto turns to his second point, an analysis of Juan Andres's history of literature or to what is better known as an Arabist theory. Andres was familiar with Giambattista Vico's *New Science* and probably also had second-hand knowledge of Ibn Khaldoun's *Muqaddimah*. In light of these readings he argued that literature, poetry in particular, could not be judged by exogenous standards but should be seen as 'the manifestation of the particular cultural development' of a given epoch. By these standards Petrarch's poetry or Spanish baroque embodied new heights of literary sophistication and excellence. In saying this, not only did Andres refute the claims of French classicism but also sought the origins of Europe's literary efflorescence in places other than ancient Greece or Rome. Likewise, the future of literature did not stop in Italy but moved in a different trajectory towards Spain.

This brings us to the final point that Dainotto makes, which had to do with the Arabist origins of European literature. True excellence in the art of letters, argued Andres, did not originate in the Frankish schools and monasteries established by Charlemagne, as claimed by Montesquieu and others. Literary scholasticism, which flourished under the Franks, was tied to the Church and was of service to a particular religious spirit. Modern European literature, argued Andres, came from Baghdad. As he noted, following Vico, 'modern literature, not only in the sciences, but also in the Belles Lettres, recognizes the Arab as its mother'.[26] The implication of this for a de-centring of Europe is considerable. As observed by Dainotto, 'Andres was not inventing the Arabist theory. He was, however, taking it away from the restricted domain of Arabists, theorists of national literature, and critics of literary genres.'[27] This rearticulating of an older theory led to the rather controversial claim that the origin of modern Europe was not in France but came from outside Europe. Southern Europe, in particular Spain, became the main receptacle of modernity, which travelled from the Arabs to the Europeans.

The de-centring of a French Europe, as carried out by Andres in his literary history, was not unproblematic. In fact, as observed by Dainotto, nowhere in his *Origins* did Andres display any empathy towards the Arabs, who he referred to as an 'itinerant, nomadic nation' and to Mohammad as 'famoso impostere'.[28] In the end, 'a true European poetry was found by Andres not in places of encounter between Europe and the Arab ... but in a second moment of translation, when whatever the Arab had given Europe was purified and codified into a modern European idiom without any trace of the Arab origin'.[29] Andres' historicism led him to posit an alternative centre of Europe in Spain rather than in France. His Arabist theory, in other words, was utilized to the ultimate end of maintaining Europe (albeit with a different centre) as the sovereign subject of all thought, history and art. It was precisely this shortcoming, concludes Dainotto, that makes Andres 'the allegory of the problems and difficulties we may still face when attempting to provincilize Europe from within its borders'.[30] Despite these problems, Andres's career and corpus highlight the limits of monolithic notions of Eurocentrism and help in reassessing 'the canon of European enlightenment, which besides Paris, and Edinburgh, could start counting ... Italian historicism and Andres' comparative history'.[31]

Postcolonial intellectual history

Where Dainotto deploys the vision of *PE* to sketch a different map of the European Enlightenment in the eighteenth century, Andrew Davison offers a different postcolonial history of Europe via modern Turkish intellectual history. In an essay on the Turkish sociologist, writer and poet Ziya Gokalp (1876–1924), Davison challenges erstwhile analyses of Gokalp's work as incompletely 'westernist' as the latter always maintained that Islam was a crucial component of Turkish identity and culture. Gokalp was a sociologist deeply influenced by the works of Emile Durkheim and Ferdinand Tonnies. 'With the self-understanding of a national sociologist', writes Davison, 'Gokalp adopted and evolved European sociological traditions – positivist idealism, ... solidaristic corporatist, egalitarian nationalism – to specify the conditions and terms under which Turkey could successfully make the transition to modernity.'[32] However, compared to Kemal Ataturk's project of Turkish modernization, Gokalp is often seen, argues Davison, as the 'not yet' in the Turkish nationalist context. Using the paradigm of postcolonial historiography provided by *PE*, Davison attempts to bring together Gokalp's modernist ideas with his championing of a Turkish–Muslim consciousness.

Scholars like Davison or Masami Arai describe Gokalp's project as one of 'modernization other than westernization'.[33] This meant fashioning an ideology of an 'up-to-date Muslim Turkism'. Gokalp executed such a project by drawing a fault line that runs through his entire corpus between the ideas of 'civilization' and 'culture'. The two ideas correspond respectively to international and national life. 'Civilization', according to Gokalp, is a 'society above societies', 'the whole that is common to various nations'.[34] If civilization represented a 'symposium' of which all nations were a part, then culture represented particularity – 'a nation's ethos', its norms regarding beliefs, morality, duty, aesthetics and ideals. It was the 'vernacular' to learn about which the elite must go to the people. For Gokalp, Turkish modernity and progress could be accomplished through 'an awareness of both poles of the civilization/culture dynamic'. Their distinction was critical in order for the Turkish nation to avoid a reductive turn down one or the other path as the 'blind roads of conservatism and radicalism propose'.[35]

Gokalp cautioned that 'It is a mistake to take Modernism as necessarily meaning Europeanism. Modernization and Europeanization are quite different things. … There is a similarity but not identity between the two.'[36] Further elaborating on this distinction, he went on to argue that the Turks should 'take from (European) civilization' the 'methods of linguistics', but 'not a national language'; the 'methods of aesthetics', but 'not standards of beauty'; the 'methods of scientific inquiry in ethics', but 'not a European moral code'. Thus Turkish progress, through the emphasis placed on learning, adhered to certain master narratives of European civilization. But the practices that filled out these narratives were culturally distinct. In Davison's words, 'The application of European concepts and practices shall not apply in the realm of culture – in taste, embodiment, and the cultural training of the senses have received over generations – where great global diversity exists, where the present in radically not-one.'[37]

Central to the assertion of coevality with Europe was a commitment to retaining Turkey's cultural and religious identity. Invoking the example of the Japanese, who 'have been able to take the Western civilization without losing their religion and national identity', Gokalp asked why the Turks 'can't accept Western civilization definitively and still be Turks and Muslims?' This gesture of invoking civilization and culture as a mark of identity with and difference from Europe was Gokalp's admission of the latter's indispensability as well as inadequacy to being the source of modes of 'thought that comes to all human beings naturally'. Indeed, he takes the point about cultural difference, plurality and translation further when he argued that institutions such as the nation, family, state and liberty carry within them a duality of 'form' and 'meaning'. Insofar as culture was a sum total of institutions, it was by definition different in different places.

In Davison's study of Turkish modernity as represented by Gokalp we see clearly a postcolonial turn mediated by the idea of provincializing Europe. To conclude this section with Davison's final reflections on Gokalp, then, political modernity meant for this Turkish ideologue an understanding of

> coeval life practices in modernity – different ways that national cultures world the earth. His critique of the West encompasses a critique of imitationism, arrogant imposition, insensitivity to contemporary sociological trends, inegalitarianism, and most fundamentally, in relation to provincializing Europe, hostility to otherness. Writing from Europe's margins but employing its master codes, he adopted those codes and put his version of the Turkish national cultural stamp … on them.[38]

Postcolonial history as minority history

So far we have demonstrated the ways in which *PE* has enabled historians to mount a critique of Eurocentrism through revisionist historical analyses of nations considered marginal to Europe or, as in the American case, by reassessing some of the ideals undergirding the West's civilizing mission. Another area where the postcolonial vision of *PE* has left a significant legacy has been in raising questions about the nature/norms of historical inquiry itself. One of the main aims of postcolonial history-writing, as mentioned earlier, is to question the hegemonic nature of state-centred narratives and the efficacy of stadial modes of thinking. These types of historical accounts have by definition a certain hierarchy built into them. Any actor/s who behave or live in ways that are at odds with the established teleology of progress (as embodied in the nation state form, or as seen through the rationalist lens of a dominant historiography) are rendered anachronistic and thereby backward in many historical accounts. Postcolonial history-writing fundamentally questions these norms of established historiographical practice. This point can be elaborated with reference to two examples, one relating to the history of magic and the other to the history of religion. A point of clarification is also in order. I do not read the two examples that follow as propagating a kind of historical relativism. Many critics have accused both the project of provincializing Europe, or postcolonial history-writing more generally, of jettisoning the notion of historical truth. It would be more profitable to understand postcolonial history-writing as an enterprise for democratizing history and thereby rendering the notion of historical truth more complex.

> The act of championing minority histories has resulted in discoveries of subaltern pasts, constructions of historicity that help us see the limits to modes of viewing enshrined in practices of the discipline of history. (*PE*, p. 106)

Postcolonial history-writing implies an ethical commitment to narrating subaltern pasts. 'Subaltern pasts' refers to aspects of past experiences or to certain practices by individuals or groups, the retelling of which through the standard paradigms of historiography can often result in a reduction of those experiences. This is especially prominent in histories of religion, occult practices or magic where the historian's anxiety about adhering to the rational codes of history-writing can unwittingly perpetrate what Gayatri Spivak calls a kind of 'epistemic violence' upon past subjects.

Reflecting on the history of magic with reference to two seminal books on the subject – Keith Thomas's *Religion and the Decline of Magic* (1971) and Anthony Grafton's *Cardano's Cosmos* (1999) – Patrick Curry remarks that both books, despite being milestones in historiography, fall short of truly representing their subject's experiences. What is privileged in these works – which are among the best on the subject – is *explanation* rather than *understanding* of past events. In Curry's words,

> They fail to fully respect and accommodate the lived experience of their historical subjects, astrologers and their clients, as *real and true* to exactly same extent, and with the same qualifications, ... as that of the historian writing about them. In a word, they lack *reflexivity*.[39]

Certain pasts, in other words, always retain a subaltern status in academic works. They are for all practical purposes well and truly dead to the point where the lives they document can only ever appear as anachronistic. The point made by historians like Curry is not so much to reject all modes of established historical reasoning, but to recognize that the objectifying mode of reasoning is one, 'albeit a globally dominant one' at present. Such a recognition, he proposes, would lead to a more reflexive historiography that recognizes its own limits. It also allows us to think about historical agency in ways that do not always add up to producing some grand narrative of progress.

The question of agency is also the subject of 'Gender, Agency, and the Divine in Religious Historiography'.[40] The author, Amy Hollywood, acknowledges the ways in which postcolonial historiography and *PE* in particular enable the historian of religion to interrogate established ways of thinking about agency – especially female agency – in medieval Europe. It is noteworthy that in this essay Hollywood returns to her own work on the thirteenth-century medieval saint Mechthild of Madgeburg to question some of her own assumptions in writing about the religious experiences of female saints. Hollywood's argument in the essay is complex, and I can only outline some of her main points here. For Mechthild, indeed for many female religious figures of the medieval period, being able to write or preach the word of God was often attributed to divine agency. In Mechthild's specific case God made her his agent on earth because her femininity made her a better conduit for communicating his message. It was female abjection and humility in Mechthild's account that made for the composition of her book *Flowing Light*. In her 1995 work, Hollywood understood Mechthild's proffered explanation as a means of feminine empowerment in a male-dominated world. Her reading, in other words, attributed a degree of instrumentality to Mechthild's own assertion of her abjectness. Only by proclaiming herself as a docile, powerless, ordinary woman, could Mechthild inhabit a role as theological writer and mystic.

This kind of historical 'explanation' is perfectly in line with existing historiography on the Christian Middle Ages. Historians such as Caroline Walker Bynum, Peter Dronke, Elizabeth Petroff and Barbara Newman have also written about medieval female saints reading their submission as a form of self-authorization and legitimation in a predominantly male-dominated world. Religious studies scholars like Wayne Proudfoot have cautioned that it is important to maintain a distinction between 'explanation' and 'understanding' in reading religious texts so that there is no epistemological haziness around questions of agency. That is to say, even if a group or individual attributed their religiosity or enlightenment to divine benediction it was important for the social scientist to make a distinction between the group or individual's understanding of the event and the analyst's explanation of it.

Hollywood notes that against such a backdrop, there are two sets of related problems that face the historian of religion: first, do all religious subjects, especially female religious subjects, act instrumentally in making God the agent of their actions?; and second, how do we reconcile (or do we need to even acknowledge) the discrepancy between explanation and understanding that is constitutive of the historian's epistemological framework?

It is with these dual dilemmas that Hollywood approaches postcolonial history and in particular Chakrabarty's analysis of agency in *PE* to point towards a novel way of thinking about the medieval female saint's religiosity. She invokes Chakrabarty's conceptualization of History 1 and 2 discussed above and refers to his discussion of an incident from colonial Indian history when some rebellious leaders deposing before a British court noted that they had revolted because

God had told them to. In previous analysis of the latter event, even the most democratic-minded historians have been unable to take the rebels' statements about their behaviour – that God made them rebel – to be the real historical cause for their actions. This inability, Chakrabarty argues, arises from the fact that to attribute agency to supernatural forces in historical analyses is at odds with the secular, universal understanding of temporality on which the discipline of history stands. Yet, the effect of rationalizing past actors' actions through a logic comprehensible to us as moderns does injustice to the historian's commitment to represent the past as accurately as possible.

The way out of this double bind for Chakrabarty, one that Hollywood adopts in her revisionist reading of Mechthild, is to maintain the 'heterogeneity of the moment'. History-writing should maintain a constant tension between the historian's contemporary value system and that of their subjects. For a medieval woman like Mechthild freedom may have had different connotations from our present-day understanding of the concept. At the same time, to completely write history from that medieval perspective may naturalize or legitimize the deep misogyny of that period.

Carolyn Dinshaw's analysis of Margery Kempe raises similar issues and demonstrates the rich yields of bringing to bear some of postcolonial historiography's, in particular *PE*'s, analysis of temporality upon medieval subjects. Margery Kempe, the author of 'the earliest extant autobiographical work in English', *The Book of Margery Kempe* (book one consisting of eighty-nine chapters written between 1436 and 1438, and book two including an additional ten chapters starting in 1438) was born in East Anglia around 1373.[41] She was married at twenty-nine, experienced a difficult childbirth, and tried her hand at business as a brewer and then as a miller. 'Failing spectacularly in these endeavors, she feels chastised by God, and is eventually converted to a passionately devout life.' Her book, which was dictated to priests who wrote it down, is to Dinshaw 'above all a spiritual autobiography', while also being a vivid sketch of the quotidian life of a woman in the Middle Ages.

For Dinshaw, the life of Margery Kempe raises a historical-feminist question: how do we as historians analyse Margery's assertions about her 'union' with Christ? Scholars like Aron Gurevich have remarked on the multiple temporal registers that people in the Middle Ages often seemed to inhabit, some of them contradictory. Thus time was experienced as 'agrarian, genealogical, cyclical, biblical, historical'. But 'Margery repeatedly experiences herself as set apart from her peers, ... joined with the holy but differentiated from her earthly companions. She is an anachronism even in her own (temporally heterogenous) time.'[42]

Herein lay Dinshaw's challenge. As a feminist historian, she feels a commitment to engage seriously Margery's own conception of time – that is, the time of the Middle Ages as well as the time of Christ. In this context Dinshaw invokes

Chakrabarty's ideas about 'good history' and 'subaltern pasts'. Good history-writing – which pushes disciplinary parameters by making the field more inclusive – must still abide by certain basic rules that govern the discipline. For this reason, historical explanation and reasoning must be secular. Academic history cannot conceivably acknowledge supernatural causes for secular, earthly events. This distinguishes history from the realms of memory and myth. And yet, Dinshaw asks, 'what if, in addition to fitting Margery into a history inclusive of gender and sexuality, we also asked following Chakrabarty: "Is [her] way of being a possibility for our own lives and for what we define as our present? Does [Margery] help us to understand a principle by which we also live in certain instances?"'[43] Let me end with Dinshaw's citation of Chakrabarty, only substituting the colonial Indian peasant with the medieval woman. This citation is suggestive of the productive engagement between postcolonial inquiry and medieval history, a theme to be explored at greater length in later pages.

> To stay with the heterogeneity of the moment when the historian meets with [the medieval woman] is, then, to stay with the difference between these two gestures. One is that of historicizing [Margery] in the interest of a history of social justice and democracy; and the other, that of refusing to historicize and of seeing [Margery] as a figure illuminating a life possibility for the present. Taken together, the two gestures put us in touch with the plural ways of being that make up our own present.[44]

Conclusion

The project of provincializing Europe, or questioning Europe's privileged position in historical (or social scientific) explanation, does not belong to the domain of postcolonial history alone. As recently observed by Sanjay Seth, scholars from different disciplinary backgrounds, such as Jack Goody, Andre Gunder Frank, Samir Amin, J. M. Blaut and John Hobson, have all in different ways sought to 'retell the history of the emergence of the modern world in such a way that Europe no longer occupies a position of centrality'.[45] To the above list may also be added historians like Ken Pomeranz, Sanjay Subrahmaniam and Christopher Bayly whose work on the eighteenth- and early-nineteenth-century China, India and the Indian Ocean world has demonstrated, among other things, that the great divergence between Europe and Asia happened long after the Reformation or Enlightenment, as is commonly assumed. The reasons behind Europe's surge were often a set of highly contingent factors (for example, Pomeranz shows how important the discovery of coal was in allowing Europe to move ahead of China) rather than some kind of European exceptionalism. In a similar vein Andre

Gunder Frank, developing his earlier position drawn from world-systems theory, argued in his 1998 book that

> Europe did not pull itself up by its own economic bootstraps, and certainly not thanks to any kind of European 'exceptionalism' of rationality, institutions, entrepreneurship, technology ... instead Europe used its American money to muscle in on and benefit from Asian production, markets, trade – in a word to profit from the predominant position of Asia in the world economy.[46]

If postcolonial histories, histories of the early modern world, as well as historical sociology, are all committed to the project of de-centring Europe or questioning Europe's position as a core or intellectual hegemon in global history, then how might we distinguish between them? Sanjay Seth's aforementioned article helps in answering this question and also enables us draw a distinction between these different methods of offering a critique of Eurocentrism. According to Seth – and I would extend his argument to Sanjay Subrahmaniam, Christopher Bayly and Ken Pomeranz, to name some of the best critics of Eurocentrism in our times – their modus of questioning Europe's privileged place as the harbinger of modernity is to come up with alternatives to 'the conventional historical narrative according to which modernity begins in Europe and then radiates outward'. These historical works are startling for the wide range of archives they tap into, and also for the ways in which they question the divide between the pre-/early modern and modern. More often than not, historians of this group carry out research in more than one language and look at more than one geographical site. The result is often a richly nuanced connected or comparative history that brings together the histories of Europe, Asia, Latin America, in the seventeenth, eighteenth and early nineteenth centuries.

Postcolonial histories, some of which we have discussed and more examples of which will follow in later chapters, start from the premise that many of the concepts driving the discipline of history (or the social sciences more generally) have their provenance in the intellectual and theological traditions of Western Europe. In other words, to recap what was said at the start of this chapter, the postcolonial historian takes very seriously the relationship between 'place' and historical thought. This is not in any way to discount the importance of European categories and concepts to the postcolonial historian's enterprise. Rather, much of their work is devoted to demonstrating the simultaneous 'inadequacy' and 'indispensability' of models derived from European thought in explaining the historical lives of non-Western actors. Postcolonial history-writing inspired by the project of provincializing Europe continues to explore both the 'capacities' and 'limitations' of European social and political categories in the context of non-European lifeworlds.

Thus even when they share the goal of rendering Eurocentric explanations problematic, the fundamental difference in outlook between postcolonial historians and others also produces a difference in the texture of their works. Postcolonial histories, in Seth's words,

> are 'thicker' histories, often based upon archival research and, partly as a result of this, usually confined to one place. ... Unsurprisingly – since their aim is to mobilize a non-Western history or a slice thereof in order to show that the categories through which we think are not fully adequate to their task – what they lack in terms of empirical range, compared to the first group, they make up for with a wider range of theoretical referents.[47]

Thus if the first group of histories contribute towards expanding our knowledge of history, postcolonial history-writing seeks to render problematic some of the governing assumptions of the historical discipline. Of course, they do not have to be competing discourses. Future historians will probably benefit from and bring together both tendencies. In upcoming chapters we will demonstrate the ways in which this critical feature of postcolonial history has been deployed in the writing of historically oriented accounts in the fields of medieval and gender studies.

Notes

1 Dipesh Chakrabarty, *Provincializing Europe: Postcolonial Thought and Historical Difference* (Princeton, NJ: Princeton University Press, 2007), p. xiii.

2 There are a number of remarkable works in South Asian history that have engaged with the ideas of *PE*, and have opened up new avenues of research and writing. Given the rich and varied corpus of this body of work, I can only cite some important books in the hope that it will encourage students interested in that region of the world to analyse them more closely. Debjani Ganguly, *Caste, Colonialism and Counter-modernity: Notes on a Postcolonial Hermeneutics of Caste* (London: Routledge, 2005); Ritu Birla, *Stages of Capital: Law, Culture, and Market Governance in Late Colonial India* (Durham, NC: Duke University Press, 2009); Sanjay Seth, *Subject Lessons: The Western Education of Colonial India* (Durham, NC: Duke University Press, 2007); Rochona Majumdar, *Marriage and Modernity: Family Values in Colonial Bengal* (Durham, NC: Duke University Press, 2009). A recent review essay by Ajay Skaria discusses the project of provincializing Europe by looking closely at *PE* as well as Chakrabarty's other work. See Ajay Skaria, 'The Project of Provincializing Europe: Reading Dipesh Chakrabarty', *Economic and Political Weekly* 44(14) (4 April 2009), pp. 52–9.

3 Chakrabarty, *PE*, p. xiii.

4 Chakrabarty, *PE*, p. 27.

5 Chakrabarty, *PE*, p. 28.

6 Chakrabarty, *PE*, p. 7.

7 Chakrabarty, *PE*, pp. 8–9.

8 Chakrabarty, *PE*, pp. 10–11. Bhabha used the 'performative' and pedagogical to invoke the dual temporality of the nation form in his well-known essay 'DissemiNation'. For him the pedagogical was 'based on the pre-given or constituted historical origin *in the past*' while the performative was 'that sign of the *present* through which national life is redeemed and iterated as a reproductive process'. Homi Bhabha, 'DissemiNation', in *The Location of Culture* (London: Routledge, 1994), p. 145 (emphasis in the original).

9 Chakrabarty acknowledges that the division between the two traditions of philosophy is artificial since most thinkers share a degree of overlap. He makes the distinction more as a heuristic device for his own analysis. Chakrabarty, *PE*, p. 18.

10 Chakrabarty, *PE*.

11 Chakrabarty, *PE*.

12 Chakrabarty, *PE*.

13 Chakrabarty, *PE*, p. 63 (words in parenthesis mine).

14 Chakrabarty, *PE*, p. 64.

15 Cited in Chakrabarty, *PE*, p. 65.

16 Chakrabarty, *PE*, pp. 65–6.

17 Chakrabarty, *PE*, p. xix. Chakrabarty is referring here to a reading of his book in Paul Steven's essay 'Heterogenizing Imagination: Globalization, *The Merchant of Venice* and the Work of Literary Criticism', *New Literary History* 36(3) (2005), pp. 425–37.

18 Chakrabarty, *PE*, p. 21.

19 Chakrabarty, *PE*, p. 182.

20 Frederick Cooper, *Colonialism in Question. Theory, Knowledge, History* (Berkeley and Los Angeles, CA: University of California Press, 2005), p. 6.

21 Julian Go, 'The Provinciality of American Empire: Liberal Exceptionalism and U.S. Colonial Rule, 1898–1912', *Comparative Studies in Society and History* 49(1) (2007), pp. 76–7.

22 Go, 'The Provinciality of American Empire', p. 102.

23 Roberto M. Dainotto, 'The Discreet Charm of the Arabist Theory: Juan Andres, Historicism, and the De-centering of Montesquieu's Europe', *European Historical Quarterly* 36(1) (2006), p. 8 (emphasis in the original).

24 Dainotto, 'The Discreet Charm of the Arabist Theory', p. 18.

25 Dainotto, 'The Discreet Charm of the Arabist Theory'.

26 Dainotto, 'The Discreet Charm of the Arabist Theory', p. 22.

27 Dainotto, 'The Discreet Charm of the Arabist Theory'.

28 Dainotto, 'The Discreet Charm of the Arabist Theory', p. 23.

29 Dainotto, 'The Discreet Charm of the Arabist Theory'.

30 Dainotto, 'The Discreet Charm of the Arabist Theory', p. 25.

31 Dainotto, 'The Discreet Charm of the Arabist Theory', p. 26.

32 Andrew Davison, 'Ziya Gokalp and Provincializing Europe', *Comparative Studies of South Asia, Africa, and the Middle East* 26(3) (2006), p. 80.

33 Arai Masami, *Turkish Nationalism in the Young Turk Era* (Leiden: E.J. Brill, 1992).

34 Davison, 'Ziya Gokalp and Provincializing Europe', p. 82.

35 Davison, 'Ziya Gokalp and Provincializing Europe'.

36 Davison, 'Ziya Gokalp and Provincializing Europe', pp. 84–5.

37 Davison, 'Ziya Gokalp and Provincializing Europe', p. 85.

38 Davison, 'Ziya Gokalp and Provincializing Europe', p. 89.

39 Patrick Curry, 'The Historiography of Astrology: A Diagnosis and A Prescription', in K. von Stuckrad, G. Oestmann and D. Rutkin (eds), *Horoscopes and Public Spheres : Essays on the History of Astrology* (Berlin and New York, NY: Walter de Gruyter, 2005), p. 264.

40 Amy Hollywood, 'Gender, Agency, and the Divine in Religious Historiography', *The Journal of Religion* 84(4) (2004), pp. 514–28.

41 Carolyn Dinshaw, 'Margery Kempe', in Carolyn Dinshaw and David Wallace (eds), *The Cambridge Companion to Medieval Women's Writing* (Cambridge: Cambridge University Press, 2003), pp. 222–39.

42 Dinshaw, 'Margery Kempe', p. 236.

43 Dinshaw, 'Margery Kempe', p. 236.

44 Dinshaw, 'Margery Kempe', p. 237.

45 Sanjay Seth, 'Historical Sociology and Postcolonial Theory: Two Strategies for Challenging Eurocentrism', *International Political Sociology* 3(3) (2009), p. 334.

46 Andrew Gunder Frank, *ReOrient: Global Economy in the Asian Age* (Berkeley, CA: University of California Press, 1998), pp. 4–5.

47 Sanjay Seth, 'Historical Sociology and Postcolonial Theory', p. 335.

4

Postcolonial medieval history

Even though it might initially appear to be an oxymoron, postcolonial histories of the Middle Ages have emerged as a thriving area of historical scholarship over the last decade. While some medieval historians have with good reason cautioned that a 'postcolonial society has a historical specificity and density that is not easily translated into premodern worlds'[1], others have demonstrated how postcolonial approaches to the European Middle Ages can yield important historiographical insights into both medievalism and postcoloniality. As was hinted at in the previous chapter, some practitioners of medieval history have engaged in a sustained dialogue with the idea of provincializing Europe. In what follows, I want to elaborate further on the nature of this engagement, by expanding it into a survey of what may be characterized as a revisionist approach to the study of medieval history. Postcolonial theory has been an important tool for medievalists who have undertaken such revisionist approaches. I say 'medievalists' rather than medieval historians because the medieval–postcolonial nexus includes a range of scholars whose disciplinary affiliations are varied. Nonetheless, their contributions, as we shall see, have expanded and enriched the history and conceptualization of the Middle Ages and the medieval, and evoked lively debates within the discipline of history.

There are three related areas in which the synergy between postcoloniality and medieval history may be considered. First, medieval historians have drawn upon postcolonial theories of temporality in order to interrogate the practice of historical periodization that is so central to the historian's craft. Periodization, they have argued, was never an innocent gesture and was always inextricably related to questions of politics. Thus, the consigning of the medieval period to the 'dark ages' of European history, neatly boxed in the millennium stretching from the fall of the Roman Empire to the Renaissance and Reformation, was, as many scholars have demonstrated, tied with questions of European imperialism, colonialism and sovereignty. The insights drawn from this body of medieval historical work make us aware of the ideological power wielded by those (peoples, institutions, nation states) who deploy the category of the medieval to critique certain social formations. Secondly, infused with a postcolonial temper, many revisionist works demonstrate the myriad ways in which the Middle Ages haunt debates about modernity from the late eighteenth to the twentieth centuries. Rather than regard the medieval and modern as hermetically sealed units of time and culture, scholars have demonstrated how ideas of the medieval were constitutive of the modern. In addition, the presence of medieval traces in the modern signals certain recalcitrant and critical currents within modernity. Finally, many medievalists have also drawn upon postcolonial critiques of Eurocentrism, calling into question the spatial conception of the Middle Ages as a purely European phenomenon. By tracking the histories of empire, nationalism and imperialism they have shown the heterogeneous territorial spread of medieval histories. In sum, it may be argued that the traffic between medieval and postcolonial studies takes many routes. For some scholars, it is not so much a question of describing the so-called Middle Ages in their own terms as asking what contemporary purpose such a periodizing device served. For many others, the project is to deploy some of the tools of post- or even anti-colonial theory to describe and analyse the so-called medieval period.

As demonstrated in previous chapters, postcolonial historiography is fuelled by a commitment to democratizing the discipline of history through a fundamental questioning of certain disciplinary parameters. Likewise, historians committed to writing postcolonial histories of the Middle Ages, through their aforementioned criticisms of temporality and spatiality, have sought to widen the disciplinary contours of medieval history. These interventions have not only informed the writing of new medieval histories but have also challenged some of the foundational assumptions of postcolonial theory. These challenges are attended to briefly in the concluding section of this chapter.

Beginnings

Kathleen Biddick's *The Shock of Medievalism*, published in 1998, was an early and controversial sounding of this critical temper in medieval history-writing. Biddick's intention in this work was to historicize medieval studies in order to bring to view some of the anxieties and presuppositions that marked the founding of the field and that still influence the work done under the aegis of medieval studies. The orthodoxy of medieval studies, she demonstrates, was a by-product of colonial and imperial apprehensions in the nineteenth century, when the historical study of the Middle Ages was founded as a discipline in England: 'In order to separate and elevate themselves from popular studies of medieval culture, the new academic medievalists of the nineteenth century designated their practices, influenced by positivism, as scientific and eschewed what they regarded as less positivist, "non-scientific" practices, labeling them medievalism.'[2] The banishing of certain areas of inquiry to a putative outside or exterior had the effect of establishing medieval history as a field marked by what many historians celebrated as the field's 'hard-edged alterity'. Biddick was also critical of the 'new medievalism', a trend of scholarship where contemporary medievalists distanced themselves from the nineteenth-century 'fathers' or founders of the discipline. These distancing gestures resulted in an ironic inversion whereby modern-day scholars reinforced 'the interior and external boundaries of the discipline' rather than questioned how these boundaries were instituted in the first place. One of the most contested and challenging intimations yet issued by a medieval historian to open up medieval studies to insights drawn from postcolonial, feminist and queer studies, Biddick's *The Shock of Medievalism* rejected historians' anxieties about presentism, their antipathy towards 'theory', and the separation of medieval studies and medievalism as it undertook the task of historicizing medieval studies.[3]

The Shock of Medievalism is a study of five wide-ranging cases. Let me discuss two of these as examples of the kind of history-writing Biddick advocated. The book opens by returning to the founding moments of medieval history as a discipline. Biddick details the events surrounding the appointment of Bishop Stubbs to the position of Regius Professor of Modern History at the University of Oxford in 1866. Stubbs's appointment marked the beginnings of the practice of scientific history in England, a mode of historical inquiry widely associated with the work of Leopold Von Ranke in the European continent. What often gets elided from the history of Stubbs's appointment is the fact that he succeeded Goldwin Smith who, according to Biddick, 'resigned' from his Oxford chair during the controversy that erupted in England after the Jamaica uprising of 1865. The Morant Bay uprising, which is discussed in some detail in the next chapter, involved the British governor, Edward John Eyre, ordering severe reprisals against 'rebels' who rioted against British land and labour policies in Jamaica. Eyre's actions roiled the British public sphere and revealed stark polarities within Britain on issues of race and colonial policy. Goldwin Smith expressed opinions against Eyre that eventually forced his 'resignation'. Smith was a historian who used his historical insights to comment on events of his own time.

Once appointed the Regius professor, Stubbs resolutely refused to teach modern history beyond the early seventeenth century and never wrote for the wider public as did his predecessor. This was a gesture calculated to show the boundaries proper to any historical inquiry. Concerns stemming out of present-day realities were definitely not within the ambit of History for Stubbs. His one 'deeply political' project was championing the Gothic architectural revival in the British Empire. This commitment to Gothic art, its renovation and preservation together with Stubbs's refusal to allow 'presentism' (an engagement with contemporary events) to contaminate historical studies makes Stubbs an important figure for an understanding of the nature of medieval history as it came to be practised in the academy. Biddick argues that at 'the center of an incipient medieval studies we thus hear the monastic-like silence of Bishop Stubbs. This silence continues to leave unspoken the conditions of his appointment in the midst of a traumatic debate over British colonial race relations conjoined with the colonial transformation of the British university.'[4]

The Stubbs story serves as a paradigm for the other examples that Biddick discusses in her book. Taken together they argue the case for historicizing medieval history by contextualizing the nineteenth century and later renewal of interest in certain themes from the Middle Ages in terms of modern colonial and postcolonial developments. One such theme centres on exploring why the leading history journal, *Past and Present,* founded in 1952, devoted a good deal of attention to the story of Robin Hood in its early years. Biddick offers an innovative and unconventional explanation of this issue by tying the historical resurgence of interest in Robin Hood to Britain's loss of India in the mid-twentieth century. Colonial India, she argues, represented for metropolitan Englishmen England's rural/pastoral past. There – so thought English civil servants, administrators and liberal thinkers – could be found the village community and land tenure processes they imagined for the Anglo-Saxon village.

As English historians in the nineteenth century embarked on the project of writing 'progressive histories of national freedom', they appropriated German scholarship on the Teutonic village community as a 'guide for imagining Saxon villages as the laboratory for democracy'.[5] But this imaginary rural past was found not in industrializing England, but in colonized India. The Teutonic village, mediated by English ideas of a rural past, was mapped on to the putative Indo-Aryan village community. Henry Maine's *Village Communities in the East and West* (1871) 'helped produce India as the rural past of England and England as the colony's constitutional future'.[6] Decolonization severed England from this imaginary rural past found in India. The surge of interest around Robin Hood was one expression of the many ways devised by contemporaries for dealing with that sense of loss. The articles on Robin Hood in *Past and Present,* in Biddick's analysis, signal a historical search for a new pastoral history of the English peasant in the aftermath of decolonization. It was an effort on the part of English historians to 'recover the medieval English village and, in so doing, to work out the problems of continuity and change for an "imperial-national" culture'.[7]

Periodization and its problems

Many of Biddick's ideas have invoked sustained and important criticisms from medieval historians. Notably, Gabrielle Spiegel faults Biddick for anachronistically applying theoretical frameworks (such as postcolonialism) to the medieval period without first demonstrating their relevance for an understanding of medieval history.[8] Related to this is Spiegel's second criticism, which has to do with questioning why medieval studies should 'create connections and pursuits in tune with contemporary interests'.[9] We will return to these concerns later on in this chapter, as they remain fundamental to any consideration of a postcolonial medieval historiography. Suffice it to say for now that *The Shock of Medievalism* remains important as an early instantiation of medieval scholarship's engagement with postcolonial criticism. Since then, postcolonial approaches to the Middle Ages have witnessed an array of important works that have furthered directions of historical inquiry. One significant intervention comes from the writings of Kathleen Davis.

Davis's *Periodization and Sovereignty* (2008) poses a radical challenge to a foundational assumption of modern historical consciousness: that a secular modernity was born out of a final rupture with a religious, feudal Middle Ages. This mode of periodization, which juxtaposes a feudal, religious, irrational Middle Ages to an enlightened, capitalist, secular modernity, provides the bulwark for the transition narratives common to much historical work. It also lies at the heart of histories of development in poorer nations, which are labelled advanced or backward depending on how much distance their economic organization and growth measure from that which is regarded as 'medieval' in their pasts. Readers will be also be aware of the rampant use of the label 'medieval' in contemporary political and media representations of countries such as Iraq, Somalia or Afghanistan – a label that signals their innate otherness from the West and heightens the urgency for military and other modes of intervention so that they may be brought in line with (Western) modernity.[10] Davis's goal is 'to address the occlusions and reifications' that underlie the historical practice of periodization. She asks: 'why in the face of all challenges to teleological and stage-oriented histories, do the monoliths medieval/religious/feudal and modern/secular/capitalist (or developed) survive and what purposes to they serve?'[11]

Davis's questions are urgent since the Middle Ages do not simply operate as a European phenomenon. They have come to be metonymic for all those areas of the world where there is a crisis or absence of a sovereign, secular state. For this reason, 'the "Middle Ages" like "modernity" before it, has been vaulted from a European category to a global category of time'.[12] The result is a certain contradiction that marks many historical works. On the one hand, we organize the political, cultural, social and economic histories of Asia, Africa, Europe or the

Middle East according to the temporal division of ancient/medieval/modern, as if the whole world 'moves in unison, in tempo with a once European story written at the height of, and in tandem with, colonialism, nationalism, imperialism, and orientalism'.[13] On the other hand, and this marks the irony of periodization, the 'Middle Ages' have become a descriptive marker for any region of the world where conditions of life do not match the normative conditions of modernity. The Middle Ages thus describe all 'backward' or 'retrograde' regions and practices that need to be pulled back into the comity of advanced nations or stamped out altogether by an exposure to enlightened views to enable the universal march towards modernization and modernity. Periodization, then, not only orders historical scholarship, and the organization of history departments in universities, but also the modern political arena. This mode of reasoning about the Middle Ages supports Davis's provocative statement in making which she states her affiliation with the postcolonial scholarship of Lisa Lowe, David Lloyd and Dipesh Chakrabarty: 'Periodization ... does not refer to a mere back-description that divides history into segments, but to a fundamental political technique – a way to moderate, divide, and regulate – always rendering its services now. In an important sense, we cannot periodize the past.'[14]

Davis elaborates on her critique of periodization by studying the history of two central concepts associated with the Middle Ages: feudalism and secularization. 'The history of periodization', she shows through a careful and wide-ranging analysis of texts, 'is juridical, and it advances through struggles over the definition and location of sovereignty.'[15]

It is a well-known historical fact that while the adjective 'feudal' has been in circulation since the tenth century, 'feudalism' as a noun that describes an entire epoch came into existence only in the eighteenth century, particularly during the tumult of ideas during the French Revolution. By this time, it became a political pejorative that stood for a European past, and the present of many European colonies. How did this come to be? Davis's analysis of legal and juridical texts from the sixteenth to the eighteenth century shows a complex two-stage process at work in the creation of a 'feudal Middle Ages'.

The first stage addresses some sixteenth-century jurists who turned to a study of feudal law – the fief, the feudal relation between the monarch, lords and subjects – in order to arrive at an understanding of the category of sovereignty. Feudal law refers to an eclectic collection of Roman law treatises called the *Libri Feudorum* dating back to the twelfth century, which contained commentaries on fiefs. Focusing on the commentaries of the *Libri* by the professional legists (or 'feudists' as they were called) Ulrich Zassius (1461–1535), Charles du Moulin (1500–66) and Francois Hotman (1524–90), Davis charts the process by which a feudal historiography was developed by these men in the context of political struggles between the Habsburgs and France, and the French civil wars.

What clearly emerges from Davis's study of these works is, firstly, that French, Italian and German legists turned to the feudal past to trace the origins of their respective national cultures. In crafting these stories, they attributed to feudal law different national origins. For du Molin, invested in forwarding France's claims to sovereignty from the Empire, feudal law was of Frankish origin. The Italian and German legists, however, argued for a Roman origin of the same law in order to safeguard Roman power and the Habsburg Empire. Secondly, these feudists also had a conflicted relationship to the Renaissance humanism of Petrarch and Lorenzo Valla. While they all wanted to follow the Petrarchan dictate of purifying feudal texts by purging them of 'postclassical barbarism', they differed on whether or not to reject outright feudal laws and legal commentaries. And finally, commentaries on the feudal relation between lord and vassal or the fief more generally served as the foundation for competing theories of sovereignty.

Even this brief summary shows that feudal law, as embodied by the *Libri*, had a vexed relationship to Roman law. This insight puts a question mark over claims that favour a clean break between the medieval dark ages and the rebirth of Europe from the Renaissance onwards. All the jurists from the sixteenth century mentioned above clearly sought their national origins in a medieval past. There, they searched for a justification for regimes in their contemporary societies.

The second part of Davis's argument about feudalism demonstrates the ways in which the yields of the juridical literature discussed above were pressed into the service of arguments about slavery. In the hands of jurists like du Molin, the interpretation of feudal law was aligned to the political goals of royal absolutism. du Molin interpreted the feudal relationship of 'homage' in such a way as to snuff out all other ties that a subject may have by insisting that the only proper relationship of subjection was the one between king and subjects. Within a generation after du Molin, this interpretation of feudal law was used by Jean Bodin (1530–96) to critique slavery and thereby to reject du Molin's account as a positive description of contemporary Europe. Feudal Europe, where those in conditions of vassalage rendered homage to the absolute monarch, became Europe's past, or was pushed outwards to places in Europe's margins or to the faraway lands of Asia and Africa.

What is discussed above constitutes Davis's argument about feudalism and periodization. In the remainder of the book she carries out a similar critique of the idea of secularism and its alleged absence from the Middle Ages. Taken together, the book shows how in the contemporary world feudalism and secularization are political concepts that are made to perform the political and cultural labour of converting vast sections of the world's population into inert masses trapped in a static past. Missing from the everyday usage of the expression 'secularization' is the awareness that 'secularism is a name Christianity gave itself when it invented religion, when it named its other or others as religions'.[16]

Likewise, feudalism shorn of its historical complexity became a story of peasant oppression and backwardness, which placed 'slavery in Europe's past and elsewhere so that Europe's, and then America's, story of rising political freedom and democracy could unfold as antithetical to that slavery and subjugation, even though the history of this democracy has developed hand in hand with the enslavement and economic oppression of millions'.[17]

Davis links the grand narrative of European progress with the ways in which particular concepts – feudalism and secularization in her case – were pressed into the service of periodization and sovereignty. Periodization, she demonstrates, is a condition for certain claims to sovereignty. This conjoining of progress and periodization reifies these concepts and erases them of their specific and complex histories. A critical 'postcolonial medievalism'[18] approaches the past to analyse the history of such erasures.

Colonialism and the Middle Ages

The complicity between ideas of the Middle Ages and practices of colonization is a theme that dominates many revisionist works of medieval history. In the Introduction to a collection of essays that appeared in a special issue of the *Journal of Medieval and Early Modern Studies* (2000), John Dagenais and Margaret Greer noted that, as metropolitan powers conquered the colonies, three processes occurred simultaneously. First, the native, his (*sic*) practices and understanding were marked out as primitive, distant and foreign in comparison to the colonizers. Secondly, this otherness was rendered comprehensible by putting it on a time map – the native's present was the colonizer's past. Ironically, even though they inhabited different spaces, peoples of the newly colonized lands and the Middle Ages were seen as belonging to the same temporal moment. Finally, the natural flow of native history was halted with the arrival of the colonial power. Much as the coming of modernity stopped the Middle Ages, so also the multiplicity of native lifeworlds came under pressure to conform to the linear, homogeneous time associated with European ideas of progress.

On the basis of these insights, Dagenais and Greer issue the following provocation: 'Is it possible to colonize a region of history, as it is to colonize a region of geography?' The response, it would seem from their analysis, is a resounding yes. Many works of medieval history have now demonstrated that the Middle Ages as a historical category were coeval with the moment of European imperial and colonial expansion. As Europe undertook to spread its 'civilizing mission' over large swathes of the world, the Middle Ages were christened as Europe's dark continent of history in much the same manner as Africa became the dark continent of geography.

> There can be no continuity, no impinging of time (and of peoples) which might threaten to link the Middle Ages in a natural way to present history. The chronological rupture cleaving the Middle Ages from history must be absolute so that any genealogies (say the Middle Ages as 'Europe's infancy') can be constructed under present control, any miscegenation carefully regulated, even if it cannot entirely be suppressed. The manifest history of the West ought to run directly from the brilliance of Antiquity to its natural successors in Petrarch and others. The thousand years which intervene are a gaping hole in history. But this gap can be made to serve in the writing of a typological history of the West.[19]

Yet, as many recent works by medievalists have demonstrated, the boundaries between the Middle Ages and modernity were just as porous as those separating colonizer and colonized. A number of books published in the last few years take a postcolonial turn to demonstrate the links between the medieval and the modern, as well the presence of the medieval in the modern.[20] Let me briefly illustrate the nature of this analysis by referring to a few select works in some detail. The yield of these works is to further nuance not only our understanding of colonialism and the Middle Ages, but also to challenge the notion of colonialism as an early modern or modern phenomenon.

In this connection it is also important to note that recent scholarly efforts have sought to extend the idea of the 'medieval' to spaces outside of Europe – to places as diverse as Mexico, West Africa, India, Australia, Lebanon and Latin America. Their authors' objective is to analyse the ways in which 'medievalism' operated in the colonies and postcolonies; to demonstrate what happened to the idea of the medieval when it was deployed in non-European sites. Such emphases not only pluralize the idea of medievalism, but also demonstrate that the Middle Ages as a category was a historical/intellectual creation that came into being in tandem with processes of imperialism and colonialism. As academic work on the 'idea of the Middle Ages outside Europe', is very much an ongoing project, I can only mention some of them at this point.[21]

In her essay 'Analogy in Translation: Rome, England, India' (2005),[22] Ananya Kabir analyses a series of literary and historical works, from the late eighteenth and early nineteenth centuries, by British scholar administrators and historians to demonstrate the way in which these writers modelled their mission in India on imperial Rome. Soon, however, the early interest of colonial Orientalist scholars ('emergent comparative linguists before the advent of Indo-European scholarship proper') gave way to the zealous Anglicist reform of men like Thomas Macaulay and Charles Trevelyan. At this point, argues Kabir, 'analogy' between Roman Britain and India became 'teleology'. For Orientalists like William Jones, John Gilchrist, James Tod, H. T. Colebrooke and Nathaniel Halhed the analogy between the English Middle Ages and early colonial India did not simply mean that they compared late-eighteenth-century India to the English Middle Ages. Rather, by making conquest the 'dynamo of cultural change' – the Roman conquest of England and the Muslim conquest of India – they put 'into the same discursive arena the relationship between Saxon and Norman on the one hand, and that between Hindu and Muslim on the other'.[23] This gesture enabled the Orientalists to map the development of English from 'the parent Saxon' on to north Indian languages such as Hindustani. Orientalists, according to Kabir, had a deep appreciation for Indian languages. To them Sanskrit or Persian were comparable to Greek or Latin while Bengali, Hindi and other vernaculars were likened to English and French. Orientalist reform in India therefore focused on the question of which of these – the classical or the vernacular – should receive state patronage. Analogy between the English Middle Ages and colonial India served a descriptive purpose for the Orientalists.

In the hands of their Anglicist successors, analogy turned more judgmental, whereby both the Middle Ages and nineteenth-century India presented historical conditions that had to be superseded in order to usher in a progressive modernity. Focusing primarily on the English government's language and education policy in India, Kabir draws attention to the implicit hierarchy in statements made by Lord Macaulay. In his (in)famous *Minute on Indian Education* (1835), Macaulay argued that just as the Renaissance brought back culture to the hitherto unrefined literatures (the chronicle and the romance) of the Saxons and Normans, so also should post-Reformation English literature be made to replace learning in the Indian vernacular or classical languages so as to usher in an Indian 'renaissance'. Unlike the Orientalists, the Anglicists regarded both classical and vernacular Indian languages as 'medieval'. State patronage, they argued, should be turned away from both these language clusters and used to promote the study of English if the Indian colony was to be marched towards modernity.

Macaulay's opinions were echoed by his contemporary Trevelyan, who noted that 'the study of English, and with it the knowledge of learning of the West, is ... the first stage whereby India is to be enlightened'.[24] Analogy was still at work in Trevelyan and Macaulay's reformism. For, just the revival of classical learning during the Renaissance elevated modern European languages from their 'barbarous' state, so also Indian vernaculars devoid of literatures had to be refined by an exposure to English. But, this time around, analogy had also become teleological. Nineteenth-century India was compared to medieval England in order to legitimize British tutelage over the colony. India, like medieval England, was backward and could only be rescued from that condition by the British to follow on a path previously charted out by them.

It must be qualified that the debate between the Orientalists and Anglicists discussed above was not a simple battle between the mutually opposed forces of indigenization and Westernization. As recently argued by the postcolonial scholar Debjani Ganguly, both groups and their Indian supporters deemed the introduction of English education in India as necessary and inevitable. The fundamental difference, argues Ganguly, lay in the way in which each group gave practical expression to their education policies and the place they accorded to the colony's existing repertoire of texts and resources. As she writes,

> to the Orientalists, India's classical and Perso-Arabic heritage was rich and capacious enough to accommodate, transfigure and even rejuvenate European knowledge forms. They favored a form of English education that could be grafted on and enhance the already existing civilizational depth of India represented by its classical Sanskrit heritage and a courtly Persian culture.[25]

For these reasons they opposed a viewpoint, one represented by the Anglicists, which regarded the introduction of English as a 'progressive' world language that would stamp out the supposedly dying linguistic and cultural remnants of India's pre-modernity. Anglicists like Macaulay saw no practical value in India's classically inspired pedagogy and culture. Labelling these as medieval, they ruled that English education was the remedy for both administrative reform and the antidote needed to rejuvenate Indian vernaculars through a process of transmission and osmosis. The English Middle Ages was the strategic metaphor, the 'analogy', as Kabir puts it, which the Anglicists deployed to make their case about Indian backwardness.

By focusing on processes of cultural translation – between the English Middle Ages and late-eighteenth and early-nineteenth-century India – Kabir demonstrates (1) the close links between the colonial enterprise and a discourse about the 'medieval'; (2) the variegated nature of the medieval in its modern deployment; and (3) the presence of the medieval in the shaping of colonial policies. Such a strategic deployment of the idea of the Middle Ages was not unique to British education and language policies in India alone. Elsewhere, Kabir illustrates the medievalism at work in British land reform policies in the Indian subcontinent.[26]

A very different articulation of a postcolonial medievalism may be found in Nicholas Howe's, 'Anglo-Saxon England and the Postcolonial Void' (2005).[27] Howe makes a case for analysing the history of Anglo-Saxon England during the years 410–597, between the times that the Roman legions withdrew from England and the arrival of Christian missionaries in the later Anglo-Saxon period, as a postcolonial society. His work, like that of Kofi O. S. Campbell, questions the established temporality of colonialism by placing it within the Middle Ages.[28]

Howe demonstrates that English identification with the Roman Empire actually began in the postcolony – that is, after the formal withdrawal of the Roman imperium from Britain. Proceeding from the premise that 'postcolonial literature is that which critically scrutinizes the colonial relationship', Howe mines authors like Gildas and Bede and poems such as *The Wanderer*, *The Ruin* and *Maxims II* for the ways in which the memory of imperial Rome was etched in these writings, particularly the references to Roman buildings, stones and spolia. These literary texts are complemented by a close study of ecclesiastical architecture of the period to demonstrate that Rome actually became the imperial capital of the province of Britannia during the years *after* the formal withdrawal of Empire. It became so 'in a spiritual and ecclesiastical fashion that was radically different from its role as imperial capital' of England, 'yet that also depended on this previous instantiation'.[29]

The Romanization of Britain was widely manifest in literary and artistic remnants from the English Middle Ages. Whether it was Gildas mourning the loss of a civilized world embodied in the stone monuments and the roads built by the Romans, now under attack from the barbarian hordes; or Bede writing about the use of stone and spolia in the monastic church at Jarrow; or the church of St John at Escomb in County Durham featuring an arch that was probably taken entirely from a Roman building – Rome was a living memory in early Anglo-Saxon England. Howe focuses on the landscape of Anglo-Saxon England as a way to study a society where literacy in Latin or Old English was a rare skill. His turn to these 'monumental accounts' is also an effort to respond to potential sceptics who would question his characterization of this society as postcolonial.

For instance, some might object to Howe's reading of the arch in the church of Escomb – a Roman arch placed in an Anglo-Saxon construction – as evidence of postcoloniality, 'as a clever playing with historical materials in an act of interpretive bricolage'. Is it plausible to think, sceptics might ask, that any Anglo-Saxon at the time would have thought in such a manner about the traces of empire in the former island kingdom? Howe offers three provisional answers to such objections. First, the artistry with which the spolia was integrated into the church demonstrated that the builders had an acute awareness of its beauty and significance. Secondly, supplementing an analysis of the architecture with the literary sources mentioned above suggests that Anglo-Saxons writing in either Latin or Old English were 'interested in the history of building stones and in the ways they demarcated historical periods'. And finally, Howe argues that there is no reason to assume that 'those who lived during the period were somehow less alert to the complications of their own history than we are some twelve hundred years later'.

Howe concludes that 'relations between metropole and colony, center and periphery, cannot be set in a single unchanging relation of the powerful and dispossessed'. Rome remained the imperial capital of Britain even after the formal departure of the Romans through the experience of Christianity as well in as in the memory of a civilization that had departed. The postcolonial thrust of Howe's analysis is strongest when he makes a case for Rome as a living memory in Britain, a memory fuelled not by anti-colonial sentiments but by postcolonial affect.

Howe's analysis highlights the natural affinity between a medievalist's methodological training and the postcolonial scholar's optic of viewing the world. The former's training makes the medievalist 'aware of the multivalent worlds that are brought together in material objects, as well as of the effects of centuries of acts of interpretation upon these objects. ... (T)exts, manuscripts, paintings, churches, maps, or other artifacts ... show the presence of temporal layers and vestiges of their multifaceted reception.'[30] These 'methodological inflections, and not just the transfer of specific insights from postcolonialism ... the careful work of embedding that we find in medieval studies' remarked Ato Quayson, is what opens up a productive conversation between the two fields.[31]

My final example of a postcolonial medievalism is drawn from the settler colonial context of Australia. Compared to Kabir's analysis, this offers a different colonial translation of Victorian medievalism. As argued by Louise D'Arcens in an essay entitled 'Antipodean Idylls: An Early Australian Translation of Tennyson's Medievalism' (2003), it is critical to extend the scope of Victorian medievalism to colonial settings in order to have a fuller understanding of the role of medievalism in colonial, imperial and national histories. Her goal in this essay is also to go beyond analyses of medievalism's role as a 'vehicle for imperialist ideals' to include an analysis of it as a discourse central to practices of colonialism. Such a reorientation shows how conventional notions of Victorian medievalism could be put into new uses in the colony.

D'Arcens's subject in this essay is John Woolley, Principal and first Professor of Classics at Sydney University from 1852. Woolley's public addresses, private letters and the syllabi he designed for the University bore marks of his deep admiration for Alfred Tennyson's *Idylls*, one of the most well-known texts associated with Victorian medievalism. Significantly, however, his reading of Tennyson's *Idylls* differed in telling ways from that of his counterparts in Britain. In the context of a settler society, Woolley recast Tennyson's literary rendering of the Arthurian past to make it relevant to the conditions on the ground in Australia. Each one of Tennyson's characters and places – Enid, Elaine, Arthur, and sites such as the forests of Devon, the castle of Astolat or the halls of Camelot – was extended to Australian parallels. Woolley preached the chivalric ideal of King Arthur's men to his undergraduates, and to various (white) founders and supporters of the University in 1852, and then again in a sermon delivered to Sydney's volunteer forces in 1862.

Woolley's invocation of medieval chivalry in a settler colonial context flies in the face of arguments that chivalry is likely to be an ideal deployed against Empire rather than for it. As D'Arcens notes, in Woolley's case he does not speak of chivalrous behaviour as the trait of a ruler, but rather of a knight who protects, or of a vassal who performed under the imperial gaze – 'the Queen is watching and her colonial champions must defend and enhance her honor'.[32] Education, poetry and duty were all depicted through a unique, if somewhat idiosyncratic reading of the *Idylls*, as part of the knightly endeavour of the settler.

Three factors emerge as most striking in D'Arcens's account of Woolley's reading of the *Idylls* and of his appropriation of Victorian medievalism in the colonial Australian context. First, his reading of Tennyson and thereafter his encouragement of poetry among students and colleagues were an attempt to stake out an independent settler voice – one that was European, but of European second-class citizens who were residing in a faraway land originally imagined as a convict colony. Secondly, Woolley's reading of Tennyson was informed by a critique of materialism and anti-mercantilism. In this sense his interpretation of the *Idylls* was different from more conventional ones that regarded the King Arthur stories more straightforwardly as a script for Britain's imperial ambitions. Woolley was no anti-imperialist. But he resorted to Tennyson's Victorian medievalism as a way of safeguarding against imminent 'cultural death' for a settler society driven by an out-and-out utilitarian and mercantilist ethos. Tennyson's land of Doorm, argues D'Arcens, provided Woolley with 'an irresistible exemplum for discussing the drawbacks of life in colonial Sydney'. Likewise his characters of Enid, Guinevere and Elaine were each read to serve as examples or warnings to settler wives as they set up homes away from the comfort and cold climes of England. Finally, the deployment of Victorian medievalism by Woolley was very much a part of settler colonial efforts to 'write over' the past of the colony. As remarked by D'Arcens, Woolley's speeches, especially his invocation of another medieval hero Alfred, depicted Australia as 'an uninhabited wilderness ripe for the introduction of European language, literature, and philosophy'.[33] Extending the cult of Alfred, Woolley exhorted his listeners

> Nine hundred and eighty years have passed since our glorious Alfred provided … a home of union and refuge for the poor and scattered scholars … Did he anticipate, with a noble pride, the Anglo-Saxon root which he had planted, not merely after a thousand years living undecayed …? Did his imagination dare her flight beyond the limits of his island home, and picture in the remotest corners of the earth the children of his race, nurtured in his institutions, bearing forth the spirit and the form which they loved into *a yet wilder solitude, and a more inaccessible wilderness?*[34]

Elsewhere, D'Arcens extends her analysis of the deployment of medievalism in the Australian settler context by looking at a different professor from Sydney University, the historian Professor George Arnold Wood. Wood, like Woolley before him, used another important medieval figure, St Francis of Assisi, to oppose Australia's involvement in the 'immoral' Boer War of 1899–1902.[35] Through these studies, D'Arcens documents how medieval pasts come alive when they are treated not simply as objects of historical knowledge but more as repositories of moral examples. Seen like this, they call into question standard historicist distinctions between what is modern and what is medieval. Both Woolley and Wood wrote as members of an emerging colonial nation, Australia, which was a part of the British imperial family. But both also invoked and wrote about medieval characters by taking them out of their specific historical context to elaborate on ideas of virtue and (in Wood's case) an immoral imperialism. Wood was inspired by works on St Francis by Arnold, Ruskin, Paul Sabatier and Walter Scott. In Wood's public lectures, St Francis became an embodiment of virtue with parallels in later-day figures like John Milton, Oliver Cromwell, Sir Thomas More and Wood's political hero, William Gladstone.

This colonial and modern use of medieval figures not only complicates the notion of the Middle Ages as a period of darkness in European history, but also puts the medieval in the service of a distinctly modern, anti-imperial politics. The catch in both Woolley and Wood's deployment of a European medievalism in shaping a white settler present in Australia at the turn of the twentieth century, however, was that it completely erased the Aboriginal population from any account of the country's past or present. While installing the European medieval as a resource in modern narratives of the nation, medievalisms such as Woolley's or Wood's effaced another medieval – that of the Australian Aboriginals – from the national narrative.

The Australian version of Victorian medievalism demonstrates two things. First, that in the mind of the white settler the medieval was a resource that could be used effectively to further the project of settlement in an unknown and untamed terrain. Secondly, that the category we call medieval glosses over a variety of social formations. In the face of the triumphalist march of settler colonialism, Victorian medievalism was posited as the putative past of Australia. The actual inhabitants of the land, their particular histories and pasts, were blotted out by the pressure of an English medievalism, via Wood or Woolley's anachronistic imposition of Europe's past upon Australia. Yet, this medievalism, while unethical in its disregard for the Aboriginal population, was ethical in its critique of imperialism, crass materialism and rampant mercantilism. Medieval values played an integral part in the moral repertoire of the modern settler, drawing attention once more to the medieval postcolonial project's emphasis on plurality of time-worlds that make up the present.

Critiques of postcolonial medievalism

Notwithstanding these manifold instances of medieval historical research in a postcolonial vein, there have been some strong objections to applying postcolonial theoretical methods to the study of the Middle Ages. Scholars like Catherine Brown, while acknowledging that the insights of postcolonial studies have been useful to medievalists, nonetheless caution against the use of a postcolonial theoretical apparatus to medieval studies. 'For one thing', Brown writes, 'the knowledge/power activities of the two disciplines in the world of the living are incommensurable in ethically crucial ways; medievalism will never affect the lives of medieval people as Orientalism has affected and continues to affect the lives of living people.'[36] Other scholars, like Dagenais and Greer, whose work was cited above, fear a 'temporal colonization' that would render the Middle Ages into a passive object analysed through the lens of contemporary knowledge apparatuses such as postcolonial theory. The introduction of postcolonial methods of analysis, they assert, might exacerbate the feeling of colonization that some medievalists already labour under. Hence 'Iberomedievalists often feel that they work under a double colonization: that represented by the colonized nature of the Middle Ages itself and that which arises from the dominant role of northern Europe, especially France and England.'[37] On the one hand, thus, fears of academic neo-colonialism haunt the enterprise of a postcolonial medievalism. On the other, medieval historians like Gabrielle Spiegel warn against 'theory hopping', arguing that 'to apply postcolonial theory to medieval society without theorizing the analogy in an explicit manner is to decontextualize postcolonial theory and medieval history alike'.[38]

If some medievalists remain wary of postcolonial theory, others have raised critical questions about certain assumptions underpinning postcolonialist writing in the course of an engaged dialogue with the field. Thus, Kathleen Davis offers a critical reading of 'a totalizable Middle Ages that serves as an unconstructed origin or prehistory to the modern nation'.[39] She further argues that despite the commitment to question a teleological nature in the past and present, and the polarized historicist sensibility of the archaic and the modern, postcolonial theorists like Homi Bhabha end up taking for granted 'the homogenizing myth of past' in his critical reading of the postcolonial nation's alleged modernity.[40] In the same vein Carolyn Dinshaw remarks that in Bhabha's work on nationalism, 'the Middle Ages is still made the dense, unvarying, and eminently obvious monolith against which modernity and postmodernity groovily emerge'.[41]

In light of these criticisms it is also useful to recall books such as *Before European Hegemony*, which questioned the historical and conceptual bases of Eurocentrism before the agenda of a postcolonial medievalism was made explicit by scholars.[42] The existence of these works testifies to the fact that

> with little or no help from postcolonial theory, … more than a few medievalists have addressed the very constellation of critical imperatives now at the center of postcolonial critique, demonstrating … the mutually clarifying capacities of medieval and postcolonial studies.[43]

Writing in a vein that emphasizes the unacknowledged overlaps between the two disciplines, Bruce Holsinger offers a medievalist's response to fellow practitioners who find it 'ethically suspect' to apply an 'anti-Eurocentric, anti-Enlightenment mode of inquiry', that is postcolonial studies, to a field whose beginnings were deeply European. He invokes the postcolonial writings of Gayatri Spivak and Dipesh Chakrabarty, among others, to demonstrate the complex relationship that postcolonial history and theory has with European thought. Chakrabarty's argument about the indispensable but inadequate nature of such thought or Spivak's caution against reading thinkers like 'Kant, Hegel, Marx … as transparent or motivated repositories of ideas' is salutary in this regard. But Holsinger's case about the natural affinity between postcolonial and medieval history is most persuasive for two further observations he makes. First, he draws attention to the *Subaltern Studies* collective's (discussed in Chapter 1) 'reflective and critical engagement' with medievalist scholarship. The works of scholars like George Duby, Emmanuel Le Roy Ladurie, Marc Bloch, Fernand Braudel, Otto von Gierke, Heinrich Mitteis, S. F. C. Milsom, Fritz Kern and Robert Brenner were widely cited in early essays by *Subaltern Studies* scholars such as Partha Chatterjee and Shahid Amin. Later contributors to the series, like Ajay Skaria and Christopher Pinney, drew on the works of Roger Chartier, Walter Ong and Erwin Panofsky. To the extent that the work of this collective

> has engendered some of postcolonial theory's most urgent conflicts, keywords, and historical reclamations over the last twenty years; the group's writings … lay out a historiographical project which, if admittedly partial, remains nevertheless rich in comparativist heuristics for a postcolonial medievalism.[44]

In their efforts to champion a mode of historiography for modern India that was anti-foundationalist and critical of the colonialist and postnationalist claims, the historians of *Subaltern Studies* turned to instances drawn from medieval European history. Theirs was a postcolonial medievalism even though it was never explicitly theorized as such. The references to the Middle Ages found in the pages of *Subaltern Studies*, perhaps unbeknown to the group, carry no whiffs of clichés about medieval backwardness, uncomprehending religiosity and static hierarchy.

Probably because the project was politically motivated towards rejecting these labels in the study of colonial India, their view of the Middle Ages was one that naturally resisted teleological/historicist readings.

Holsinger's second observation broadens this argument from *Subaltern Studies* to the range of philosophical and theoretical literature that is widely referred to in much postcolonial theory and history. He notes that social theorists and philosophers as varied as Max Weber, Martin Heidegger, Jean Lyotard, Georges Bataille and Giles Deleuze all engaged intensively with medieval texts, and writes,

> These and many other instances of what we might call theoretic medievalism suggest that it may be time for medievalists to finally jettison the defensiveness and resistance that can still so often accompany the so-called importation of various theoretical vocabularies into the study of premodern eras.[45]

Holsinger's remarks draw attention to a natural affinity between the fields of postcolonial and medieval history. Works such as Ranajit Guha's 'The Prose of Counter-insurgency', which discusses a case of a mid-nineteenth-century Indian peasant uprising against British rule, and Steven Justice's *Writing and Rebellion*, an account of rural protest in late-fourteenth-century England, proves this affinity even at the level of method. Both scholars emphasized new ways of reading and writing in order to penetrate the silence of elite archives for evidence of peasant agency. Ultimately, then, what brings together medieval and postcolonial history is not only a mutually shared commitment to criticize stadial historical thinking and the value judgments that inhere in historical periodization but also a methodological emphasis on reading existing archives against the grain to uncover new materials that would challenge the canon – both colonial and/or medieval.

In his recent book *Irish Times*, the postcolonial theorist David Lloyd remarks that the 'simultaneous coevality and incommensurability of the modern and medieval is by no means one that we have outlived'.[46] Let me close this chapter by briefly discussing the implications of Lloyd's comment for it draws attention to the fact that the term 'medieval' designates much more than simply a time period in history-writing. For Lloyd, the medieval is a site characterized by intractable ambiguity. In its colonial and neo-colonial usage, 'the medieval' is often used to designate social formations that will in the fullness of time become modern. We have repeatedly witnessed this invocation of the medieval in different colonial settings where the colonized is depicted as medieval and therefore as a figure of lack. In our contemporary world, we often hear populations and countries described as medieval, a description that draws strength from the analogy between these countries and the popular imagination of the medieval Dark Age chaos of failed states, warring lords and starving peasants. But these descriptions elide the fact that these so-called medieval formations are both contemporaneous and indeed co-emergent with our own. Sometimes, they are the products of historical processes in which 'we' (the West) played no small part.

Lloyd's characterization of the medieval in this manner draws on the works of both medievalists and postcolonial historians. It also challenges a conceptualization of the medieval as a site of 'hard-edged alterity', and views it rather as part of a present 'formed by multiple temporalities'.[47] Thinking of the medieval in such a manner means that we acknowledge that 'the medieval is a point of origin that is also a space of transition', or 'a set of transitions that yield continually to one another'. It implies that modern social formations carry in them a palpable trace of the medieval. Sometimes, these traces may be sublimated into the modern condition and disappear. But, frequently, the medieval persists in modernity as social formations that are resistant or recalcitrant to such absorption. How do we as historians regard the presence of the medieval in contemporary life? 'Do such sites of resistance represent merely the persistence of an obdurate backwardness or do they … represent the possibility of as yet unexhausted alternatives to the unidirectional progress of modernity?'[48]

This manner of characterizing the medieval goes against the thesis of its alterity; it favours instead the view that acknowledges its lack of clarity as precisely a sign of the multiple possibilities for historical transition that the so-called medieval may contain. Thus we often hear of manifold transitions: from the 'Dark Ages' to the 'early medieval' to the 'late medieval', and so on. A postcolonial medievalism draws attention to this composite, contradictory and many-stranded phenomenon that is the medieval – 'its Janus-face turned at once forwards and backwards, its connotations at once negative and positive' – and thus helps us to see that the naming of historical transition is always a phenomenon in which passions and interests are both invested. Postcolonial medievalism, much like the postcolonial analyses of modernity, calls into question the received 'names' of history.[49]

Notes

1 Gabrielle M. Spiegel, 'Epater les Medievistes [Impressing the Medievalists]', *History and Theory* 39(2) (May 2000), p. 250.

2 Kathleen Biddick, *The Shock of Medievalism* (Durham, NC: Duke University Press, 1998), p. 1.

3 Biddick, *The Shock of Medievalism*, p. 4.

4 Biddick, *The Shock of Medievalism*, p. 9.

5 Biddick, *The Shock of Medievalism*, p. 65.

6 Biddick, *The Shock of Medievalism*.

7 Biddick, *The Shock of Medievalism*, p. 66.

8 Spiegel, 'Epater les Medievistes', pp. 243–50.

9 Nadia Altschul, 'Postcolonialism and the Study of the Middle Ages', *History Compass* 6(2) (2008), pp. 588–606. Altschul offers a detailed critique of Spiegel in this essay.

10 For a rich and complex reading of how medievalism works in rhetoric of politically conservative and fundamentalist forces, see Bruce Holsinger, *Neomedievalism, Neoconservatism, and the War on Terror* (Chicago, IL: University of Chicago Press, 2007).
11 Kathleen Davis, *Periodization and Sovereignty: How Ideas of Feudalism and Secularization Govern the Politics of Time* (Philadelphia, PA: University of Pennsylvania Press, 2008), p. 2.
12 Davis, *Periodization and Sovereignty*, p. 5.
13 Davis, *Periodization and Sovereignty*.
14 Davis, *Periodization and Sovereignty*.
15 Davis, *Periodization and Sovereignty*, p. 6.
16 Gil Anidjar, cited in Davis, *Periodization and Sovereignty*, p. 133.
17 Davis, *Periodization and Sovereignty*.
18 This expression was coined by Bruce Holsinger whose work is discussed in the forthcoming pages.
19 John Dagenais and Margaret Greer, 'Decolonizing the Middle Ages', *Journal of Medieval and Early Modern Studies* 30(3) (Fall 2000), p. 435.
20 Jeffrey Jerome Cohen (ed.), *The Postcolonial Middle Ages* (New York, NY: St Martin's Press, 2000); Patricia Clare Ingham and Michelle R. Warren (eds), *Postcolonial Moves: Medieval through Modern* (New York, NY: Palgrave Macmillan, 2003); Ananya Kabir and Deanne Williams (eds), *Postcolonial Approaches to the European Middle Ages: Translating Cultures* (Cambridge: Cambridge University Press, 2005); Kathleen Davis and Nadia Altschul (eds), *Medievalisms in the Postcolonial World: The Idea of 'the Middle Ages' Outside Europe* (Baltimore, MD: The Johns Hopkins University Press, 2010).
21 The expression 'idea of the "Middle Ages" outside Europe' comes from the title of Kathleen Davis and Nadia Altschul's recent book *Medievalisms in the Postcolonial World: The Idea of 'the Middle Ages' Outside Europe* (Baltimore, MD: The Johns Hopkins University Press, 2010).
22 Ananya Kabir, 'Analogy in Translation: Rome, England, India', in Ananya Kabir and Deanne Williams (eds), *Postcolonial Approaches to the European Middle Ages* (Cambridge: Cambridge University Press, 2005), pp. 183–204.
23 Kabir, 'Analogy in Translation', p. 187.
24 Kabir, 'Analogy in Translation', p. 193.
25 Debjani Ganguly, 'The Language Question in India', in Ato Quayson (ed.), *Cambridge History of Postcolonial Literature* (forthcoming).
26 See Kabir's analysis of the role that Chapter 26 of Tacitus's *Germania* played in the moulding of the European imagination of the village community in India: *Medievalisms in the Postcolonial World*, pp. 51–79.
27 Nicholas Howe, 'Anglo-Saxon England and the Postcolonial Void', in Ananya Kabir and Deanne Williams (eds), *Postcolonial Approaches to the European Middle Ages* (Cambridge: Cambridge University Press, 2005), pp. 25–47.
28 Campbell argued that by the twelfth century England had been colonized several times. He also noted that English colonial interests in Scotland began sometime around the tenth century, and made a case for the rise of literary English from time of Chaucer to English attempts to stave off French cultural domination. Clearly, 'colonialism' operates as a fairly capacious category in Campbell's case. Yet, it is only by including coloniality into disciplinary thinking on the Middle Ages, as Nadia Altschul has usefully noted, that we can start to analyse the differences between medieval and modern colonialisms (and the different postcolonial conditions to which they gave rise).
29 Howe, 'Anglo-Saxon England and the Postcolonial Void', p. 42.
30 Altschul, 'Postcolonialism and the Study of the Middle Ages', p. 10.
31 Ato Quayson, 'Translations and Transnationals: Pre- and Postcolonial', in Ananya Kabir and Deanne Williams (eds), *Postcolonial Approaches to the European Middle Ages* (Cambridge: Cambridge University Press, 2005), p. 260.
32 Louise D'Arcens, 'Antipodean Idylls: An Early Australian Translation of Tennyson's Medievalism', *Postcolonial Moves: Medieval through Modern* (New York, NY: Palgrave Macmillan, 2003), p. 245.
33 D'Arcens, 'Antipodean Idylls', p. 251.

34 D'Arcens, 'Antipodean Idylls' (emphasis in the original).
35 Louise D'Arcens, '"Most Gentle Indeed, But Most Virile": The Medievalist Pacifism of George Arnold Wood', in Kathleen Davis and Nadia Altschul (eds), *Medievalisms in the Postcolonial World* (Baltimore, MD: The Johns Hopkins University Press, 2010), pp. 80–108.
36 Cited in Bruce W. Holsinger, 'Medieval Studies, Postcolonial Studies, and the Genealogies of Critique', *Speculum* 77(4) (October 2002), p. 1202.
37 Holsinger, 'Medieval Studies, Postcolonial Studies, and the Genealogies of Critique', pp. 1202–3.
38 Spiegel, 'Epater les Medievistes', p. 250.
39 Kathleen Davis, 'National Writing in the Ninth Century: A Reminder for Postcolonial Thinking about the Nation', *Journal of Medieval and Early Modern Studies* 28(3) (1998), p. 613.
40 Davis, 'National Writing in the Ninth Century', p. 629.
41 Carolyn Dinshaw, *Getting Medieval: Sexualities and Communities, Pre- and Post-Modern* (Durham, NC: Duke University Press, 1999), p. 16.
42 Janet L. Abu-Lughod, *Before European Hegemony: The World System A.D. 1250–1350* (New York, NY: Oxford University Press, 1989).
43 Holsinger, 'Medieval Studies, Postcolonial Studies, and the Genealogies of Critique', p. 1200.
44 Holsinger, 'Medieval Studies, Postcolonial Studies, and the Genealogies of Critique', p. 1209.
45 Holsinger, 'Medieval Studies, Postcolonial Studies, and the Genealogies of Critique', p. 1224.
46 David Lloyd, *Irish Times: Temporalities of Modernity* (Dublin: Keough-Naughton Institute for Irish Studies, University of Notre-Dame/Field Day, 2008), p. 74.
47 Altschul, 'Postcolonialism', p. 8.
48 Lloyd, *Irish Times*, p. 76.
49 Lloyd, *Irish Times*, p. 77.

5

Empire and postcolonial history

In the last three chapters we have noted the ways in which historians of the *Subaltern Studies* collective and a range of medievalists used postcolonial theory in history-writing. Postcolonial theory served, in these instances, as both a heuristic and a hermeneutic that enabled historians to overcome the drawbacks they criticized in their respective fields of study. We noted how ideas of postcoloniality were deployed and fashioned anew as historians critically interrogated the implications of stadial thinking, of certain Eurocentric assumptions about civilization, nationalism and historical difference as they wrote revisionist accounts of nationalism, colonial thought and medieval history. In a slight departure from this mode of analysis, in this and subsequent chapters I want to draw attention to the way in which postcolonial historiography developed much more as the historian's response to certain political imperatives in the contemporary world. The historian, in what follows, will be seen as both responding to issues arising from within the parameters of the academic discipline of history, but also as political observer, responding to crises in contemporary conditions. By contemporary I mean the years from the mid-twentieth century to the present.

Readers should not assume that the accounts of postcolonial history-writing presented so far were necessarily apolitical. Quite the contrary. *Subaltern Studies* and the project of provincializing Europe, as we noted, were partly a response to the perceived failure of the sovereign Indian nation state to live up to the promises it made during decolonization, to established modes of historiography to adequately represent the 'subaltern' in the narratives of nationalism, and most important to the refusal in hitherto existing historical works to acknowledge that subaltern thought could positively contribute to modern knowledge apparatuses. History, like the state, it was argued, was blinkered by the biases of elite groups, both European and Indian. Likewise, medievalists drew attention to the political assumptions underlying periodization, to the hierarchy inherent in labels such as 'medieval' or 'modern'.

What will be taken up in the following pages are trends in postcolonial history that followed from developments in the former metropolitan centres of the world. The burden of my explication will be to demonstrate that history-writing was an engagement with changing political currents in these countries from the decolonization years to the present. This is not to argue that historians simply projected contemporary realities into the past. Such an exercise would be anachronistic. Rather, the past, particularly the past of colonial empires, became a site that historians revisited in order to better understand the present by establishing points of continuity and rupture.

In the most general terms, the conditions that enabled the body of work discussed in the following pages were the end of colonial empires. Globally, the decolonization era and the years thereafter witnessed the arrival of the ex-colonized races, both an educated, professional middle class as well as working-class groups to the ex-colonizing countries. This was due in large measure to changes in immigration rules in the early postwar years that contributed to increasing population mobility across the world. Members of these groups settled in the 'West'. Some among them and the generation that followed gradually became a thriving presence in Western institutions – government agencies, industry, colleges, schools, universities and hospitals. Even in instances where material success eluded many of the new migrants they remained in the West, often under ghettoized conditions. The presence of second- or third-generation migrants, by now full British, American, French or Australian citizens, changed forever any conception of these countries as 'white'. Troubled by the responses – including chauvinism, racial panic, incomprehension and disengagement – in public and political circles to the presence of the 'colonies' at 'home', historians turned their attention to the history of empire and colonialism for a better understanding of the deep racial fissures that were rending apart the fabric of former metropolitan societies.

Political context

Before discussing in detail the academic debates that generated postcolonial histories of Empire, it would be useful to briefly rehearse the global political climate following the end of the Second World War, and of national liberation struggles in different countries. This larger context is critical for an understanding of the rise and changes in postcolonial modes of thinking. The 1960s marked the end of the decolonization era. The Bandung conference of 1955, 'that daunting quest for a nonaligned postcolonial world', as Homi Bhabha put it, represented a significant moment in global history.[1] Twenty-nine free nations of Asia and Africa, with some 600 delegates, came together from 18 to 24 April 1955 in Bandung, Indonesia to mark their commitment to a post-imperial world. But, the euphoria about the end of colonialism was slowly corroded in many newly decolonized countries, and by the late 1960s large parts of the world saw the rise of peoples' struggles against the nation state – in South Africa, Palestine, India, Bangladesh, Vietnam, parts of the Middle East and the various nation states of Europe – many of which are still ongoing.

To many postcolonial thinkers, 1989 marked another turning point in global history. The fall of the USSR and the Berlin Wall, the end of state communism and the bloody battles in Eastern Europe signalled the birth of a unipolar world where a market-driven capitalism reigned supreme. The end of apartheid in South Africa raised utopian hopes about new beginnings in 'that newest first-world nation'.[2] But the new postcolony of late capitalism with its huge numbers of 'unwaged citizens' also witnessed 'crime as an increasingly banalized mode of production and income redistribution, terrifying violence of various kinds, the demonization of immigrants, and the attachment of blame for social disorder to young black males; as if none of this had anything to do with the legacy of apartheid'.[3]

For historians and other social scientists analysing this tragic dialectic acquired new urgency. Was it possible, asked many, to understand the shifting contours of racial and economic policies in the postcolony by turning back to the dynamics of race and imperialism in different sites of the colonial world? The absence of cultural homogeneity within the national body was not a new development but was a fact of life from the age of eighteenth- and nineteenth-century colonialisms. Yet, were these earlier imperial models comparable with contemporary ones? As different countries set up stringent (and often brutal) immigration regimes, or sought to quell dissonant voices within their territorial boundaries, it became clear that the nation state was in many of its practices the legatee of former imperialist/colonialist regimes. But the nature of the legacy remains to be worked out in different postcolonial sites.

Although 'colonialism' was acknowledged as a thing of the past, state repression, discrimination and control of populations in different parts of the world – both in the so-called global north and south – resonated with colonial practices. To put it slightly differently, the fissures between the many nations or peoples that inhabited the state became increasingly prominent in multiple sites in a manner where (for many) the state could no longer be said to represent the nation – a belief that had sustained decolonization struggles in the early part of the twentieth century. It became apparent by the late 1980s that policing and immigration checks were critical features of state policy in the prosperous nations of the world. The gap between elite ruling groups and the rest of the population in terms of wealth, livelihood questions and power has only widened in the post-1970s decades. Where these mid- and late-twentieth-century regimes differed from their colonial predecessors was that state control was now exercised in the name of a sovereign nationhood. As population mobility increased across the world, so did national and international security measures. It was against this backdrop that there was a veritable explosion of histories that sought to analyse the contemporary, post-decolonization crisis of the nation state and to trace the genesis of repressive state acts. Constructions of nationhood, argued many, are 'contradictory and crisis-riven, serving diverse forms of legitimation'.[4]

The global political situation acquired the pitch of emergency following the 11 September 2001 attacks in the United States. The US invasion of Iraq, the rise of global Islamic militancy and bombings in London, Madrid, Bali all contributed to a sense of political panic. The response of different Western countries to this sense of panic, one that state authorities played no small part in fanning, as well the continued political turmoil in large swathes of the world – the Middle East, South Asia, the US–Mexico border, to name just a few – destabilized easy certitudes about the end of Empire. While there is no question that, unlike eighteenth- and nineteenth-century empires, present-day military invasions were not geared towards permanent settlement in the countries invaded, it was precisely this difference that needed to be debated and analysed.

Finally, it was (and is) argued that systems of state welfare in European countries and in places like Canada, Australia and New Zealand were being stretched to breaking point by the influx of immigrant groups into these countries. Yet, in some places such as France, as one scholar observed, while 'public discussions are now unproblematically about a deluge of immigrants pouring into the country, … immigration has not increased … over the last twenty years'.[5] What begs analysis therefore are the causes behind the rise of xenophobic tendencies and the demonization of immigrants in recent years, attitudes bound to worsen in the wake of the ongoing global financial crisis. For historians in particular, the main concern was to analyse the continuities, if any, between colonial racial practices and postcolonial ones; to question if the work of decolonization was ever completed or if national sovereignty in different parts of the world simply entailed a transfer of state power; and finally to find the tools with which to analyse the resurgence of imperial and racial politics in today's world. The American invasion of Iraq made the spectre of Empire, thought to have ended with the era of decolonization, a present-day reality. It is to this issue about Empire that I shall devote the rest of this chapter.

Postcolonial history, 'new' imperial history and empire

Over the last decade or so, a rich body of historical work has emerged, which is described by its practitioners as the 'new imperial history'. Not all the work conducted in this field would fall under the rubric of postcolonial history. Indeed, some scholars working in the field of new imperial history have been strongly critical of postcolonial historiography. But the contributions by Catherine Hall, Kathleen Wilson, Antoinette Burton, Ann Laura Stoler and Nicholas Dirks, to name a few notable examples, also speak to the close linkages between postcolonial history-writing and new imperial history. These works also illustrate that many of the charges levelled against postcolonial historiography by some historians of empire are often based on a misunderstanding of both the projects of 'new' imperial and postcolonial history.

According to Antoinette Burton, a leading practitioner in both fields, new imperial history developed as a response to 'the imperial turn', which she defines as 'the accelerated attention to the impact of histories of imperialism on metropolitan societies in the wake of decolonization, pre- and post-1968 racial struggle and feminism in the last quarter century'.[6] The similarity in the intellectual genealogies of new imperial and postcolonial histories, evident in Burton's statement, is clarified further by Kathleen Wilson in the Introduction to a volume of essays she edited in 2004. Wilson thus summarized the arc of the essays collected in that volume: 'Energized by the political and imaginative wakes of postcolonial and cross-disciplinary scholarship, … the kind of "new imperial history" at work here has at its heart the importance of difference – in historical settings and forms of consciousness as well as in historiographic and critical practice – that supports and extends the pluralities of historical interpretation.'[7] She cites Catherine Hall, whose work is discussed below in some detail, arguing that 'new ways of theorizing difference are central to the task of writing new imperial histories'.[8]

Difference was central to imperial projects and policies, and was often the ground on which European ideas of domination were justified. New imperial historians analyse the historical deployment of difference as a hierarchical category that separated colonizer from colonized. They are also committed to analysing the ways in which empires led to the circulation of European peoples, institutions, customs, laws and religions around the globe, and the 'contribution of these extended territories and peoples' to the formation of 'national' cultures within Europe. Such an orientation produces a critical stance among new imperial historians towards other practitioners of imperial history. For example, new imperial historians of the British Empire are critical of projects such as the five-volume *Oxford History of the British Empire*. Wilson, for instance, questions the validity of the claim made by the volumes that the British Empire was a 'series of discrete components of limited relevance to the study of Britain, rather than … a permeable web or network shaped by global and regional currents, that impacted metropolitan as much as colonial culture'.[9] Furthermore, new imperial historians are particularly committed to studying the internal difference between imperial projects. For example, eighteenth-century accounts abounded in references to 'the empire of the seas', 'the empire of the east' or the 'New World Dominions'. These 'empires' were by no means identical, even though there were points of commonality, and all of them profoundly shaped the formation of British metropolitan identity.

Readers will recall that the question of historical difference – both its existence and blurring – is central to the project of postcolonial history-writing. Postcolonial historians do not treat the difference between the colonizer and colonized as a Manichean separation. Related to this is a deep investment in understanding the processes of translation of universal categories in particular locales and languages across different historical time periods. Finally, colonialism, as both postcolonial and new imperial historians demonstrate, was far from being a monolithic and coherent process. The emphasis of the revisionist scholarship is to explore the 'tensions' of Empire, rather than its triumphs alone.

Before turning to a more detailed analysis of some postcolonial approaches to the history of empire let me point out a slight difference in emphasis between new imperial historians and their postcolonial counterparts. For the new imperial historian the main focus of attention is the imperial formation(s) – a term used first by Mrinalini Sinha – a model that allows for the different trajectories of metropole and colony while insisting that both were constituted by a history of imperialism, a point that has since then also been made by Frederick Cooper and Ann Laura Stoler.[10] The historians in question strenuously argue in favour of shifting analytical focus away from the nation form – both colonizing and colonized – to Empire seen as an organic (if uneven) relationship between metropole and colony. They are critical of notions of splendid isolation of any colonizing nation state, and are committed to demonstrating the close linkages, indeed the mutually constitutive role, between ideas of empire/colony and nation/empire.

Postcolonial historians in turn take colonialism, decolonization and neo-colonial practices as their object of study. But their fundamental unit of analysis is the nation state, not so much as an entity they celebrate, but as an apparatus that often fails to live up to its promises for a series of endemic historical reasons. Postcolonial historians are committed to critical analysis within a national frame, informed by global perspectives. As argued by the historian Gyan Prakash, postcolonial histories question the 'leaden understanding of colonialism as History'.[11] His use of history with a capital 'H' is a challenge to the dominant narratives that have long structured university and college curricula. The latter are informed by the commonsense, teleological understanding of the arrival of modernity to different parts of the contemporary world through the vehicle of colonial rule. This narrative may be summarized as follows: As European powers colonized less-developed regions of the world they also brought to these disparate and far-off lands the light of reason and science. Enlightened by Western knowledge, the colonized population eventually arose against colonial domination. National liberation struggles ensued, inaugurating the era of decolonization. The result of this mode of representing the past, notes Prakash, was to sequester 'colonialism tightly in the airless container of History' and present 'postcoloniality as a new beginning'.[12] The task of postcolonial history-writing, among other things, is to reveal the limits of such neat periodization. Even in the aftermath of colonialism, most countries still display the operation of colonial categories albeit in a different guise – colonizer/colonized; white, black, brown; civilized and uncivilized; modern and archaic; cultural identity; tribe and nation.[13]

Demonstrating the existence of neo-colonial practices is not where postcolonial history-writing stops. Rather, postcolonial historians also focus on the ways in which colonial categories were operationalized on the ground by the natives, often described by the colonizers as uncivilized or backward. But at that moment of encounter 'colonial oppositions were crossed and hybridized'.[14] Thus every colonial category has written into its history the story of the native's appropriation, resistance and translation. The task of postcolonial history is to read these hybrid pasts for a richer understanding of the present. And it is their mutual commitment to analysing the history of colonialism as one of encounter that brings together postcolonial and new imperial histories.

It follows from the above that both schools of history-writing have left behind the spirit of anti-colonial criticism where the colonizer and colonized represent totally opposed forces locked in struggle. They view the colonial world as one of 'hybridity' and 'mimicry', to use the words of Homi Bhabha. Even though the history of decolonization struggles is a matter of the past for these historians, the struggles remain relevant for an analysis of the present. As Edward Said remarked, the work of postcolonial criticism was fuelled by the recognition

> that even though a hard and fast line separated colonizer from colonized in matters of rule and authority (a native could never aspire to the condition of the white man), the experiences of ruler and ruled were not so easily disentangled. On both sides of the imperial divide men and women shared experiences – though differently inflected experiences – through education, civic life, memory, war.[15]

Said's argument, I propose, is equally applicable to new imperial histories.

Case studies

In an essay that was originally delivered as a lecture in 2003 on the twenty-fifth anniversary of the publication of Edward Said's *Orientalism*, and later published as an article after Said's death in September of that year, Catherine Hall offers some important reflections on what she refers to as 'Britain's version of postcoloniality'.[16] It is important to recount this postcolonial context in some detail as it provides the critical backdrop for Hall's important study on Britain and Jamaica in particular, as well as for new imperial history more generally.

At issue is what Hall and others identified as a 'long-term crisis over British identity'.[17] There are considerable debates about the chronological origins of the British Empire. Many would date it back to the twelfth century and Britain's activities on the Celtic fringe, others to the sixteenth century and England's interactions with the Irish. Still others would consider the beginning to be Britain's colonizations in America and the Caribbean in the seventeenth century. The second British Empire, as many have argued, began in the nineteenth century, following Britain's recovery from the loss of America and with the establishment of settler societies in Australia, New Zealand and the Cape on the one hand, and with the setting up of dependencies in India, parts of the Caribbean, East and West Africa, and Ceylon on the other. Britain's self-conception, in the nineteenth century, was inextricably linked to these varied colonial ventures and to its identification as an island race whose providential career was to govern peoples in far-flung areas of the globe. Already in the 1820s, that is, even before the second British Empire was fully established, Britain ruled 26 per cent of the world's population, a proportion that expanded considerably as the century progressed.[18]

From 1945, the British Empire disintegrated with the rise of national liberation struggles and decolonization. But the significant changes in immigration policies that began in the decolonization era brought waves of South Asian and West Indian migrants to Britain. The latter, who 'had come to stay has changed forever the demographics and cultural and political identities' of the British Isles.[19] Prior to this period there was no noticeable non-white population in Britain. Hall notes that the Irish or the Eastern European Jews were 'sometimes racialized', but 'their presence never threatened the imagined whiteness of the nation'.[20] But the immigration of large numbers of non-whites from the former colonies challenged the self-understanding of Britain as a white nation and of the British as an imperial race. Starting in the 1960s, and intensifying during the prime ministership of Margaret Thatcher, race (the empire coming home, as it were) became a critical issue in British society. 'This was Britain's postcolonial moment, the time of transition, as Simon Gikandi puts it, when the foundational histories of the metropole began to unravel, a disjunctive moment when imperial legacies came to haunt English and post-colonial identities.'[21]

New imperial historians have invoked this moment in Britain's contemporary history as also being the time when works by Edward Said, Paul Gilroy and Stuart Hall started to gain currency in the British academy, alongside a resurgence of interest among black activists, feminists and historians in the writings of Frantz Fanon, C. L. R. James and W. E. B. Du Bois. Despite the wide currency of works by the aforementioned scholars and intellectuals within the academy, there still remained widespread opposition to ideas of Orientalism, or to studies that sought to 'rematerialize the presence of non-white Britons in the United Kingdom before 1945'. Notable instances of such opposition included the influential intervention made by the well-known imperial historian Peter Marshall in his 1993 article in the *Times Literary Supplement* entitled 'No Fatal Impact? The Elusive History of Imperial Britain'. The reception accorded to Niall Ferguson's *Empire* (2003) in the British mainstream press also testified to the longing for an imperial race and to notions of glory associated with the white man's burden. These works demonstrated (1) that for many historians developments in the empire were hardly seen as relevant to the trajectory of British history at home; and (2) there prevailed among many – both historians and the public – a belief in the beneficial effects of empire. Ferguson was hailed in the popular press in Britain as the Errol Flynn who saved the British Empire from historiographical calumny. In the five years that followed the events of 11 September 2001, a number of books on the British Empire were published that illustrate the fissures dividing the historical discipline on this issue. Books such as David Cannadine's *Ornamentalism: How the British Saw Their Empire* (2001) attempt to show that British society in the nineteenth century developed in relative isolation from imperialist efforts away from home. Others like Linda Colley's *Captives* (2002) presented imperial history from the perspective of the colonizer as victim, and downplayed the significance of empire to British domestic life. Taking stock of these revisionist histories of Empire, Edward Said noted,

> A generation ago the influence of Fanon's typology of empire ensured that one could only be either very much for or very much against the great imperial structures that disappeared piece by piece after the Second World War; now, after years of degeneration following the white man's departure, the empires that ruled Africa and Asia don't seem quite as bad. The perplexingly affirmative work of Niall Ferguson and David Armitage scants, if it doesn't actually trivialise, the suffering and dispossession brought by empire to its victims. More is said now about the modernising advantages the empires brought, and about the security and order they maintained. There is far less tolerance for the disorder and tyranny that people like Nkrumah, Lumumba and Nasser instigated in the name of anti-colonialism. A crucial tactic of this revisionism is to read present-day American imperial power as enlightened and even altruistic, and to project that enlightenment back into the past.[22]

These developments, when put in the context of the history of political developments in Britain – including Enoch Powell's 1968 'rivers of blood' speech; Powell's 1985 statement that Britain, with an increasingly multiracial population of Asian or African descent, will be 'unimaginably wrecked by dissension and violent disorder, not recognizable as the nation as it had been, or perhaps as a nation at all'; the 1995 declaration by a British minister of efforts to elevate figures like Olaudah Equiano and Mary Seacole to the status of British heroes as a 'betrayal'; the furore surrounding the publication of the Runnymede Trust report *The Future of Multi Ethnic Britain* (2000); riots, like the one in Bradford in 2001, that beset the country – demonstrate that history-writing takes place in an atmosphere that is fraught with political tensions.

Catherine Hall's *Civilizing Subjects: Metropole and Colony in the English Imagination, 1830–1867*, a book that brings a postcolonial outlook to new imperial history, offers a sharp contrast to the aforementioned works on imperial pasts. Hall begins by explaining the genesis of her project on an autobiographical note. We learn of her early childhood in a missionary household in Kettering, a small English town where the Baptist Missionary Society was founded in 1792. The family subsequently moved to Leeds where Hall grew to develop a more agonistic relationship with the Baptist mission. While she approved the individual autonomy that Baptists seemed to grant to members of that faith via the practice of adult baptism, she simultaneously became uneasy about the 'narrow-minded and self-righteous aspects of this nonconformist culture'.[23] This personal ambivalence around the Baptist mission informs Hall's reading of the Baptist mission in nineteenth-century Jamaica. A main component of *Civilising Subjects* is missionary activity in Jamaica, particularly Baptist efforts to civilize the natives, oppose slavery, but its ironic failure to respond positively to the call for citizenly rights issued by the ex-slave population.

Hall's marriage to the Jamaican cultural studies scholar and historian Stuart Hall, her days as a student in Birmingham and the multiracial political atmosphere of Britain in the 1960s and 1970s, she notes in retrospect, all had a silent impact on her intellectual persona as a postcolonial historian. It grew more articulate after the completion of *Family Fortunes*, a magisterial account of middle-class women and family in Birmingham, co-authored with Leonore Davidoff. As she began searching for a future research project, Hall arrived in Jamaica in 1988 with her husband and two children. In a country that she had visited intermittently since 1964, she discovered the namesake of her birthplace and much more.

A realization that dawned upon her during her Jamaican sojourns in the late 1980s, writes Hall, was that 'the Christian version of the family of man and the Left's universal humanism had both acted as screens for me, allowing me to avoid full recognition of the relations of power between white and black, the hierarchies that were encoded in these two paradigms'.[24] *Civilising Subjects* was the labour of Hall's recognition that while decolonization resulted in the expulsion of the colonizing power from newly liberated lands, it had done little to decide the fates of people from the ex-colonized countries who 'came home to roost' in the old mother country and made very different claims upon it. It was in the context of understanding herself anew as a white woman, born in a missionary household, married to a black man naturalized in Great Britain, who identified more as English than as Jamaican, and as the mother of mixed-race English children that Hall conceived this book. As she noted,

> My reasons for choosing to work on Jamaica are perhaps self-evident by now: it was the site of empire to which I had some access. It was the largest island of the British Caribbean and the one producing the most wealth for Britain in the eighteenth century. ... It was through the lens of the Caribbean, and particularly Jamaica, that the English first debated 'the African', slavery and anti-slavery, emancipation and the meanings of freedom.[25]

Jamaicans in postwar Britain presented a very different picture. They, like her husband Stuart Hall, were those who had left the island to 'come to Britain, ... had settled, had children and claimed full national belonging'.[26] But claims to national belonging do not mean that 'belonging' was an accomplished fact. *Civilising Subjects* is a working-out, through history-writing, of problems that Hall encountered deeply at an everyday existential level. As she noted,

> England was no longer at the heart of a great empire, and its domestic population was visibly diverse. One historical power configuration, the colonial, had been displaced by another, the post-colonial. ... It was this new configuration with its repetition, the same but different, which made possible both the return to the past and a rewriting of connected histories.[27]

The book sets out a cast of diverse characters – officials, abolitionists, traders and philanthropists like Edward Eyre, Joseph Sturge and William Morgan; Baptist missionaries like William Knibb, John Henderson and John Angell James; major writers and thinkers of the day like Thomas Carlyle and John Stuart Mill. Its chronological frame is flanked by the two reform bills passed in England between 1832 and 1867, which gradually expanded the franchise among British male citizens. At the heart of the book is the Morant Bay rebellion of 1865, and the controversy that ensued in Britain over Eyre's order to open fire on the 'rebels' to quell the uprising.

What emerges clearly from Hall's account is that while many Baptist missionaries went to Jamaica with the ostensible goal of civilizing the colony, they were in the process also remaking themselves through the encounter with a new race. Yet, the process of refashioning the self reached its limit point when it came to imagining the black ex-slave as a citizen. For liberals like John Stuart

Mill or William Morgan the ideal of equality did not include in its ambit the coloured island peoples. This, as Hall argues, was the result of the conditions under which the principles of liberalism were produced in the first place. Mill and his lesser-known contemporary Morgan were products of an imperial England, and even their most radical ideas were coloured by that context. Unlike their more overtly racist contemporaries like Carlyle and Eyre, to the Baptist missionaries empathy for the poor black Jamaican was an article of faith – but one that sadly stopped short of full equality. It was ironical that these occurrences coincided with the expansion of franchise in Britain.

A comparison of Jamaica and Birmingham (Hall's focus in the book is on this particular English city) proves that what was deemed appropriate for England was not so for Jamaica. The people there needed to be in history's 'waiting room' until the time was ripe for them to be admitted to full citizenly rights. Hall demonstrates the deeply textured quality of racial discourse in reformist Britain. She also shows how the ambiguity that some Baptist missionaries experienced in the early and mid-nineteenth century about treating Jamaicans as lesser individuals was completely replaced by a strident biological racism that believed in the superiority of the whites as the century progressed. The book offers a searing critique of imperialism but also usefully acknowledges its fraught nature by highlighting the difference and ambivalence that divided the colonial Briton on the race question.

Hall's book qualifies as *new* imperial history in its scholarly commitment to think of the histories of the metropole and colony in the same analytical frame. Events in Jamaica left their deep imprint on British thinking, just as much as the latter was shaped and incited by political currents in England. Its postcolonial outlook is highlighted by its nuanced treatment of the relationship between the colonizer and colonized, a position that was no doubt shaped by the political climate of Hall's own contemporary England. The Baptist missionaries, white settlers or metropolitan thinkers were by no means identical in their attitudes towards the island races. Despite these differences, however, in the context of the Morant Bay uprising colonial civility and altruism reached its limit. The civilizing mission faltered irrevocably over the hurdle of race. The challenge facing contemporary multiculturalism is to avoid the fate of the past.

The tensions of empire also figure as an important area of inquiry in the South African context. The historical anthropologists John and Jean Comaroff's *Revelation and Revolution* is a classic study of the gnarled histories of British missionaries, Boer settlers and the indigenous population in the northern frontier of South Africa in the nineteenth century. The narrative of colonialism in their account is replete with internal differences. This does not diminish in any way, as John Comaroff qualifies,

> the brute domination suffered by the colonized peoples of the modern world. ... Nor is it to deconstruct colonialism as a global movement ... it

> is to treat as problematic the *making* of both colonizer and colonized in order to understand better the forces that … have drawn them into an extraordinarily intricate web of relations.[28]

Let me briefly discuss here an essay by John Comaroff as it clearly demonstrates the yield of a postcolonial standpoint to the study of empire. One of the main contributions of Comaroff's study is to link the missionaries, as agents of colonialism in South Africa, to their English pasts. It is through missionary eyes that he analyses the colonial enterprise in South Africa and highlights the polarization among different white groups in the Cape. The members of the London Missionary Society and the Wesleyan Methodist Missionary Society in South Africa came from the lower rungs of the English bourgeoisie – 'the ideological core yet the social margins of bourgeois Britain' – in the early years of the industrial revolution.[29] That past, argues Comaroff, shaped their South African mission where they sought a 'neat fusion of three idealized worlds'.[30] This meant first, a desire to shape the South African colony on a rational, capitalist model 'wherein unfettered individuals were free to better themselves'.[31] Secondly, they tried to recreate an idyllic countryside in the colony, one that was irrevocably lost in England, thanks to the incursion of the factory into rural areas. The colonial agrarian landscape of the missionary's imagination would be laboured upon by 'hardworking peasants, equipped with suitable tools and techniques', producing 'gainfully for the market'. Finally, the colony would also be transformed into 'a sovereign Empire of God, whose temporal affairs remained securely under divine authority'.[32] The missionaries' civilizing mission was a combination of granting rights to the natives as they were also modernized and proselytized into proper Christian subjects.

These missionary visions collided violently with the erstwhile occupants of the Cape. Apart from the native Africans and the men of God, three different cast of characters were present, each favouring a different 'model' of colonial rule. There were first, British administrative officials, usually men of elite rank and/or birth. Secondly, there were the British settlers, mostly respectable, middle-class men settled in Cape Town and big farmers in the colony. Thirdly, there were the 'rude' (in missionary eyes) Boers (lit. farmers) of Dutch, French and German descent. Each group subscribed to a particular ideology of rule. While there was some overlap between each group, they nonetheless represented a different template of colonial domination.

To the missionaries, the Boers represented a model of settler colonialism whose ultimate end was the total subordination and dispossession of the blacks. The latter were destined to remain as lesser beings *vis-à-vis* the Boer with no right of ownership of their lives and labour. 'Baboons and Bechuanas' was their frequent invocation of the natives. The British bureaucracy's attitude was not as hostile even though they remained disinterested in questions of civilizing the African. To the British administration, *pax Britannica* was the need of the hour. This necessitated some limited negotiation and pacification of the 'tribes', which, it was hoped, would be achieved through the extension of trade. The arc of official rhetoric was geared towards the transformation of 'blacks into labourers', as epitomized in a statement by the prime minister of the Cape, Sir Gordon Sprigg, in 1878, when he declared that his goal was to teach the natives 'to work, not to read and write and sing'.[33] Teaching the native to read, write and sing was precisely the goal of the missionaries. Theirs, in Comaroff's words, was a 'civilizing colonialism' – an effort to bring to fruition the energies of a Christian utilitarianism that had failed to run its course in the metropole.

Comaroff's analysis concludes with several observations. First, that the three models of colonialism eventually confronted each other in struggles to expand their respective sway in South Africa. The missionaries were accused, sometimes rightly, of supplying arms to the tribes, which resulted in the destruction of mission properties by the Boers. Colonial rule, in other words, was far from being unified. If the British bureaucracy represented a politico-juridical face of the colonial project, the Boer settlers highlighted the socio-economic logic of race relations in the colony. The missionaries carried the values of bourgeois European culture to the colonies, which they struggled to disseminate through their conflicts with both the aforementioned groups. Secondly, despite these variations – 'the niceties of competing colonialisms' – the fact of native subordination remained a brute fact. Yet, the struggles among the ruling elites also created, albeit in a limited manner, 'spaces and places in which some blacks were to discover new, if limited, modes of empowerment; others ... were to find novel sources of enrichment at an almost Faustian cost'.[34]

Both Hall and Comaroff demonstrate the limits of imperial altruism and civility in the face of racial difference. Together they reveal the deep sediment of racial categories in the making of British and other European identities through the colonial encounter. By tracking what designated race in the past, they alert

> us to the fact that even those quintessential forms of racism honed in the colonies were never built on the surefooted classifications of science, but on a potent set of cultural and affective criteria whose malleability was a key to the sliding scale along which economic privilege was protected and social entitlements were assigned.[35]

If the two examples discussed deal primarily with the public life of empire politics, historical research on issues of intimacy over the last decade or so has established the linkages between the domestic and sexual order between metropole and colony. Ann Laura Stoler's writings have been pioneering in this regard.

Stoler, a historian and an anthropologist, together with Frederick Cooper characterized colonial history as one of entanglement between apparently discrete entities. Her work, like that of many others, has informed the processes by which binary categories such as colonizer/colonized, metropole/colony, bourgeois/primitive, arose in the first place in the colonial/imperial context. This is not to suggest that Stoler, like Hall and Comaroff, does not see the serious inequities in power relations between empire and colony, or that she is not sensitive to the internal differences between colonial ventures. It is true, she argues, that 'colonial studies scholarship identifies striking similarities in policy and practice: patterns of panic, discourses reiterated, outrages rehearsed, and fantasies shared'. She also notes that 'no one would argue that the former Dutch East Indies, British India, French Indochina, and the Belgian Congo looked everywhere and from anywhere the same'.[36]

Stoler's main argument, made in the context of histories of intimacy and sexual regimes in the Dutch Indies and (to a lesser extent) French Indochina, is complex. She draws attention to the anxieties that many Europeans expressed about their domestic arrangements once they moved to the colonies. European women, who were for a long time allowed restricted access to colonial lives, were eventually allowed in those faraway lands as gatekeepers of 'white prestige'. At the same time it was common for white men to take on colonial companions. While some of these liaisons were legitimized through marriage, others remained live-in relationships with household servants or concubines. Many of the unions resulted in offspring – children of 'mixed blood' or metissage. Many of the latter were allowed into the metropoles as full citizens while others were denied such access. How are we to comprehend these shifting boundaries to intimate lives? How did people fix the boundaries of what constituted proper intimacy? Stoler's conclusions suggest that concerns about intimacy were inextricably linked with the political project of colonial governance. Ideas such as 'white prestige' or 'mixed blood' were not set in stone. Rather they evolved alongside ideas about colonial bourgeois subjecthood.

In this context, Stoler raises some critical questions from what I would read as a postcolonial standpoint, about Michel Foucault's hugely influential work *History of Sexuality* and offers important insights into his 1976 lectures delivered at the Collège de France. Readers will recall Foucault's provocation: Why from the seventeenth century to the late nineteenth century had there been a proliferation of discourse surrounding sex and sexuality in Europe, when by most accounts these three centuries were a time of sexual repression and prudery? In his words, 'when one looks back over these three centuries with their continual transformations … around and apropos of sex, one sees a veritable discursive explosion'.[37] In this 'discursive explosion' the couple had a central place. As reproductive sex, 'carefully confined' to the home, was legitimized as the norm 'the image of the imperial prude is emblazoned on our restrained, mute, and hypocritical sexuality'. Transgressive sex was put in its proper place – the brothel. And in the event it got out of hand, the task of sexual normalization was entrusted to the mental asylum. Sexuality, in other words, was not simply a biological instinct. It was something saturated with conceptions of control, 'a result and instrument of power's design'. Foucault argued that the nineteenth century witnessed an incitement to talk, control and incessantly argue over the fact of sexual control and management. This was the core of the repressive hypothesis – that the 'truth' about people could be ascertained by understanding and controlling them as sexual subjects.

Sexuality in Foucault's exposition was about 'biopower'. He explained the latter as a dual process that involved the *disciplining* of the body in order to optimize its capacities and usefulness and as a *regulatory* mechanism that regarded the human as a species body, and produced knowledge about its longevity, morality and health. 'The disciplines of the body and the regulations of the population constituted the two poles around which the organization of *power* over life was deployed.'[38] The history of sexuality was therefore a history of power in modern life. Biopower marked, for Foucault, a fundamental transformation of humans in modernity. He argued, 'For millennia man remained what he was for Aristotle: a living animal with the additional capacity for a political existence. Modern man is an animal whose politics places his existence as a living being in question.'[39]

Stoler's critique, or in her words, her 're-reading' of Foucault, is based in the main on two observations. First, 'Europe's eighteenth- and nineteenth-century discourses on sexuality, like other cultural, political, or economic assertions, cannot be charted in Europe alone.'[40] The colonies were in fact the laboratories of modernity where the workings of biopower were clearly articulated. The presence of different races in the colonies acted as a stimulus to erect sharp contrasts between 'other' bodies and healthy, normal, bourgeois bodies, coded as European. Stoler's postcolonial gesture lies in her argument that the history of a normative European sexuality should be traced along a 'circuitous imperial' route rather than one whose genesis and elaboration was metropolitan. Using the Dutch Indies, and in later works examples from French Indochina, she demonstrates how ideas about bodily control, intimacy and family life 'were refracted through the discourses of empire and its exigencies, by men and women whose affirmations of a bourgeois self, and the racialized contexts in which those confidences were built, could not be disentangled'.[41] Secondly, she argues that discourses on sexuality 'do more than define the distinctions of the bourgeois self'. Once again, by focusing on 'poor whites' in the colonies, as well as creolized populations of mixed blood, Stoler demonstrates how ideas of 'marginal populations' and indeed the 'interior frontiers' of the metropole were 'secured through and … in collision with … the boundaries of race'.

One can argue with Stoler's reading of Foucault. Moreover, since the publication of her book in 1995, numerous others have worked extensively on the 1976 Collège de France lectures, discussing at some length Foucault's ideas on race and the way in which Western, liberal societies have attempted to contain the racial wars that make up the fabric of these societies. None of this, however, diminishes the importance of Stoler's seminal contribution to postcolonial history-writing, which rests in her analysis of the history of European bourgeois culture and imperial race relations through the lens of regimes of intimacy in the colonies.

More recently, scholars working on other colonial contexts have also considered the complexities of interracial relationships, as well as the implications of these relationships to questions of citizenship, national belonging and identity. Important in this regard are Jean Pederson and Alice Conklin's work on mixed-race children and ideas of being French, and Lora Wildenthal's analysis of gender in the German colonial empire. While many of these historians have not self-identified as postcolonial and are more likely to think of themselves as new imperial historians, their work both draws upon and furthers certain assumptions of postcolonial historiography.

Let me close this section by briefly discussing one recent example, Durba Ghosh's *Sex and Family in Colonial India*. Ghosh offers a revisionist account of the race relations between the British rulers and their Indian subjects by looking into the history of domestic relationships in the India during the first century or so of English rule. She analyses three types of interracial relationships and households. The relationships range from domestic slavery and concubinage to marriage. Ghosh's attentiveness to archival records on these relationships, especially the manner in which women's names were gradually elided from these records, offers important insights into the shaping of metropolitan and colonized identities. Her analysis reveals that there was a steady decline in archival records about 'colonial companions' between the late eighteenth and late nineteenth/early twentieth centuries. The absence of records should not be interpreted as a direct correlate of ground reality; European men and Indian women continued to have relationships and parent mixed-race children well into the nineteenth century, several decades after the Cornwallis code of the 1790s banned these liaisons. 'This suggests', argues Ghosh, 'not that the number of interracial relationships declined, but that men and women were careful to suppress any archival traces of these relationships in their letters, wills, diaries, and other written accounts' in order to shield themselves from the censorious gaze of the state.[42]

Let me outline in brief the kinds of relationships described by Ghosh in *Sex and Family*. First, there were liaisons between women of pedigree whose families belonged to erstwhile courtly groups in India, and high-ranking European officials. The relationship between Khairunnissa and James Kirkpatrick, the British resident at the court of the Nizam of Hyderabad, is one of the cases representative of this group. The second category included women whose conjugal (or concubine-like) relationships with European men commenced once they had been sold or bartered to these men. Companionship, in other words, came after an economic transaction that inducted these women into domestic service. By far the most complex in the array of relationships that Ghosh analyses, these bonds were remarkable because many of these women continued to assert their fidelity to their European consorts even after being abandoned or being offered the option to return to their natal families. Their stories are also littered with events of abuse and violence, some of which were presented before colonial law courts. The slave girl who lived with and was eventually abandoned by Robert Grant and the powerful Begam Samru are examples in this second category. The colonial state did not sanction the relationships in question. Indeed, cohabitation and/or marriage with Indian women was a source of much anxiety to the Court of Directors of the English East India Company. Yet, to regard these relationships purely through the lens of domination and subjugation of Indian women by European men misses the negotiations that these women engaged in as well as their rich, affective links with their lovers/husbands. Some came into property, others secured material wealth and still others managed to send their mixed-race children 'home' to be acculturated into proper racial and cultural norms.

The picture changes, however, when Ghosh turns to analyse lower-class women. They mostly linked up with low-ranking European soldiers, or other members of the colonizing underclass. Their children, much like their counterparts in the Dutch Indies, ended up in state-run orphanages or found careers in travelling bands, or joined the Company's service in lowly positions. They did not enjoy the mobility of members of the two aforementioned groups. In all three categories, however, there occurred moments when cross-cultural intimacy produced conjunctures that cannot be readily absorbed into either an 'Indian' or 'British' repertoire of cultural practice. For instance, the wills and testaments that Ghosh discusses articulate a desire by women, who had cohabited with white men and mothered their children, to be given a Muslim burial. Likewise, it is difficult to understand the pain of mothers who let go their mixed-race children, often under duress, so that the latter could be properly socialized in the 'home' country. Do we read into these gestures an assertion of female agency? Or do they reflect a desire to restore some semblance of cultural propriety in death or solitude after transgressing established gender norms?

It would be impossible to give definitive answers to these questions. What does emerge conclusively from Ghosh's analysis of interracial relationships in early colonial India is the innate fallacy that characterized much nationalist and colonialist thought about the family being the zone of a pure, unsullied spiritual home of the nation. Instead, by excavating fading traces of the 'female transgressor' from the colonial archive Ghosh 'complicates the development of the fiction of "respectable" domesticity so central to British colonial authority and later, in a different way, to the Indian nationalist imagination'.[43] The archival denial of indigenous women's conjugal (or other) bonds with the whites testifies to the anxiety and 'focus on social and racial regulation' that characterized imperial formations. Finally, the presence of mixed-race children at 'home'; interracial relationships that happened despite the fear of state reprisal; and campaigns by Indian widows of European men and the Eurasian community for financial and citizenly rights makes clear that the history of the metropole as a multicultural and multiracial space can be pushed far beyond the era of decolonization.

Postscript

'Many historians who call themselves "postcolonial" have taken it for granted that colonial rule was always evil and colonialist motives always bad,' runs an observation by David Gilmour, an imperial historian who has done considerable work on the British Empire in India. 'A reading of their work', he continues, 'leaves the impression that the best of the colonialists was less worthy than the worst of the colonized, unless the latter was an ally of the imperial power, in which case he is dismissed as a "lackey" or "collaborator".'[44] Gilmour's remarks end up attributing to postcolonial history precisely those Manichean binaries against which this body of work has defined itself. As we have noted in the preceding analysis, postcolonial historians have devoted themselves to understanding the workings of the colonial world in terms that call attention to the inadequacy of the binary logic of colonizer/colonized. The works discussed above not only demonstrate the inchoate, yet inexorable nature of the colonial enterprise. They also draw attention to the altruistic aspects of the colonial project while underscoring its ability to dominate and command.

In his 2005 *Colonialism in Question*, Frederick Cooper levelled more serious charges against postcolonial scholarship. As Cooper's criticisms are made from a historian's standpoint, it would be apposite to consider them in some detail. One caveat, relevant for our purposes, is that Cooper addresses a wide range of work conducted under the rubric of postcolonial studies, often by scholars who are not historians by training. The principal shortcoming of such work, he argues, is that it looks at 'history ahistorically'.

Cooper elaborates four aspects of postcolonial work that produces ahistorical history: 'story plucking, leapfrogging legacies, doing history backward, and the epochal fallacy'.[45] Story plucking refers to the collapsing of differences between colonialisms – ignoring the materiality of 'context, struggle, and the experience of life in the colonies' by simply laying stress on the fact of being colonized.

Leapfrogging is a tendency he notes in some scholarship not to pay adequate attention to causality. In Cooper's own words, it is claiming that 'something at time A caused something in time C without considering time B, which lies between'. Doing history backwards is another name for presentism; that is to say, the attempt to understand the present by looking to the past. Not only does this leave scholarly accounts open to the charge of anachronism, but it pays scant attention to 'paths not taken, the dead ends of historical processes, the alternatives that appeared to people at the time'.[46] Finally, by 'epochal fallacy', Cooper sees postcolonialists producing 'history as a succession of epochs', which 'is to assume a coherence that complex interactions rarely produce'.[47] He submits that the 'post' in postcolonial 'can usefully underscore the importance of the colonial past to shaping possibilities and constraints of the present'. But 'such a process', he argues, 'cannot be reduced to a colonial effect, nor can either a colonial or a postcolonial period be seen as a coherent whole, as if the varied efforts and struggles in which people engaged in different situations always ended up in the same place'.[48]

The analysis presented in this chapter (and in previous ones) raises doubts about Cooper's criticisms. Postcolonial historians discussed so far have been attentive to the internally variegated character of colonial projects. Not only have postcolonial histories engaged the differences of different colonial cultures; they have also focused their energies towards exhuming histories of individuals and groups in the metropole and colony who 'renounced the privileges of imperialism and elected affinity with victims of their own expansionist cultures'. Leela Gandhi's study of *fin-de-siècle* radicalism in late Victorian Britain is an excellent case in point. Postcoloniality, as John Comaroff usefully noted in an interview with Homi Bhabha, invoked 'a state of being, defined by its place in the passage of epochal history'.[49] This would be consonant with Cooper's understanding of the postcolonial as implying a time period when 'decolonizations of the postwar era extinguished the category of colonial empire from the repertoire of politics that were legitimate and viable in international politics'.[50]

But Comaroff and Bhabha also saw the postcolonial as 'a critical orientation toward reading the past, not least of its textual traces'.[51] It was in this second sense that they described the postcolonial as a diachronic condition – one that is still evolving. They demarcated two phases of the postcolonial condition, both of which are relevant to our preceding discussion on empire. The first encompassed the era of decolonization and the birth of independent nation states, while the second had its genesis in 1989, 'with the end of the Cold War, the "triumph" of neoliberal capitalism, democratization movements, and the rise of a new wave of post-revolutionary societies in Central Europe, South Africa, and elsewhere'.[52]

Many of the works discussed above may be read as attempts to write histories of colonialism as a conversation between these two periods of modern history.

This is not the same as submitting that they have smuggled present-day concerns and categories back into the past. Rather the concerns of the present encouraged and enabled historians to view the past through a postcolonial optic.

Notes

1 Homi Bhabha, 'Foreword', *The Wretched of the Earth* (New York, NY: Grove Press, 2004), p. ix.
2 Homi Bhabha and John Comaroff, 'Speaking of Postcoloniality in a Continuous Present: A Conversation', in David Goldberg and Ato Quayson (eds), *Relocating Postcolonialism* (Oxford: Blackwell Publishing, 2002), p. 34.
3 Bhabha and Comaroff, 'Speaking of Postcoloniality in a Continuous Present', p. 35.
4 Anne McClintock, Aamir Mufti and Ella Shohat, *Dangerous Liaisons: Gender, Nation, and Postcolonial Perspectives* (Minneapolis, MN: University of Minnesota Press, 1997), p. 4.
5 Ann Laura Stoler, 'Racist Visions for the Twenty-first Century: On the Cultural Politics of the French Radical Right', in David Goldberg and Ato Quayson (eds), *Relocating Postcolonialism* (Oxford: Blackwell Publishing, 2002), p. 109.
6 Antoinette Burton (ed.), *After the Imperial Turn: Thinking with and through the Nation* (Durham, NC: Duke University Press, 2003), p. 2.
7 Kathleen Wilson, *A New Imperial History: Culture, Identity and Modernity in Britain and the Empire, 1660–1840* (Cambridge: Cambridge University Press, 2004), pp. 2–3.
8 Wilson, *A New Imperial History*.
9 Wilson, *A New Imperial History*, p. 14.
10 Mrinalini Sinha, *Colonial Masculinity: The 'Manly Englishman' and the 'Effeminate Bengali' in the Late Nineteenth Century* (Manchester: Manchester University Press, 1995), p. 182.
11 Gyan Prakash (ed.), *After Colonialism: Imperial Histories and Postcolonial Displacements* (Princeton, NJ: Princeton University Press, 1995), p. 4.
12 Prakash, *After Colonialism*, p. 5.
13 Prakash, *After Colonialism*.
14 Prakash, *After Colonialism*, p. 3.
15 Edward Said, 'Always on Top', *The London Review of Books* (20 March 2003).
16 Catherine Hall, 'Remembering Edward Said', *History Workshop Journal* 57 (2004), p. 238.
17 Hall, 'Remembering Edward Said'.
18 Hall, 'Remembering Edward Said'.
19 Hall, 'Remembering Edward Said', p. 239.
20 Hall, 'Remembering Edward Said'.
21 Hall, 'Remembering Edward Said'.
22 Said, 'Always on Top'.
23 Catherine Hall, *Civilising Subjects: Metropole and Colony in the English Imagination, 1830–1867* (Chicago, IL: University of Chicago Press, 2002), p. 3.
24 Hall, *Civilising Subjects*, p. 6.
25 Hall, *Civilising Subjects*, pp. 10–11.
26 Hall, *Civilising Subjects*, p. 11.
27 Hall, *Civilising Subjects*.
28 John Comaroff, 'Images of Empire, Contests of Conscience', in Frederick Cooper and Ann Laura Stoler (eds), *Tensions of Empire* (Berkeley, CA: University of California Press, 1997), p. 165.
29 Comaroff, 'Images of Empire, Contests of Conscience', p. 168.
30 Comaroff, 'Images of Empire, Contests of Conscience', p. 169.
31 Comaroff, 'Images of Empire, Contests of Conscience'.
32 Comaroff, 'Images of Empire, Contests of Conscience'.
33 Comaroff, 'Images of Empire, Contests of Conscience', p. 180.
34 Comaroff, 'Images of Empire, Contests of Conscience', p. 192.

35 Ann Laura Stoler, 'Racist Visions for the Twenty-first Century', p. 119.
36 Ann Laura Stoler, *Carnal Knowledge and Imperial Power: Race and the Intimate in Colonial Rule* (Berkeley, CA: University of California Press, 2002), p. 209.
37 Michel Foucault, *The History of Sexuality: An Introduction*, vol. 1 (New York, NY: Vintage Books, 2003), p. 17.
38 Foucault, *The History of Sexuality*, p. 139 (emphasis mine).
39 Foucault, *The History of Sexuality*, p. 143.
40 Ann Laura Stoler, *Race and the Education of Desire: Foucault's* History of Sexuality *and the Colonial Order of Things* (Durham, NC: Duke University Press, 1995), p. 7.
41 Stoler, *Race and the Education of Desire*.
42 Durba Ghosh, *Sex and Family in Colonial India: The Making of Empire* (Cambridge: Cambridge University Press, 2006), p. 253.
43 Ghosh, *Sex and Family in Colonial India*, p. 251.
44 David Gilmour, 'Surprises of the Empire', *The New York Review of Books* (2 November 2006).
45 Frederick Cooper, *Colonialism in Question: Theory, Knowledge, History* (Berkeley and Los Angeles, CA: University of California Press, 2005), p. 17.
46 Cooper, *Colonialism in Question*, p. 18.
47 Cooper, *Colonialism in Question*, p. 19.
48 Cooper, *Colonialism in Question*.
49 Homi Bhabha and John Comaroff, 'Speaking of Postcoloniality in a Continuous Present', p. 15.
50 Frederick Cooper, *Colonialism in Question*, p. 19.
51 Bhabha and Comaroff, 'Speaking of Postcoloniality in a Continuous Present', p. 15.
52 Bhabha and Comaroff, 'Speaking of Postcoloniality in a Continuous Present'.

6

Postcolonial history and settler contexts

This chapter continues to address the theme of empire, but with a different accent from that of the previous discussion. My focus here is on settler colonial contexts, the dismantling of these bastions of European colonialism through decolonization, violent and non-violent, and the movements for rights unleashed by these processes. Taken together, they created a new postcolonial European world and crystallized enduring features of politics and society in many of the former white colonies such as Australia, Canada and New Zealand. The processes I analyse in this chapter are part of a burgeoning historiography and point towards future directions that postcolonial history-writing might take in years to come. The common thread that binds the forthcoming analysis is made up of the twin phenomena of settler colonialism and postcolonial conditions that follow when this form of social, political, economic and cultural domination comes to an end or is seriously challenged.

The case of settler colonial countries has given rise to new turns in postcolonial history showing both overlaps with and divergences from *Subaltern Studies* type approaches discussed in Chapter 1. What, then, was settler colonialism?

> White men who live beside, but not among, a colored proletariat will insist that they cannot afford to deal in ethics that do not relate to that predicament. That they choose to stay in it is beside the point. They resent the social analyses that issue from a commentator's armchair, because they see in them only a menace to their own security, to preserve which is, and must always be, their first duty.[1]

Thornton's suggestion that the settlers perceived the subject population as a 'menace' forces us to think about the relationship between settler colonialism and conquest. Numerous studies by scholars on the antipodes or Algeria have documented long years of armed, bloody conflict between settlers and indigenous groups, which makes it clear that colonial occupation in these countries did not happen peacefully. While in some places, such as New Zealand and North America, armed conquest was accompanied by treaties between settlers and native groups, in others such as Australia settlement occurred in the absence of treaties. The presence or absence of treaties has important ramifications upon postcolonial developments in these countries, a theme explored at some length in recent postcolonial history. It is striking, however, that while much work has been carried out by historians on settler colonialism – both postcolonial and others – rarely have settler contexts been analysed in a comparative frame. This chapter is an effort to undertake such a comparative analysis.

In order to highlight the specificity of the settler colonial context, David Prochaska, author of the well-known postcolonial history of Bone, *Making Algeria French*, usefully separates this form of colonialism from concepts such as 'plural society' and 'internal colonialism'. The former concept was first used by J. S. Furnivall to describe colonial situations in South and South-east Asia, particularly Burma and Indonesia. Plural society in Furnivall's usage was 'one in which a European colonizing minority lived alongside an indigenous colonized majority with, in addition, intervening ethnic and racial groups which provided labor that the Europeans and natives either would or could not perform themselves'.[2] The concept of internal colonialism, Prochaska notes, was first used by Lenin and then Gramsci. It was elaborated more fully by writers working on Latin America to analyse Indian–Latino relations, as well as by those studying various ethnic groups within national societies, such as the Blacks in the United States and South Africa, or the Irish in Great Britain.

While settler colonialism has much in common with both of these formations, what distinguished it from other varieties of colonialism was that 'whereas in the majority of colonial situations there are two primary groups involved – temporary migrants from the colonizing country (colonial administrators, military personnel, merchants and traders, missionaries) and the indigenous people – in settler colonies the settler constitutes a third group'.[3] This is significant because it draws attention to a particular 'life choice' that settlers made to live and work in a place that was far removed from their place of birth. It also explains the overwhelming importance of land control in settler colonial histories compared to other types of colonialism. Whether one is studying settler groups such as tea planters in Sri Lanka, rubber planters in Malaysia and Indonesia, tobacco farmers in Zambia, cattle farmers in Kenya or wine growers in Algeria, land remains a central issue in settler colonial history.

To summarize, then, a settler colony was one where large groups from the colonizing community laid down more or less permanent roots in the colony.

It is this feature that distinguished them from economic colonies or trading posts where the European presence was much smaller in comparison. Some scholars have argued that the pattern of colonial rule often determined the nature of decolonization movements. The end of settler colonialism, it is noted, was usually marked by large-scale violence and large numbers of returning European migrants to the metropole. While it is no doubt true that some settler colonies witnessed massive violence at the moment of decolonization, some others such as Canada, Australia and New Zealand did not experience a decolonization movement *per se*. Yet, as I will demonstrate, these countries also share some of the predicaments of postcolonial nations. To draw attention to the differences between different settler colonial situations and demonstrate the way this is reflected in history-writing are the main aims of this chapter.

Making Algeria French

David Prochaska's study of colonial Bone (present-day Annaba, and historically better known as Hippo), a city in north-eastern Algeria near the border of Tunisia, offers an excellent starting point for analysing what a postcolonial outlook can contribute to writing an urban history of a settler colonial city. Algeria was the 'premiere settler colony' of the second French Empire, which also included Indochina (present-day Vietnam, Laos and Cambodia), New Caledonia, the protectorates of Morocco and Tunisia, and several more '*colonies d'exploitation*' across sub-Saharan Africa.[4] By the mid-nineteenth century, Algeria was incorporated into metropolitan France as three states or *départements*. Other smaller overseas French *départements* included Guadeloupe, Martinique and Réunion.

As a postcolonial historian, Prochaska trains his analytical lens upon the formation of settler society in colonial Algeria. Instead of focusing on the metropole or on indigenous Algerians, Prochaska's attention to the mediating link between the two – the settlers – demonstrates the ways in which colonial Algeria came to enjoy near sovereign status from metropolitan France. It was the settlers, and not influences from the metropole, that made Algeria 'French'. His work is also critical as a historical backdrop for understanding the alienation experienced by the *pieds-noirs* (singular *pied-noir*, black foot, a name by which the settlers came to be known) who returned to the metropole in large numbers at the end of the Algerian war of 1958–62. Prochaska does not address this reverse migration issue in his work. His focus is on the actual process of settlement, and on the processes by which European settlers became Algerians. This settler identity came undone over the course of the Algerian war that ended in 1962. Let me discuss in some detail the processes entailed in settler colonialism, using Prochaska's analysis of Algeria as a case study.

The Algerian settlers were not, as one might assume, a group made up only of people of French origin. Rather they were a diverse medley consisting of Italians, Spaniards and Maltese, the *petits blancs*. There was in addition to these European groups a highly populous group of Jews in Algeria who were granted French citizenship in 1870. The status of the Jews, according to Prochaska, was somewhat ambiguous. While they were definitely not part of the settler community they were, for the most part, better off in their relations with the settlers than the Muslim population. As a social group they continued to have monetary and trading links with both settlers and Muslims. In 1870, military rule in Algeria was replaced by civilian rule. Hereby the three coastal provinces of Algeria – Algiers, Oran and Bone – became *départements* of mainland France. This did not, however, mean that all Algerians became French citizens with equal electoral and other political privileges. 'And there precisely was the rub,' writes Prochaska. Despite being members of a French *département*, local Algerians did not become French citizens. The situation instead was one where,

> A *département* of metropolitan France in which non-citizens outnumbered citizens but in which citizens counted for more at the polls, that is some people were more equal than others. Thus, Algeria was a French colony – the colonizers maintained hegemony over the colonized, and at the same time Algeria was not a French colony – it was an integral part of France. In short, Algeria had been incorporated but not integrated into France in 1870, ingested but not digested.[5]

As an aside, it should be noted that scholars working on the history of women's rights in France have remarked upon the similarity between the status of the colonized in Algeria and the status of women in the metropole under the Third Republic. Frenchwomen under the Third Republic were citizens but without voting rights. In fact, some women's groups protested against the possibility of granting the vote to the colonized prior to the extension of suffrage among women in France.

The establishment of civilian rule signalled recognition on the part of metropolitan France of Algeria's special status as a colony – where the settlers comprised of the French as well as other European groups were present in huge numbers compared to other colonial situations. Yet colonial Algerian politics was not the mirror image of domestic French politics. While 'the replacement of the illiberal Second Empire by the liberal Third Republic' may have ushered in an era of republicanism within France, it resulted in increased settler power in Algeria. 'Settler power was turned mainly against Algerians to create an increasingly illiberal regime in Algeria only nominally controlled by a liberal regime in France.' So while 1870 did not result in an increased European presence in

Algeria in absolute numbers, that year marked a 'tilt in the colonial equation of power in favor of the settlers'.[6]

The ways in which this 'tilt' was registered at the level of everyday life were manifold. Starting in the 1870s, but really picking up pace in the period between 1890 and 1920, a settler colonial culture crystallized in Algeria. Henceforth it was the settlers who reserved the moniker 'Algerian' for themselves. The native Algerians were simply known as the *indigenes*. 'At one blow the settlers proclaimed their hegemony in Algeria and at the same time obliterated the native Algerians in the very terms they used to describe themselves.'[7] The category 'Algerian' came to signify from the late 1890s the 'native and naturalized French, the Spanish, Italians, and Maltese who had or were in the process of giving up one collective identity and assuming another'. These new Algerians created a new language, Pataouete, which is a dialect of French spoken in Algeria but with about 600 foreign words – 210 from Arabic, 180 from Spanish, 60 from Italian and 70 from the patois spoken in southern France from Provence to Languedoc. Around the turn of the twentieth century there also emerged a *pied-noir* literature. While Albert Camus remains the colonial Algerian writer of world renown, there were also many lesser-known authors who contributed regularly to settler journals and newspapers, producing a thriving literary culture. The latter testified to the existence of an 'Algerian melting pot' – a settler colonial culture drawing upon traditions of diverse groups of Europeans who defined their power and status by strictly distancing themselves from and discriminating against the local Muslims and Jews.

Discrimination was manifest in the physical organization of settler life. Settler groups were concentrated in the urban regions of Algeria where they largely outnumbered the locals. Residential segregation began from the earliest days of French colonization and continued throughout the 130 years or so of colonial rule. Not only were the Europeans segregated from the Jews and local Algerians, but the Europeans 'also were segregated in their own colonies within the larger French colony'.[8] In Bone, for example, most of the native French lived in the new city while the other Europeans lived in the working-class neighbourhoods of Colonne Random. Furthermore, the 'recently naturalized French' had more in common with 'their Italian and Maltese confreres' than with the native French in terms of residential patterns. Thus, even within the segregated French neighbourhood there remained racial tensions. Despite these internal differences, 'the non-French' (that is, the whites) 'were significantly less segregated from the French than from the Algerians or the Jews'.[9]

Prochaska's analysis of the physical layout of the settler city confirms Frantz Fanon's famous observation in *The Wretched of the Earth*. 'The colonial world is a world cut in two,' wrote Fanon. 'The settler's town is a strongly built town, all made of stone and steel. It is a brightly lit town; the streets are covered with asphalt, and the garbage cans swallow all the leavings, unseen, unknown, and hardly thought about.' It was a 'town of white people, of foreigners'. The colonized or native people's quarters were a different landscape altogether. 'It is a world without spaciousness; men live on top of each other, and their huts are built one on top of the other. The native town is a hungry town, starved of bread, of meat, of shoes, of coal, and of light.'

Certainly, the division of the colonial city into native and white quarters was not unique to Algeria. But what marked out a settler colonial city like Bone, Algiers and Oran from Delhi, Cairo or Calcutta was the sheer numbers of settlers among the urban population. The latter outnumbered the local Algerians by huge percentages.[10] Indeed, by 1896 settlers born in Algeria were more numerous than *émigrés* coming from the metropole – a feature that distinguished the settler city from other colonial cities. This fact impacted on the development of infrastructure and the myriad ways in which the local population was marginalized.

Prochaska demonstrates that the bulk of streets names in Bone carried some reference to the French colonization of Algeria in general and of Bone in particular. The military flavour of street names spilled over to the names of villages around the Bone region. Only three streets in the old city were named after figures predating the French occupation of 1830, and only two had Muslim names – a striking fact for a city with a 2,000-year-long history where Muslim, Christians and Jews had lived together through peace and conflict. Prochaska sees in this quirky but highly interesting history of street names 'the hand of colonialism' set in stone. Residential segregation was mirrored in the cultural division of labour. In the Algerian labour market the native French colonized the best jobs and businesses, with the Italians and Maltese after them and the native Algerians far below either group. There was unequal pay for equal work, and the native French remained at the top of the job hierarchy.

Ironically, 'the Muslims received the colonialist message' for in postcolonial Annaba every French street name was changed, French monuments defaced or neglected and Muslim ones maintained. The same bias marked the historiography of Algeria, which remained divided between those who argued from a metropolitan perspective and those who sought to represent the native's side of the story. Yet, to comprehend the ways in which these biases were formed one needs to take a step back and regard colonial Algerian history from a postcolonial vantage. An analysis of French colonialism in Algeria as a story mediated by the settlers (who became Algerian and made Algeria French) represents one such vantage point. Such a perspective demonstrates that '(T)he Bone past is not only part of the Annaba present, it is not even past.' It helps to explain some of the ferocity with which what is today called Annaba was created with the fundamental goal of erasing any signs of French occupation.[11] Yet, that drive to remake colonial Bone into postcolonial Annaba, from a French to an Algerian city, is oddly reminiscent of its settler origins. Just as the settlers made Algeria French by erasing or denying therein the presence of the Muslim Arabs, Berbers and Jews, so also postcolonial Annaba was created through a process of historical amnesia about its 130-year-long French past.

The close circuitry between metropole and colonies implies that there was a fairly regular traffic in people and goods between the mainland and colonies. Staying with our example of colonial/imperial France, we notice an increasing dependence of the metropole upon the colonial markets, especially in the aftermath of the First World War. Other kinds of social circulation also expanded. People from the mainland travelled on administrative, ethnographic and educational ventures to the colonies. Likewise, non-Europeans arrived in France as educational, labour and military migrants. Non-Western troops served in the French army during the Great War and many stayed back in France during the armistice. North African, Malagasy and labour migrants from Indochina filled French factories and docks. Finally, there was an educated sector of Antillean professionals and university students, 'an expatriate colonial population' that continued to grow through the 1920s and 1930s.[12] Let me turn then in the next section to people from the colonizing and colonized groups as they moved/returned to the metropole during and after the end of colonial rule.

Postcolonial peoples

The two groups of people analysed below experienced colonialism quite differently – the first came from the body of the colonized while the next was comprised of ex-settlers. In each case, I shall explain why I have characterized these individuals or groups as postcolonial. The first was a diasporic group whose members came from different parts of French Africa, Martinique and Antilles. Identified in historical scholarship as the pioneers of Negritude – on account of their shared interest in Africa and their investment in an ideal of a global Pan-Africanism – members of this group are often seen as an elite black diaspora who lived in Paris during the interwar years. The second group analysed is more disparate. It includes ex-settlers and natives who fought in metropolitan armies and migrated to different parts of Western Europe, the United States of America and Australia following the decolonization movements from the 1940s onwards. By discussing these quite different sets of people as 'postcolonial' it is also my intention to draw attention to the diversity inherent in that label.

The Negritude movement never constituted a formal organization. Its main figures included men like Aimé Césaire, Léopold Sedar Senghor, Léon-Gontran Damas and René Maran, and women like Paulette and Jane Nardal. They were all born in different French colonies and engaged intensely with French republican ideals, African history and culture in their writings and speeches in salons and discussion groups in Paris. They followed contemporary developments in black culture such as the Harlem Renaissance in the United States. Césaire, Damas and

Senghor read and translated the works of poets and writers like Langston Hughes, Richard Wright and Claude McKay, and followed African-American journals such as *The Crisis* and *Opportunity*. Through these engagements, Negritude writers sought 'to elaborate a shared Panafrican identity among a transnational community that could then be linked to an alternative black humanism'.[13]

Gary Wilder's insightful study of Negritude writers demonstrates the overlaps between the cultural and aesthetic articulation of experiences of racism by blacks in Paris and those in Harlem. But Negritude, he argues, must also be distinguished from parallel movements of 'radical Panafricanism'. The latter included more militant groups in metropolitan France that tried to 'organize colonial workers, overturn the colonial system, and support a worldwide communist revolution'. Like the Negritude writers, the radical pan-Africanists also struggled to find their own ways of participating in French civil society and sought to mobilize a transnational black public sphere. They found allies among the French Communist Party. Lamine Senghor, a radical pan-Africanist and a distant cousin of Léopold Senghor, in 1926 founded the Comité de Défense de la Race and its affiliated newspaper *La Voix des Nègres* with support from the French Communist party. Despite the commonality between Negritude writers and the pan-Africanists in their commitment to black internationalism, they differed in their attitudes to the metropole, their ideas about black identity and violence. Negritude's aims are perhaps best summarized as an attempt, on the one hand, to 'elaborate a common ideal, born of the accord between their native civilizations and the demands of the modern world'. On the other was also a commitment to 'assimilate' and 'appreciate the richness of French culture' while 'remaining close to [their] own people' and avoiding 'mechanical and bleached imitation'.[14]

This is not to imply, however, that Negritude writers agreed with one another on all issues. For example, Césaire called upon black youth to emancipate themselves by struggling against 'assimilating colonizers, against other blacks who support assimilation, and against their own impulse to assimilate'.[15] Wilder does not read Césaire's declaration of racial particularity as a disavowal of universalism. Rather, he argues that Césaire believed that only by expressing their particular *colonial* experience could black writers 'contribute to universal life, the humanization of humanity'. In Wilder's words, Césaire's polemic against 'assimilation and insistence on natural racial differences … concludes with a universal vision of racial humanism'.[16] Contra Césaire, Senghor rejected the concept of racial purity and argued that all *nègres* are 'biologically *métis*'. If Césaire found his universal in blacks writing about their racial experience, Senghor argued that 'the very project of universal humanism compels blacks to inquire into their culture'.[17] His was a project of black humanism that tried to ally racial self-discovery with universal humanity.

Wilder insists that Negritude writers were neither the precursors of an anti-colonial resistance movement whose fruition lay in independence from colonial rule, nor were they invested solely in culture rather than politics. Theirs was a politics of culture. Canonical scholarship has treated Negritude, as did many of its founders in later life, as a turn to nativism. Negritude has been celebrated as an instance of anti-colonial resistance that prefigured the development of a full-blown nationalism in many African countries. Others have treated the exponents of Negritude as a Francophilic, colonized elite. Wilder demonstrates that colonialism for men like Senghor *et al.* represented a double bind. It was the vehicle through which they were exposed to universal ideas but also a power structure that prevented the realization of these ideas. They sought to combat cultural alienation through their novel engagement with ideals of republicanism that came to them through their metropolitan education. Cultural particularism – in this case, African culture – would flourish, they thought, within the framework of a reconstructed colonial rule. Wilder states:

> Their two-sided formulations of Franco-African identity, black humanism, Panafrican republicanism, and cultural politics implicitly challenged the grounding dichotomies (modern-primitive, individual-collective, rational-racial, national-global, political-aesthetic) on which the distinctiveness of France's civil society and public sphere depended. By embracing both sides of these pairs at once, (these) colonial subjects practiced a transformative imperial citizenship that simultaneously followed and challenged the republican rules for engaging in civic activity and public politics.[18]

Negritude intellectuals were, in effect, demanding 'membership *within* Greater France *as* Negro-African citizens'.[19] It was in this sense of being both profoundly African and European that these people were postcolonial. They rejected the sharp divide between colonizer and colonized and yet were part of an anti-colonial Zeitgeist in their strident critique of colonial racism. Their engagement with French republican thought highlighted what Chakrabarty has described as the indispensable and yet inadequate nature of European thought when used by the colonized for analytical ends. For republicanism and racism were two sides of the same coin in the lives of these intellectuals. Negritude intellectuals embraced republican thought that came to them via the vehicle of colonial rule, but criticized the modus of imperial rule.[20]

Let me close this discussion of postcolonial peoples with an analysis of populations that have received far less scholarly attention than the figures of the Negritude movement. My focus here is on ex-settler groups who migrated back to the metropole during the turmoil of decolonization. Given that this is an emerging area of scholarship, it may be useful for the reader to have some basic demographic facts that have come to light as a result of research conducted since the late 1990s. Scholars who have studied return migrations to France, the Netherlands and Portugal in the wake of decolonization estimate that some 5 to 7 million people came to these countries as these European empires collapsed one after another in different parts of the world. To call these people repatriates is a misnomer. For, as argued by the anthropologist, Andrea Smith, many of the settlers who migrated to Europe, or to other places such as the United States or Australia, were not born in these countries. Many of them were descendants of European ancestors who were colonials and lived in the colonies for several generations. Furthermore, national origin did not necessarily determine the country to which the returnees migrated. The Maltese, who had acquired French citizenship during the colonial occupation of Algeria and then returned to France around 1962, are a case in point. Many of the migrations were voluntary and not mediated by the assistance of the states to which the returnees went. They were not prisoners of war, nor were they all administrators and government officials returning after the fall of a colonial regime.

In the Introduction to a volume of essays on European returnees from Indonesia, Algeria, Angola and Mozambique entitled *Europe's Invisible Migrants*, Andrea Smith notes that the first to leave the colony were those who had arrived there most recently, soldiers or administrators – that is, people who had designated jobs but enjoyed no real ties to the place. The second group consisted of a wealthier segment of the European settler population, many of whom did not necessarily consider their journeys in terms of a 'return'. They usually had close kin or friendship ties in the metropole and often 'thought they were only leaving temporarily', only to find that returning to the colony had become impossible on account of the tumultuous political conditions there.[21] Most of them left property and possessions behind in the colonies. Finally, the most populous group consisted of those who had lived in the 'colony/former colony the longest ... those of few means, people with the longest family histories there, and those with few or no ties to the metropolitan country; in other words people who had the most to lose by leaving'.[22]

The demographics of the ex-settler groups varied widely depending on the degrees of miscegenation between colonizers and colonized in the different sites of empire. People classified as 'European' in the former Dutch Indies included whites, Asian wives of European men (discussed in the last chapter) as well as Turks, Japanese and Christian Africans from West Africa who had been recruited to fight in the Dutch armies. Immigration to the Netherlands started during the Japanese occupation of Indonesia in the 1940s. At the time there were approximately 300,000 individuals recognized as European. Of them some 80,000 had been born in the Netherlands or the Indies (contemporary Indonesia) of Dutch parents, 170,000 were 'indo-Europeans' of mixed ancestry and 14,000 were people of mixed indigenous origins. There were in addition to these figures some 12,000 Amboinese or South Moluccans who had fought in the Dutch military and 7,000 Peranakan-Chinese. Not all these people were permitted entry into the Netherlands, and thousands migrated to the United States and Australia.

In the French case, from Algeria alone there were over 1 million people who had arrived back in France during the years 1958–62, many of whom were the third to fifth generation born overseas. Unlike the Dutch, there were fewer cases of intermarriage between the Europeans and Algerians. There were, moreover, 450,000 'repatriates' who came into France from Indochina, Morocco and Tunisia. Finally, the influx of populations from Algeria after the end of war in 1962 also included approximately 100,000–200,000 Muslims, known as the *harkis*, who fought in the French army and had held positions in the colonial administration.

The Portuguese Empire (one of the first European maritime empires) was the last to decolonize. During the late 1940s and throughout the 1950s, when most European countries were pulling out of their colonial possessions, the Portuguese government encouraged emigration to Angola and Mozambique. During 1974–6, in the wake of decolonization, some 800,000 *retornados* (returnees) arrived in Portugal from these countries. Interestingly, while Portuguese law defined who counted as 'indigenous' in 1954, the law was not extended to smaller Portuguese colonies of Macao, Goa, Diu and Cape Verde whose inhabitants were '*de facto* Portuguese citizens and therefore able to migrate to Portugal regardless of origin'.[23] In the larger colonies, however, the 1954 law did apply. The legal definition of Portuguese made it difficult for people of 'mixed' and African origin to receive the certificate of *assimilado* (assimilated). In Angola in 1956, approximately 30,000 people of African origin were given this status out of a total population of 4.3 million.

Given the large numbers cited above it is curious that these migrations have not received much scholarly attention until very recently. This may be owing to the fact that the ex-settlers are difficult to identify as a group. We are told that many of them socialize with each other in secluded enclaves of social clubs in present-day France, Australia and other adoptive countries. But since being a returnee usually brought with it the status of citizenship, they don't readily show up in government documents such as the census as anything but European. But, as the above account of the composition of the returnees makes evident, the category European in the postcolonial world was far from homogeneous or white.

There are similarities between these returnees and other refugees or labour migrants. 'Like many refugees they left the colony suddenly, at the chaotic end of a specific political order, usually without the possibility of return. Like many labor migrants, most were migrating to a place they had never seen.' Yet, unlike these two categories, many of the returnees knew the language of the metropolitan countries they went to and were used to metropolitan legal and educational institutions. At the same time, scholars working on these groups repeatedly emphasize the difficulties they faced in assimilating to their new countries on account of different economic, social and geographical conditions. In Frederick

Cooper's analysis, for instance, the lack of interest in these peoples may be related to precisely their postcolonial status:

> The very distinctiveness that the Indonesian Dutch, Angolan Portuguese, or Algerian French had asserted no longer had legitimacy in a decolonizing world: they were people who had no right to exist. To the extent that their identification with a place – with the sights, sounds, and smells of a tropical or Mediterranean land – had any significance, that identification would have to be shared with the majority of inhabitants of those places, whose majoritarian claims to political power were precisely what the repatriates were fleeing. And to the extent to which they could claim someplace to flee to, it was not on the basis of the profound sentiments associated with life in the shared space of France, Portugal, or the Netherlands, but of the more abstract affinities of race and citizenship.[24]

Elaborating on the question of why the returnees have been neglected both by scholars as well by the populations of the countries to which they went, Cooper makes one final point that is crucial for an understanding of a postcolonial European community. This has to do with the 'changing significance of Europe from the 1950s onwards'. This period saw the rise of a more (Western) *European* ideology, witnessed, for instance, in the idea of a European Economic Community. Thus, argues Cooper,

> the politics of particularity of the returnees was played out not just against a national citizenship, but against a population increasingly seeing itself as 'European,' and for whom the discarding of colonies was part of looking toward greater interaction within the European continent, both economically and socially.[25]

It comes as no surprise that, for most of the returnees, settling back into life in the metropole was difficult. Most contributors in Smith's volume document the unpreparedness on the part of the French, Portuguese and Dutch states to receive large numbers of migrants within the space of a few years when the countries in question were reeling under the combined pressures of bad economies, rising unemployment, fear of criminality and loss of empires.

In a study of returnees to the city of Marseilles, Jean Jacques Jordi documents the difficulties faced by them ranging from travelling to the port city in boats that were packed beyond capacity to landing in a city that was unprepared to house them or even acknowledge them as anything but 'seasonal workers looking forward to their holidays'. While non-governmental groups such as the Red Cross, Catholic, Protestant and Jewish groups, and the Salvation Army offered some initial assistance, their support collapsed under the sheer weight of returnee numbers. In Marseilles, whose total population was 770,000 in 1962, the number of repatriates was 194,117. While the government was intent on shifting the repatriates to the north, the latter often refused to budge from the spot where they first arrived 'for what they perceived to be a hostile if not foreign country beyond'.[26] The irony of French citizens feeling 'foreign' on French soil should not be lost on us. Nor were these fears unjustified. The French state, fearful of OAS infiltration in the country, carried out widespread police operations, leaving the repatriates with the impression that the government considered them 'criminally suspect'. Local Marseilles residents also 'feared that the *pieds-noir* would carry with them to France the turmoil of Algeria'.[27]

The accounts of metropole negligence persist as we turn our attention to the Netherlands. Historians Elsbeth Locher-Scholten and Wim Willems approach the problems faced by Dutch peoples returning from Indonesia during the period from 1945 to the 1960s. As mentioned above, there was more intermarriage among the Dutch and the local Indies population, with the result that 'Dutch' in the postcolonial period included a group of people who were both white and of mixed origins. The Netherlands government in the initial years of Dutch migration refused to grant entry permits to those of mixed origins. Even when granted entry, migrants were encouraged by the government to leave for the Indies once the sovereign state of Indonesia was established in 1949. Eventually, under the combined pressure of publicity against the discrimination faced by the Dutch in Sukarno's Indonesia, lobbying by migrant groups in the Netherlands and rising political tensions between the Netherlands and Indonesia following the refusal of the former to recognize Indonesian claims to Dutch New Guinea, the Dutch government gradually relaxed its policy towards allowing migrants into the Netherlands. Yet, for many who came to the Netherlands not only were climate, diet, housing and employment a challenge, even the Dutch language they spoke was quite different from the native Dutch spoken on the mainland. Many disillusioned migrants therefore left the Netherlands for countries such as the United States of America and Australia. There was also an added slight for many Indies-Dutch migrants who felt that in a post-Second World War Netherlands there was little, if any, public acknowledgment of the tribulations they faced during the Pacific War. Their experiences of internment in Japanese camps or of lives severely torn apart during the Japanese colonization of the Indies went unremarked in the Netherlands. Only as recently as the 1990s, thanks to an initiative by the University of Leiden, have the Indies Dutch been the focus of scholarly and subsequently state attention. Willems is actually one of the historians who were appointed by the Dutch government to write a 'coherent history' of the Indies Dutch in the colonial and postcolonial periods.

Willems's research probes into the details of the lives of Dutch migrants in the Indies, in the Netherlands, as well as in America and Australia. With reference to the latter two places, there are interesting differences in the history of Dutch migrants. While they were professionally successful in both places, the story of postcolonial Dutch settlement in Australia was rendered complex by demands on the part of now Dutch-Australians that their suffering during internment in Japanese war camps during the Second World War be recognized by the state, either the Netherlands or Australia. The Dutch government made it clear in 1988 that no one but Indies Dutch permanently settled in the Netherlands was eligible for a one-off compensation of 7,500 guilders under the Indies Camp Detainees Welfare Act. Likewise the Indies migrants were also ineligible for benefits that the Australian government extended to prisoners of war as many of them were 'civil detainees'. Moreover, the claims for compensation and recognition of their victim status also came into conflict with compensation claims being made by the Australian Aboriginal population from the state. Willems cites one revealing quote, presumably by a Dutch-Australian, who asked,

> How far back will we go to attribute guilt? Before you know it situations arise like the mess in the Balkans where families have been acting out feuds for centuries. If we aspire to a tolerant, modern state, we cannot go on blaming the current generation in Japan. ... Nobody is blameless. I don't feel called upon to dole out billions to the Aborigines now for what Australians did before the great postwar migrations. As newcomers, that's not our responsibility, is it? Should the taxpayers of 1998 pay off the debts of the English?[28]

The speaker in question clearly identified as a 'modern' Australian, even as he acknowledged his status as a newcomer. His statement testifies to a desire to assimilate. But this also requires, as he argues, that the history of past wounds – both Dutch and aboriginal – be buried. The same denial was upheld by the right-wing, conservative government in power in Australia in the 1990s. The latter was in favour of a policy of assimilation of the Aboriginal population into mainstream Australian society but was opposed to acknowledging a history of past injustices inflicted by 'white Australia' upon that community. Let me close this chapter by exploring the relationship of 'historical wounds' to writing postcolonial history.

Postcolonial history and the politics of recognition

In her much-acclaimed book *Postcolonial Theory: A Critical Introduction*, Leela Gandhi takes issue with some postcolonial theorists who argue that settler societies such as Australia or Canada 'stand in the same relationship to colonialism as those societies which have experienced the full force and violence of colonial domination'.[29]

These claims, she argues, render the experience of colonization homogeneous and 'confer a seamless and undiscriminating postcoloniality on both white settler cultures and on those indigenous people displaced through their encounter with these cultures'.[30] Gandhi is right in urging postcolonial theorists to differentiate the experience of colonialism in countries like Canada, Australia and New Zealand, from places like India. As mentioned above, these places did not witness a decolonization movement that involved a transfer of power from the colonizer to the colonized. Why, then, do we invoke them in this analysis of postcolonial history-writing? To put it briefly, even though countries such as Australia, Canada and New Zealand did not go through a political decolonization movement, settler culture there has been seriously called into question by a process of what the historian Miranda Johnson has described as 'ethical' decolonization – a sustained and continuing process of questioning the past assumptions of white supremacy by dialogue between and across different socio-cultural communities. The discipline of history has played no small part in this process as historians have undertaken to revise and challenge existing records of settler–indigenous relations, probed the violation of treaty histories and (together with other scholars and activists) helped build up cases of Native Titles, that is, the claims by indigenous peoples to ancestral lands.

This is where one can identify two postcolonial characteristics of revisionist historiography produced in and about these countries. One relates to points of convergence between something like, say, *Subaltern Studies* and revisionist histories of white settler colonies. The other relates to phenomena unique to these countries where the option of complete decolonization is not available to indigenous peoples. I shall illustrate the two characteristics by reference to the works of Dipesh Chakrabarty and Miranda Johnson.

In a recent essay on the Australian historian Henry Reynolds, Dipesh Chakrabarty comments on the similarities between the historical projects of Aboriginal history, which became a separate discipline in Australian universities from the 1980s and *Subaltern Studies*, discussed in Chapter 1. Reynolds himself commented on these overlaps, albeit in retrospect, in his Introduction to the 2006 edition of *The Other Side of the Frontier*, where he wrote:

> It was only much later that I realized that what I was trying to do closely paralleled the contemporaneous work of the historians of South Asia who launched the school of subaltern studies. A month or two after *The Other Side of the Frontier* was published in Townsville, in Canberra Ranajit Guha wrote the preface to the first volume of *Subaltern Studies*, which he explained would deal with those who were subject to subordination … [and] the failure of traditional history to acknowledge the subaltern as the maker of his own destiny.[31]

The similarities between *Subaltern Studies* and Aboriginal history (in the hands of historians like Reynolds), argues Chakrabarty, signal that both projects are products of a 'postcolonial condition'.[32] Both Ranajit Guha, the founder of *Subaltern Studies*, and Henry Reynolds challenged the narratives of nationalism and national progress that elided socially marginal groups from the history of the nation. While Guha took Indian nationalist historiography to task for not including the contributions of peasants, workers and tribals into the making of Indian nationalism, Reynolds challenged Australian national histories written between 1955 and the 1980s for celebrating the success with which 'free' British institutions had been transplanted to the settler state. In his celebrated book, *The Other Side of the Frontier*, he wrote, 'This is the first book to systematically explore the other side of the frontier, *to turn Australian history, not upside down, but inside out.*'[33] These words challenged narratives of settler freedom from which Aboriginal agency and dispossession had been erased. But there was also a second, more complex move, entailed in this gesture of seeing the subaltern/Aboriginal as agents of history.

Both Guha and Reynolds refused to treat the Aborigine as a 'pre-political' figure whose absence of class consciousness precluded purposeful political action. For example, refuting earlier historical works that regarded Aboriginal practices as inherently primitive, Reynolds in his *Fate of a Free People*, analysed Aboriginal resistance in Tasmania in the early to mid-nineteenth century as a nationalist enterprise. Walter Arthur, the leader of the movement, was in Reynolds's reckoning 'the first Aboriginal nationalist'. Chakrabarty argues that it was not as if Reynolds was unaware of the European roots of the modern idea of nationalism. But, his deliberate gesture of reading Tasmanian Aboriginal resistance through the idiom of nationalism tore away that idea 'from all its anchorage in the history of modern institutions'.[34] Reynolds was explicit that he was not writing 'blackfella history'. His work was aimed at non-indigenous Australians intended as a challenge to the way white Australia looked upon its Aboriginal past. In doing this, he made a classic postcolonial move of stretching categories of European thought by displacing them from their places of origin to colonial locations and peoples. Chakrabarty argues that, for Reynolds (as also for Guha),

> politics and nationalism are under-determined, part-sociological and part-rhetorical categories ... not completely open to the demand for clarification. And it is their rhetorical imprecision that actually enables Reynolds to let us see something new in history. He has, in Gayatri Spivak's terms, successfully brought the word 'nationalism' to a catachresis, which is the only way subalterns appropriate the categories of the dominant.[35]

Thanks to the efforts of historians like Reynolds and others, 'history has become a matter of fierce public debate in the three settler states of Australia, Canada, and New Zealand'.[36] Aspects of indigenous–settler relations are often the subject of public debate in the media, documentary and feature films. The case of the so-called 'stolen generations', Aboriginal children forcibly removed from their parents and raised by settlers, is a telling example of a subject that has most recently fuelled 'history wars' in Australia.[37] These efforts have undoubtedly gone a long way towards transforming these settler states into postcolonial states by helping raise public awareness of colonial/Aboriginal issues. Also significant is the way in which the protocols of the historical discipline have been challenged in these countries as academic historians worked together with indigenous peoples and activists in preparing their land claims and native titles.

Academic historians acknowledge the differences between indigenous histories and their own. But taking these differences seriously has led historians to write academic histories more creatively without compromising on the issue of historical objectivity.[38] For instance, indigenous histories are often oral narratives whose author is a collective 'we' rather than the putative 'I', which is the subject of most Western historical records. Indigenous accounts, 'especially "myth-narratives," are often framed by a radically different sense of reality, causation and time'. As observed by Bain Attwood and Fiona Magowan, 'events can be sequenced in ways other than those usually demanded by history … while chronologies are either absent or follow a different logic (for example, in one Captain Cook story Ned Kelly [a nineteenth century outlaw] precedes Cook)'.[39]

It would, however, be a mistake to argue that the acknowledgment of indigenous people's grievances by settler states – both at the material and symbolic level – has produced the same postcolonial condition in all the three countries under consideration. Miranda Johnson's recent researches into the work of courts and tribunals in Australia, Canada and New Zealand to which indigenous people have brought their claims highlight some of these differences. Two critical insights emerge from Johnson's study, which shed new light on the way in which indigeneity operates in relation to settler identity in a postcolonial world.

'In all three countries under consideration,' writes Johnson, 'there have been wide-ranging moral arguments about what happened in the settler colonial past and what the traumatic effects of the actions of the settler state were for indigenous communities.' Historians, lawyers, activists and government officials argue about the 'responsibility' of settler states and settlers to indigenous groups. In working out the meaning of responsibility courts and specially created commissions of inquiry in those three countries examine indigenous claims. Johnson sees these legal sites as places in which a variety of strategies are used to transform the relations between settlers and indigenous peoples – something akin to partial decolonization. There are, however, significant limitations on any such transformation. Although being indigenous is actually a modern identity category, in legal sites indigenous claimants must establish their authenticity by establishing how traditional they really are.[40]

In New Zealand and Canada, two countries where settlers made treaties with indigenous groups, debates about the meaning of 'historical compensation' raise questions about what it means to be indigenous in a modern nation state. As Johnson asks, 'Are governments settling the past, and therefore dispensing with their responsibilities? Or are they recognizing that rights that were not properly acknowledged in the past have to be acknowledged now?' These questions are important because often indigenous scholars and activists argue that the 'very act of making treaties in the past' underscored 'recognition of indigenous political authority and even sovereignty'.[41] Thus, recognition of treaties on their own terms implies that indigenous rights pre-exist the settler state. It also raises questions about whether or not indigenous peoples' collective differences go beyond or are resolvable by their rights as national citizens. Whatever the outcome of the legal disputes, the existence of treaties in New Zealand and Canada actually allows for recognition of indigenous peoples, from the time of conquest, as historical actors. In 1969 the Canadian Cree political leader Harold Cardinal criticized the Trudeau government for its proposal to scrap pre-existing treaties that recognized Indians as special wards of the state by arguing that treaties bore a national historical significance, for they were 'signed by honourable men on both sides'. Indigenous peoples in these two countries can claim special privileges from the state on the ground that their treaties – signed between different but equal actors – were violated.[42]

In the case of Australia (or the province of British Columbia in Canada) where there is no treaty history, the status of indigenous peoples is markedly different. Through a close analysis of land rights or native title cases in Australia, Johnson argues that in order to be successful in their claims Aboriginal people must successfully establish their indigenous, cultural authenticity. For example, in the landmark Gove land rights case, Justice Blackburn admitted Yolungu testimony even where it 'might fall foul of heresy rules', that is, where it 'consisted of second- or third-hand statements'.[43] Even though Blackburn did not rule in favour of the plaintiffs, 'his sympathetic treatment of the Yolungu worldview is now represented as the beginning of the decolonization of Australian law'.[44] Yet, there was a deep irony underpinning this gesture. Blackburn admitted Yolungu testimonies on the grounds that they were 'traditional in form and content' and therefore not subject to the same kinds of evidentiary proof that eyewitness testimony or other primary records are. Yolungu people were thus established as a people with tradition, frozen in time and space, lacking in historicity. In Johnson's words, 'the more indigenous you show yourself to be through the performance of tradition, the less historicity or historical agency you can claim'.[45] This was clear in the failure of the Yorta Yorta claimants in their 1998 Native title claim where the plaintiffs demonstrated that their ancestors protested their loss of land rights in the nineteenth century through a petition to parliament. Ironically, the claimants' engagement with 'modern' political forms such as petition and litigation 'signified to the federal court the inauthenticity of their claim to traditional continuity'. The absence of treaties in Australia throws up a curious problem for postcolonial Aboriginal communities. It 'shows how difficult it is for indigenous people to establish a modern personhood and still be recognized as properly indigenous'.[46]

Conclusion

Postcolonial history-writing clearly demonstrates that the end of empire made 'the politics of recognition' a central feature of modern democracies. The political struggles around decolonization and civil rights movements from the 1960s onwards have powerfully fuelled this politics. Yet, as the analyses presented in this and the last chapter make clear, not all groups have been successful in their calls for recognition. The success or failure of a group in being recognized by the state, both as national citizens but also as individuals marked by a specific community identity, depends on the extent to which there is consensus around the fact that they have been wounded by the past actions of dominating powers.

Let me close this discussion of postcolonial history-writing and empire with a brief analysis of what Dipesh Chakrabarty calls 'historical wounds'. Chakrabarty develops the idea of historical wounds from the philosopher Charles Taylor's discussion of 'the politics of recognition' in multicultural societies. 'Misrecognition', writes Taylor, 'can inflict a grievous wound, saddling its victims with a crippling self-hatred'.[47] Furthering Taylor's notion of wound, Chakrabarty argues that 'for a person or group so "wounded," to speak of the wound or to speak in its name is already to be on the path to recovery'.[48] A historical wound in Chakrabarty's particular usage is a historical phenomenon that comes into being when there is broad social consensus that particular groups in society owe their marginalization to discrimination and oppression suffered during the colonial past. This recognition by both the sufferers and those who caused the suffering paves a way towards the redressing the grievance and reconciliation. We see this in evidence in the cases mentioned above as well as in postcolonial South Africa. In order for a historical wound, in the sense that Chakrabarty writes about it, to be recognized there needs to be a degree of consensus between both academic historians, the state and other social groups.

Herein lies a challenge that the postcolonial condition poses for academic history-writing. For a historical wound is different, although not entirely divorced, from the notion of a 'historical truth'. The latter consists of 'facts', which are open to verification and refutation, and its veracity is not dependent upon experiential claims. Historical wounds, however, fall somewhere between history and memory. Historical truths endure, but the notion of a wound is more fragile and can change if there is a change in political alignments. Chakrabarty cites the example of the 'stolen generations' to demonstrate the difference between the two ideas of historical wound and historical truth.

> That there had been such a removal of Aboriginal children was a piece of historical truth, a generalization open to empirical verification. But the epithet 'stolen' packed into the expression an emotional intensity that could not be measured by the historian's scale. Its instant popularity in the nineties, however, was due to a broadly emergent social consensus about the historical plight of the Aboriginal people.[49]

The fact that Canadian Indians, Maoris or Australian Aboriginals have succeeded in making their respective governments and societies conscious of their past and present grievances was to a large degree enabled by historical (and other scholarly) works, most of which were authored by non-indigenous historians, which were devoted to the writing of histories whose sympathies were pro-Aboriginal. Yet, the same kinds of histories written about minority groups in other democratic settings, such as India or the United States, for example, do not produce the same results politically. In the latter instance, 'there are ... sub-disciplines within history departments or programmes devoted to studying the pasts of these groups but the fierce battles over the intellectual consequences of identity politics shows that these sub-disciplines have never achieved the commanding heights' of a field like Aboriginal history in the Australian context.[50] We live in a world where it is no longer possible to ignore the politics of identity. Multiculturalism now operates without the domination of imperial authority. But it is also continually challenged within different nation states by the ideology of assimilation. The contemporary world is one where everywhere numerous groups jostle with state authorities and other global organizations for rights and recognition. In these postcolonial conditions, history-writing can no longer remain disengaged from issues of memory and experience, nor can the historian's agenda be driven simply by these latter factors. The discipline of history in postcolonial times has to take into account a careful and considered negotiation of archival materials, as well as other kinds of knowledge gleaned from the realm of experience and social memory – oral histories, myths, films and other mass media.

Notes

1 Thornton, cited in David Prochaska, *Making Algeria French: Colonialism in Bone, 1870–1920* (Cambridge: Cambridge University Press, 1990), pp. 6–7.

2 Prochaska, *Making Algeria French*, p. 7.

3 Prochaska, *Making Algeria French*, p. 9.
4 After the loss of settlements and territories in North America, the Caribbean, India and in some islands on the Indian Ocean a new wave of French colonialism began in the nineteenth century.
5 Prochaska, *Making Algeria French*, p. 137.
6 Prochaska, *Making Algeria French*, p. 138
7 Prochaska, *Making Algeria French*, p. 223.
8 Prochaska, *Making Algeria French*, p. 165.
9 Prochaska, *Making Algeria French*.
10 For more details, see Prochaska, *Making Algeria French*, p. 22.
11 Prochaska, *Making Algeria French*, p. 247.
12 Gary Wilder, *The French Imperial Nation-state: Negritude and Colonial Humanism between the Two World Wars* (Chicago, IL: University of Chicago Press, 2005), p. 27.
13 Wilder, *The French Imperial Nation-state*, p. 175.
14 Wilder, *The French Imperial Nation-state*, p. 185.
15 Wilder, *The French Imperial Nation-state*, p. 188.
16 Wilder, *The French Imperial Nation-state*.
17 Wilder, *The French Imperial Nation-state*.
18 Wilder, *The French Imperial Nation-state*, p. 197.
19 Wilder, *The French Imperial Nation-state*, p. 212 (his emphasis).
20 Wilder invokes postcolonial theorists such as Chakrabarty and Chatterjee at different points in his work. See Wilder, *The French Imperial Nation-state*, pp. 80, 159, 203, 257.
21 Andrea L. Smith (ed.), *Europe's Invisible Migrants* (Amsterdam: Amsterdam University Press, 2003), p. 12.
22 Smith, *Europe's Invisible Migrants*, p. 13.
23 Smith, *Europe's Invisible Migrants*, p. 15.
24 Smith, *Europe's Invisible Migrants*, pp. 169–70.
25 Smith, *Europe's Invisible Migrants*, p. 173.
26 Smith, *Europe's Invisible Migrants*, p. 68.
27 Smith, *Europe's Invisible Migrants*, p. 69
28 Smith, *Europe's Invisible Migrants*, p. 55.
29 Gandhi was addressing the works of postcolonial theorists I. Adam and H. Tiffin in their book, *Past the Last Post: Theorizing Postcolonialism and Postmodernism*. Leela Gandhi, *Postcolonial Theory: A Critical Introduction* (NSW: Allen & Unwin, 1998), p. 168.
30 Gandhi, *Postcolonial Theory*, p. 167.
31 Henry Reynolds, *The Other Side of the Frontier*, new edition (Sydney: University of New South Wales Press, 2006), p. 4.
32 Dipesh Chakrabarty, 'Aboriginal and Subaltern Histories', in Bain Attwood and Tom Griffiths (eds), *Frontier, Race, Nation: Henry Reynolds and Australian History* (Melbourne: Australian Scholarly Publishing Limited, 2009), p. 57. For a gloss on the 'postcolonial condition', see Introduction.
33 Reynolds, *The Other Side*, p. 199 (emphasis mine).
34 Chakrabarty, 'Aboriginal and Subaltern Histories', p. 68.
35 Chakrabarty, 'Aboriginal and Subaltern Histories'.
36 Miranda Johnson, 'Making History Public: Indigenous Claims to Settler States', *Public Culture* 20(1) (2008), p. 97.
37 For more details on the history wars and debates on aboriginal history, see Stuart Macintyre and Anna Clark (eds), *The History Wars* (Melbourne: Melbourne University Press, 2003); Bain Attwood, *Telling the Truth about Aboriginal History* (NSW: Allen & Unwin, 2005); Robert Manne (ed.), *Whitewash: On Keith Windschuttle's Fabrication of Aboriginal History* (Melbourne: Black Inc, 2003); Dirk Moses (ed.), *Genocide and Settler Society: Frontier Violence and Stolen Indigenous Children in Australian History* (New York, NY: Berghann Books, 2004); Patrick Wolfe, 'Settler Colonialism and the Elimination of the Native', *Journal of Genocide Research* 9(4) (2006), pp. 387–409.
38 For an example of this kind of historical writing, see Judith Binney, *Redemption Song* (Auckland: Auckland University Press, 1995).

39 Bain Attwood and Fiona Magowan (eds), *Telling Stories: Indigenous History and Memory in Australia and New Zealand* (NSW: Allen & Unwin, 2001), p. xv.
40 Miranda Johnson, 'The Gove Land Rights Case and the Problem of History in a Decolonizing Australia', in Bain Attwood and Tom Griffiths (eds), *Frontier, Race, Nation: Henry Reynolds and Australian History* (Melbourne: Australian Scholarly Publishing Limited, 2009), pp. 305–29.
41 Johnson, 'Making History Public', pp. 99–100.
42 Quoted in Miranda Johnson, 'Struggling over the Past: Decolonization and the Problem of History in Settler Societies' (Ph. D. dissertation, University of Chicago, 2008), p. 79.
43 Johnson, 'The Gove Land Rights Case', p. 307.
44 Johnson, 'The Gove Land Rights Case'.
45 Johnson, 'The Gove Land Rights Case', p. 308.
46 Johnson, 'The Gove Land Rights Case'.
47 Charles Taylor, cited in Dipesh Chakrabarty, 'History and the Politics of Recognition', in Keith Jenkins, Sue Morgan and Alan Munslow (eds), *Manifestoes for History* (London: Routledge, 2007), p. 77.
48 Chakrabarty, 'History and the Politics of Recognition'.
49 Chakrabarty, 'History and the Politics of Recognition', p. 78.
50 Chakrabarty, 'History and the Politics of Recognition', p. 79.

7

Postcolonial and gender histories

The Martinique-born anti-colonial intellectual Frantz Fanon's scathing indictment of French colonialism, *A Dying Colonialism*, begins with a chapter entitled 'Algeria Unveiled'. The main focus of the chapter is to discuss the role of women, in particular the veiled Algerian Muslim woman, in the armed struggle for Algerian liberation. The veil (and by implication the woman under the veil), argued Fanon, constituted the ideological battleground between the colonizer and colonized, the colonizer often seeing himself as the champion(s) of progress and the colonized as representing stasis. To liberate the Muslim woman from the layers of cloth that hid her from the world was used by the colonizer as a challenge whose purpose was to tame and shame Algerian patriarchy. 'The method of presenting the Algerian as a prey fought over with equal ferocity by Islam and France with its Western culture reveals the whole approach of the occupier, his philosophy and his policy.'[1] The prey in question, of course, was the veiled woman. Fanon's discussion on the veil is instructive for our purposes. It raises a set of related issues that will constitute the core of this concluding chapter, namely, the place of gender and necessarily linked to it questions of race and nation in the colonial encounter and the postcolonial historian's approach to these issues.

If the symbol of the French civilizing mission in Algeria was premised upon the unveiling of the Algerian woman, Algerian male strength and honour too got inextricably wrapped up in the symbolic virtue of the veil. In Fanon's words, 'It is the white man who creates the Negro. But it is the Negro who creates Negritude. To the colonialist offensive against the veil, the colonized opposes the cult of the veil.'[2] Needless to say, the Algerian woman, as the wearer of the veil acquires huge symbolic currency in this entire discourse. Fanon discussed the revolutionary conditions under which the Algerian woman shed the veil or *haik*. This unveiling, he argued, made her feel stripped and naked before the eyes of her male (both European and native) beholders. Yet, it was a gesture of defiance, imbuing her body with a coded message. Then again, as the war became more intense, it became necessary for women to don the veil again, this time to smuggle weapons, grenades and false papers under its layers. In a statement that remains relevant to postcolonial discussions on the veil to this day, Fanon noted,

> There is thus a historic dynamism of the veil that is very concretely perceptible in the development of colonization in Algeria. In the beginning the veil was a mechanism of resistance, but its value for the social group remained very strong. The veil was worn because tradition demanded a rigid separation of the sexes, but also because the occupier was bent on unveiling Algeria. In the second phase ... (T)he veil was abandoned. ... What had been used to block the psychological or political offensives of the occupier became a means, an instrument. The veil helped the Algerian woman to meet the new problems created by the struggle.[3]

As evidenced by this brief discussion of 'Algeria Unveiled', questions of tradition, modernity, patriarchy, racialism, agency and oppression are all intimately bound up with the colonial discourse about gender. The problem of the veiled woman appears like a microcosm that contained many of the themes that postcolonial historians of gender continue to grapple with. On the one hand, the category of the 'veiled woman' raises questions about representation and the particular condition of subalternity for the 'third world woman', which in turn fold back into the problem of empire. On the other, historians critical of the stereotype of the veiled or third world woman have expended their energies in searching for the 'real' woman (behind the veil/or unveiled). These efforts have produced a whole raft of possibilities for thinking through postcolonial modernities. Despite their differences, the many approaches to the history of gender signal that this has been an area in which postcolonial historians have had a noticeable imprint. In what follows, I want to identify and elaborate upon certain themes that have given the discussions of gender in postcolonial historiography its distinct cast. Briefly, these may be summarized as the question of the third world woman; the role of gender in the so-called 'civilizing mission'; gender in nationalist discourse; gender as the site for a 'clash of civilizations'. Let us briefly assess how each of these areas of inquiry has been dealt with by historians. In conclusion, we will discuss some emergent areas of inquiry in postcolonial historiography with regard to gender.

The third world woman and liberal feminism

In her 1993 book, which offered one of the most cogent introductions to postcolonial theory, Leela Gandhi analysed some of the cleavages that divided postcolonial and feminist theorists of gender. Briefly, these have to do with the category of the 'third world woman' and the discursive and actual collusion between imperialism and liberal feminism that is implied in positing such a category. Related to this, Gandhi also drew attention to the ideological task in which certain 'feminist criteria' were deployed in justifying colonialism's 'civilizing mission'.[4] In the nearly two decades that have elapsed since the publication of Gandhi's book, many feminist scholars – including Rajeshwari Sunder-Rajan, Mrinalini Sinha, Anne McClintock, Lila Abu-Lughod and others – have revisited the schism between liberal and postcolonial feminism, and the question remains one of the most fertile areas of inquiry in the academy. It is therefore important that we understand what is implied by these theoretical considerations and simultaneously illustrate how they have shaped historical writing.

'The most significant collision and collusion of postcolonial and feminist theory', notes Gandhi, 'occurs around the contentious figure of the "third world woman".'[5] Parsing out the implications of Gandhi's statement, we realize that the vantage of the third world woman is often one that allowed for the most incisive critiques of imperialism and nationalism. Historians working on a range of colonial contexts have demonstrated that women often suffered the might of double colonization – by imperial rulers, and by indigenous patriarchs. In that sense the third world woman was the 'victim *par excellance*' and scores of feminist writers have challenged the gender blindness of both imperialism and nationalism. At the same time, positing a category such as the third world woman has the effect of rendering homogeneous groups that are internally variegated and heterogeneous. This insight constituted the core of Chandra Mohanty's influential article, 'Under Western Eyes: Feminist Scholarship and Colonial Discourse'. In a wide-ranging survey of liberal feminist writings, Mohanty delineates six ways in which the 'third world woman' emerged as a category of analysis in Western feminist discourse on the third world. These are: women defined as victims of male violence; as universal dependants; as victims of colonial process; as victims of Arab or Oriental familial systems; as victims of the Islamic code; and finally, as victims of the economic development process.[6] Irrespective of what the subject of analysis was, women invariably emerged as victims of institutions and systems. The result, argued Mohanty, was the production of an image of the 'average third world woman'.

> This average Third World woman leads an essentially truncated life based on her feminine gender (read: sexually constrained) and her being 'Third World' (read: ignorant, poor, uneducated, tradition-bound, domestic, family-oriented, victimized, etc.). This, I suggest, is in contrast to the (implicit) self-representation of Western women as educated, as modern, as having control over their bodies and sexualities and the freedom to make their own decisions.[7]

The creation of a category such as the third world woman also produced an archetype that relegated actual historical actors to a status of inescapable marginality. Gayatri Spivak has noted that the relentless emphasis on the third world woman's marginality often produced something like a reverse colonialism or a 'new Orientalism'.[8] As she noted, 'When a cultural identity is thrust upon one because the center wants an identifiable margin, claims of marginality assure validation from the center.'[9] Others, like Sara Suleri, have argued in a similar vein that the trope of the third world woman brings race and gender together in such a way that the female subject gets endowed with an 'iconicity' that is almost 'too good to be true'.[10] Suleri noted elsewhere, 'The coupling of *postcolonial* with *woman*, ... almost inevitably leads to the simplicities that underlie unthinking celebration of oppression, elevating the racially female voice into a metaphor for "the good".'[11]

In two essays, 'Can the Subaltern Speak?' and 'Subaltern Studies: Deconstructing Historiography' which are now grist for the mill of many postcolonial analysts, Gayatri Spivak introduced the notion of 'epistemic violence', a (sometimes unintended and often unconscious) by-product of well-intentioned attempts at representations of marginal, colonized and ex-colonial populations.[12] To speak of epistemic violence is to demonstrate how Western/colonial knowledge systems occluded the non-Western/colonized by subordinating to themselves other modes of knowing the world. Representation became more a matter of the colonizer's own concerns and identity than of the colonial subject(s) in question. To draw attention to epistemic violence is to show how paradoxical the act of historical representation is. Even as her goal was to rescue the third world woman from oblivion, the historian/scholar can end up erasing that *real* woman from history. Spivak elaborated on this notion with reference to Julia Kristeva's *About Chinese Women* and developed and furthered the idea in the two essays mentioned above.[13]

Let us turn now to some of the ways in which these critiques have been developed, and in some instances challenged, by postcolonial historians. Lata Mani's essay 'Contentious Traditions: The Debate on Sati in Colonial India'[14] focused on the debates on the abolition of *sati* between Indian and British reform-minded men and their more conservative opponents. *Sati* – an abbreviation for *satidaha* – referred to the Hindu practice of the immolation of widows on their husband's funeral pyre. A woman whose life ended in this tragic manner was hailed as a *sati*, seen as the epitome of selfless and virtuous action, following the myth of the Indian goddess Parvati (or Durga), also known as *sati*. The British government, under Governor General Lord William Bentinck, enacted a law banning the practice in 1829.[15] In doing this the British were aided and inspired by Indian reformers like Raja Rammohun Roy (1774–1833) who analysed scriptural writings on *sati* in order to demonstrate its illegitimacy. Indian opponents of *sati* abolition argued that the law was a travesty of Indian tradition and that it sanctioned the English East India Company's meddling in indigenous social and religious practices.

Mani's essay, which was further developed in her monograph by the same title, demonstrated how women had no voice in deciding the fate of a practice that deeply influenced their life. Women, she argued, were simply the site upon which Indian and British men jostled with each other about the normative parameters of tradition and modernity. The woman whose destiny was being decided by the conservative and reform lobbies was reduced to an abstraction – voiceless and unreal. Mani's argument had far-reaching consequences for gender history. Her postcolonial outlook threw into sharp relief the commonality between colonial and nationalist leaderships that legislated in the name of subjects with scant attention to the feelings or opinions of the groups who stood to be deeply affected by these reforms. The postcolonial state that followed in the wake of independence replicated these colonial attitudes in large measure.

Mani also highlighted the importance of colonial discourse analysis in writing the history of gender. First, she demonstrated the ways in which the colonial state generated knowledge about India. Reminiscent of Edward Said's *Orientalism*, or even of Fanon's veiled Algerian woman, Mani's analysis demonstrated how the discourse on widow burning became a trope for the retrograde nature of Indian civilization. The widow became a summary for the condition of Indian women in general, whose plight was seen as an index of India's backwardness. Colonial intervention was thus deemed necessary to rescue the Indian woman from such unmitigated misery. Secondly, by emphasizing the near-absent role of women in the making of laws that would impact on their lives, her analysis highlighted the patriarchal character of both colonial and Indian reformism. Finally, she demonstrated the ways in which colonial (and subsequently postcolonial) discourse made an equation between women, tradition, and the nation.

The last point has been exemplified further by historians writing about histories of violence against women during riots and other moments of political strife. Women's bodies, as these histories document, have often been regarded as symbolic of the nation. Historians like Tanika Sarkar, Gyanendra Pandey and others have shown how during riots that accompanied the partition of India in 1947 and in more recent times there was a discursive equation made between the violence perpetrated upon women and that unleashed upon the national body.[16] Violence, as historians working on different contexts the world over have demonstrated, reduced women's bodies to carriers of a sacred national tradition, emptied out, as it were, of their lived present.

'Contentious Traditions' resonates with the argument proposed by Gayatri Spivak in the essay 'Can the Subaltern Speak?'. Spivak argued,

> One never encounters the testimony of the women's voice-consciousness. Such a testimony would not be ideology transparent or 'fully' subjective, of course, but it would have constituted the ingredients for producing a countersentence. As one goes down the grotesquely mistranscribed names of these women, the sacrificed widows, in the police reports included in the records of the East India Company, one cannot put together a 'voice'. The most one can sense is the immense heterogeneity breaking through even such a skeletal and ignorant account.[17]

Mani, however, pushes further at the implications of Spivak's argument in her book. She asks whether, the 'cannot' in Spivak's claim 'the female subaltern cannot speak' implies that the female subaltern 'does not know how to' speak as opposed to being 'unable to (speak) under the circumstances'.[18] Furthermore, is it the case, she asks, that the female subaltern cannot speak only in official records, such as 'police reports' mentioned above, or that she is unable to speak 'in any voice, however refracted?' In answering these questions, Mani turns to an analysis of women's testimonies on *sati*. Reading this account, it becomes clear that while the dominant male (both British and Indian) view regarded *sati* as a primarily religious practice, women's accounts testified to the numerous material hardships and social denigration faced by the Hindu widow, to the point where she often chose to willingly end her life than face a life of complete social abnegation. This reading of women's archives enables Mani to critically rephrase Spivak so that we 'remain vigilant about the positioning of women in colonial discourse without conceding to colonial discourse what it did not, in fact achieve – the erasure of women'.[19]

Postcolonial historians like Mani have demonstrated the ways in which female agency can often disrupt narratives of progress that marked colonial and nationalist accounts of the nation. Considerations of gender challenge liberal accounts of a colonial nation's march towards modernization and sovereignty. Nowhere was this proposition more clearly demonstrated than in Partha Chatterjee's influential essay 'The Nationalist Resolution of the Women's Question'.[20]

Gender and nationalist discourse

Chatterjee, as we know from previous chapters, writes out of the context of colonial and postcolonial Indian history. His work offers important insights to historians writing on other regions, such as the Middle East, whose encounter with the modern was mediated by Western colonialism. In the essay under consideration, Chatterjee begins by remarking on the 'sudden disappearance' of the women's question from the agenda of Indian nationalists at the turn of the twentieth century. If an early generation of social reformers, such as Rammohun Roy mentioned above, or Ishwar Chandra Vidyasagar (1820–91), devoted their lives to the removal of certain injustices that crippled women's lives, namely, the burning of widows, the ban on widow remarriage, the prohibition on women's inheritance rights and female education, and widespread child marriage, latter-day nationalists appeared little concerned with women's issues. As he probes the reason behind the apparent suspension of interest in matters concerning the uplift and modernization of women's conditions, Chatterjee argues that it was hardly the case that late-nineteenth-century nationalists in India were disengaged with the so-called 'women's question'. On the contrary, 'nationalism did in fact provide an answer to the new social and cultural problems concerning the position of women in "modern" society'. But 'this answer was posited not on an identity but a difference with the perceived forms of cultural modernity in the West'. Readers will be reminded of the discussion on Chatterjee's theory of nationalism in Chapter 1. In a similar vein, this time with particular reference to the history of gender, Chatterjee argued that towards the end of the nineteenth century Indian nationalist discourse had successfully positioned the women's question in an 'inner domain of sovereignty far removed from the arena of political contest with the colonial state'.[21]

Chatterjee's analysis of nationalist discourse runs along the following lines. In the colonized world of late-nineteenth-century India, nationalist men effected a discursive separation between the home and the world. The 'world' corresponded with the material sphere of life. Here the Indian/non-European experienced subjugation at the hands of the British/European owing to the latter's ascendancy in science, technology and capitalist progress. The 'home', however, was the domain of the spiritual, unsullied by foreign values. In the inner sanctum of the home – represented by the native woman in her role as wife and mother – no encroachments by the colonizer would be tolerated. 'Once we match this new meaning of the home/world dichotomy with the identification of social roles by gender,' wrote Chatterjee, 'we get the ideological framework within which nationalism answered the women's question.'[22] He adds further, in what would be a powerful postcolonial critique of liberal feminism, that

> It would be grave error to see in this, as liberals are apt to in their despair at the many marks of social conservatism in nationalist practice, a total rejection of the West. Quite the contrary: the nationalist paradigm in fact supplied an ideological principle of selection. It was not a dismissal of modernity but an attempt to make modernity consistent with the nationalist project.[23]

Chatterjee's essay evoked much discussion and debate among feminist scholars. One of the yields of his analytical framework was to help us understand why so many nationalist movements in different parts of the colonized world manifest such contradictory approaches to questions of women's modernization. For example, in India, Egypt and Iran, to name a few places, there was a great deal of emphasis placed on women's education. Yet, the thrust of the education was towards making women 'good' and 'modern' wives and mothers. Women's traditional gender roles were not challenged by nationalists even if they were recast to some degree. One could argue that this was a model of education followed in the Victorian period in the West too – where education was expected to remake the wife as a helpmeet to her husband. But what makes the non-Western instance different was the fact that education was often delinked from the project of a secular modernity. Nor did women's modernization necessarily imply freedom in terms of the body and sexuality. Chatterjee would argue that this was not a contradiction as such. His historical framework helps us see these changes – which he christened the 'new patriarchy' – as a constitutive feature of nationalism's attempt to stake its sovereignty *vis-à-vis* the West by retaining the autonomy of the familial sphere. Furthermore, Chatterjee challenges a unilinear notion of modernity in the realm of gender relations and the family by demonstrating that cultures have different ways of being modern that do not correspond neatly to Western, liberal ideas of modernization and progress. Rather, it is an active engagement with certain liberal ideas that results in the principle of critical 'selection' he considers germane to the modern condition in the non-West. This insight of postcolonial gender history, the notion of modern but different from the West, is particularly useful when we consider why some cultures to this day privilege practices such as arranged marriage; or why definitions of modern personhood are inextricably linked to caste, religious virtue and piety. Instead of regarding these practices as reactionary or traditional, the postcolonial optic allows the historian to analyse them as coeval with the West but not necessarily identical with it.

Take the widespread practice of arranged marriage in modern India.[24] Arranged marriage refers to marriages that are negotiated by the families of the bride and bridegroom. Historical and popular accounts often depict them as a sign of a frozen tradition. Men and women married in this manner are seen as deprived of the freedom of choice that appears to be the basis for 'love' marriages in the West. Historical research demonstrates, however, that far from being a static or unchanging practice, arranged marriage in India underwent a series of transformations from the late nineteenth century. For example, marriages were often arranged through matrimonial advertisements (reminiscent of present-day dating columns, only put out by the guardians of the bride or bridegroom) where the marriageable candidates were described in short, pithy, condensed phrases such as 'civil servant, seeking fair, educated, bride'. This manner of describing men and women as a series of traits shows the commodification and impact of print culture on this system of matrimonial negotiation. Furthermore, to assume that arranged marriage was completely antithetical to ideas of romantic love is a mistake. A closer look at the matrimonial culture of late colonial India brings to light use of new technologies like photography to lend a romantic aura to the wedding couple. Similarly, while nationalist literature on domesticity often emulated Victorian ideals of companionate marriage, it would be inaccurate to assume that bourgeois forms of domesticity and coupledom were wholeheartedly embraced in India. What we see instead is a process of certain bourgeois ideals modifying, but not replacing, certain pre-existing norms of the extended family. The result was a form of matrimony that continues to flourish to this day. However, to argue that arranged marriage is a modern phenomenon does not deny the inequities that characterize the institution. Just as there remain serious inequities in the institution of marriage anywhere in the world, so also arranged marriages display patriarchal privilege and hierarchy through practices such as dowry. But by squarely locating arranged marriage as a part of Indian modernity we are better able to analyse the specific strengths and weaknesses of that practice.[25]

Another area of postcolonial scholarship that radically challenges liberal, feminist analysis has developed around the history of caste in India. Anupama Rao's eloquently titled book *The Caste Question* demonstrates, among other things, the impossibility of delinking gendered identity in modern India from that of caste. Rao draws attention to a tension that was constitutive of many reformist endeavours towards women's empowerment in India. *Dalit* (ex-untouchable) women, she argues, suffered from a double stigmatization. They suffered in the hands of an upper-caste patriarchy on account of their caste status (or the lack thereof). They also bore the brunt of more intimate forms of control exercised upon their bodies and labour by *dalit* men. Through an analysis of the writings and achievements of *dalit* leaders from the late nineteenth century to the present, Rao argues that their works offer

> possible avenues for rethinking the genealogy of Indian feminism to engage meaningfully with *dalit* women's 'difference' from the ideal subjects of feminist politics. By drawing attention to the relationship between caste ideology and gender relations in the intimate and public sphere, by arguing, in fact, that the regulation of gender and sexuality constituted an integral aspect of the ideology of caste, *dalit-bahujan* feminists have demanded a changed politics of feminism …[26]

Interestingly, the postcolonial scholarship on caste has in recent years allied itself to other areas of radical scholarship on human rights and racial discrimination.

This is an emergent area of study and points to ways in which postcolonial and globalization discourses can often come together in the service of human rights. Rao writes about the petition put forth by *dalit* representatives at the UN World Conference against Racism, Racial Discrimination, Xenophobia and Related Intolerance held in Durban, South Africa from 31 August until 7 September 2001. Equating caste violence with racial violence, particularly along the axis of gender they stated,

> We declare that *dalit* women are victims of caste and gender violence, used by landlord, middlemen, and contractors, on construction sites and policemen to 'inflict political lessons' and crush protests, struggle and dissent against centuries' old discrimination being inflicted on their whole community. *Dalit* women are raped and mutilated before being massacred and used as hostages to 'punish absconding relatives.'[27]

The internationalization of women's issues is not a by-product of the era of globalization. Feminism from the moments of its earliest articulation was bound up with issues that went beyond the nation state. Ironically, its internationalism also made the feminist project an unlikely bedfellow to projects of imperialism and colonialism.

Feminism and the civilizing mission

Antoinette Burton's significant intervention in British imperial history was to demonstrate the linkages between British feminist work and thought to the ideological work of British imperialism. Feminists and suffragists from the 1860s onwards – women like Mary Carpenter, Josephine Butler, Frances Cobbe, Millicent Garrett Fawcett, Eleanor Rathbone and Margaret Cousins – used the trope of the hapless Indian woman, trapped in the *zenana* (women's quarters), or oppressed by 'timeless' casteist practices, as a justification for their participation in empire's civilizing mission. A critical insight gleaned from Burton's early work, *Burdens of History*, is that imperial feminism's championing of the cause of colonized (in this case Indian) women constituted an important plank in their agenda towards their own reform. The Englishwoman's demand for suffrage, for example, was justified on the grounds that she required full membership in her own nation in order to be able to shoulder the responsibility of her colonized sisters. The latter in turn was necessary if Britain was to live up to its imperial responsibilities.

Imperial feminism's goals cannot be divorced from the context of the British Empire. In this there was a similarity between British feminists, Indian nationalists and imperial statesmen. For all these apparently separate groups, the Indian woman, whom they imagined variously and to suit their own purposes, was 'one of the universals upon which their liberal and "liberating" reform projects depended'.[28] The implications of such a study for an understanding of some of the postcolonial predicaments of liberal feminism are salient. Imperial feminists could only champion the cause of colonial women on the moral ground of a global sisterhood. But they projected their own norms on to the women of India and found them wanting. The situation brings to mind Chandra Mohanty's observation that such notions of universal sisterhood are 'predicated on the erasure of the history and the effects of contemporary imperialism'.[29] Burton's study of British feminism in the age of empire shows how and why the 'modern British women's movement produced a universal female "we" that continues to haunt and, ironically, to fragment feminists worldwide'.[30]

Likewise, scholarship on the history of settler contexts demonstrates feminism's rootedness in settler, racial ideologies. Work by Fiona Paisley, Marilyn Lake, Ann Curthoys, Heather Goodall and others shows on the one hand that the campaigns by pro-indigenous women for improving the conditions of Aboriginal women – securing them property rights, preventing the forcible removal of Aboriginal children by settlers and taking steps against sexual exploitation of Aboriginal women by white male settlers – during the interwar years constitutes an important 'episode in the contestation of settler colonialism by settler colonists themselves'.[31] On the other hand, however, their arguments for greater independence of the Aboriginal woman 'inevitably contributed to new levels of intervention in Aboriginal lives'.[32] Settler feminists, observed Marilyn Lake, 'travelling between the New World and the Old understood their position as one of a "double difference", standing between the "barbarism" of the Old World and the "primitivism" of Aboriginal society'.[33]

The legacy of these feminist efforts is not inconsiderable for an understanding of the postcolonial politics of reconciliation in Australia. As argued by Fiona Paisley in her study of Australian feminists during the interwar years, these women's championing of the rights of Aboriginal women and children was one of the earliest instances when the hegemony of biological theories of race was interrogated within the Australian public sphere and also in the international forum of the Commonwealth. By challenging settler society's right to forcibly remove Aboriginal children to white homes these women simultaneously challenged the certitude of creating a white Australia through assimilation. The 1997 report by the Human Rights and Equal Opportunity Commission entitled *Bringing Them Home* explored the effects 'of removal upon Aboriginal individuals and communities'. Reflecting on the said report, Paisley notes that by '[d]rawing on the testimony from Aboriginal women and men who were subject to policies of removal and dispersal' the report 'provides a wealth of evidence of the impact of government assimilationism on successive generations of Aboriginal women, men, and children, but also the ways in which Aboriginal individuals and communities lived on through these experiences and often became empowered despite or even because of them'.[34]

Paisley, it appears, is drawing an analogy between the early humanitarian work by pro-indigenous white women in Australia and the efforts of postcolonial scholars and acitivists, both non-indigenous and indigenous. Both these efforts go some way in urging 'non-indigenous Australians to listen with "open heart and mind" to the impact this past has had upon individuals' so as to forsake the earlier policy to assimilation in order to begin a process of reconciliation.

Anne McClintock's *Imperial Leather* expands the postcolonial historiography of gender to mount a critique of the very structures of thought that bolstered Victorian and Edwardian notions of imperial virtue. She shows the triangulated relationship between imperialist expansion, the new cult of bourgeois domesticity that unfolded in the metropole and was then exported to the colonies, and the emergence of new ideas of labour, racial idleness and the market. From the exploratory journeys undertaken from the time of the Enlightenment, argues McClintock, there has been a 'persistent gendering' of the 'imperial unknown'.

> As European men crossed the dangerous thresholds of their known worlds, they ritualistically feminized borders and boundaries. ... Cartographers filled the blank seas of their maps with mermaids and sirens. Explorers called unknown lands 'virgin' territory. Philosophers veiled 'Truth' as female, then fantasized about drawing back the veil.[35]

As colonization unfolded, the virgin territory is populated and civilized with a new ethic of labour and the market. Not only did this deny history to the indigenous people, it also put the colonized and women in an analogous relationship. Like women, the colonized too were to be 'discovered, entered, named, inseminated, and above all, owned'. It is important, however, to note that the 'gendering of imperialism took very different forms in different parts of the world'.

> India, for one, was seldom imaged as a virgin land, while the iconography of the harem was not part of Southern African colonial erotics. North African, Middle Eastern and Asian women were, all too often, trammeled by the iconography of the veil, while African women were subjected to the civilizing mission of cotton and soap. In other words, Arab women were to be 'civilized' by being undressed (unveiled), while sub-Saharan women were to be civilized by being dressed (in clean, white British cotton). These sumptuary distinctions were symptomatic of critical differences in the legislative, economic, and political ways in which imperial commodity racism was imposed on different parts of the world.[36]

Islam and women in postcolonial historiography

Women and Islam has emerged in the last two decades as one of those topics in which the yields of feminist postcolonial historiography are striking. Scholars working on a variety of sites – France, Egypt, Iran, India – have all in different ways sought to understand, what at first glance appears to be an embrace, particularly by women, of Islamist ways and religiosity. The most visible icon of this return to faith, which is also simultaneously cast as a lapse into a static tradition, is the veil. This article of women's clothing has been a subject of much controversy in different parts of the world, and has come to stand in for the putative backwardness of Muslim women compared to their Western counterparts. Little attention is given to the internal variety of Islam or indeed to the many different ways that the veil can be worn.

In a fascinating article entitled 'The Veil in Their Minds and on Our Heads' Homa Hoodfar argues that the Western preoccupation with the veil as an object that shrouds the Muslim woman in backwardness can be dated to the late eighteenth and early nineteenth centuries. Numerous writings prior to this period reported on Muslim women's 'lack of morality and shamelessness based on their revealing clothes and … free mobility'.[37] The veil, it would appear, was constitutive of the West's colonial enterprise to orientalize the East. 'Images of Muslim women', argues Hoodfar, were a 'major building block for the construction of the Orient's new imagery, an imagery that has been intrinsically linked to the hegemony of Western imperialism, particularly that of France and Britain.' Work by scholars like Edward Said, Leila Ahmad, Malek Alloula and others shows that the veil was bound up with Western beliefs about the oppression of Muslim women, and that this image was bolstered by travel narratives and historical and anthropological accounts on the region. By a conservative estimate, during the years 1800–1950, there were some 60,000 books published in the West on the Arab Orient. The central focus of many of these books was 'to depict the colonized Arabs/Muslims as inferior/backward and urgently in need of progress offered to them by colonial superiors. It is in this political context that the veil and the Muslim *harem*, as the world of women, emerged as a source of fascination, fantasy, and frustration for Western writers.'[38] No doubt these depictions of the world of Muslim women served as an ideological justification of the West's civilizing mission highlighting the need, in Gayatri Spivak's words, for white men to save brown women from brown men.

Ruby Lal's study of the Mughal *harem* during the sixteenth and seventeenth century shows that far from being the overly sexualized, domestic retreat for women's exploitation and male debauchery, the *harem* in fact was a politicized arena where Mughal women made serious decisions about the polity and its governance. Furthermore, as Hoodfar argued, arguments about the West's colonizing and civilizing mission neglected to take into account the changes that were taking place in women's conditions and family life in Western Europe and England during the same period. Lila Abu-Lughod, Omnia Shakry, Afsaneh Najmabadeh and several others have drawn attention to the ways in which ideas of Victorian morality, women as the managers of the home and hearth, and new ideals of modesty for the middle-class, bourgeois woman congealed during this period. The colonial encounter between the West and different parts of the Middle East and Asia led to a percolation of many of these ideas among the colonized populations. Omnia Shakry, writing on Egyptian ideas of motherhood at the turn of the twentieth century, observes that these reforms 'need to be situated at the cusp of colonial and anti-colonial discourses of modernity'. But, as noted by Hoodfar,

> ... Western writers zealously described the oppression of Turkish and Muslim women, with little regard for the fact that many of these criticisms applied equally to their own society. Both Muslim oriental and Christian occidental women were thought to be in need of male protection and intellectually and biologically destined for the domestic domain.

Western women too appeared quite blinkered in this regard. Many women travellers from Europe noted the 'boredom and the limitation of domestic life' experienced by their Oriental sisters, with little attention to the fact that it was these factors that motivated them to escape their own homes and lives to undertake long sojourns in the East. Hoodfar's analysis is instructive in pointing to the ways in which writers from both the Orient and Occident were struck by the foreignness of the other's conditions. An incident she cites from Mabro's *Veiled Half-truths* is instructive in this regard.

> When Lady Mary Montague was pressed by the women in a Turkish bath to take off her clothes and join them, she undid her blouse to show them her corset. This led them to believe that she was imprisoned in a machine that could only be opened by her husband. Both groups of women could see each other as prisoners and of course they were right.[39]

Under conditions of colonialism, however, impressions of foreignness could, and did, rapidly slide into generalizations about the overall condition of women. And it was in this context that the veil emerged as an object laden with negative connotations about women's social position. Thus, in 1936 the father of the Shah of Iran made a decision to outlaw the veil as part of his modernization programme. So did Kemal Ataturk, although he did not stop with the veil alone and declared all traditional clothing, including the *fez* (a male headgear), to be against the modernization of Turkey. In Cairo, in 1923 women's organizations publicly removed the veil.

Postcolonial feminist scholars have documented that during the colonial encounter the veil was in a sense decontextualized. There was little appreciation for the freedom of movement and association it allowed women. Nationalist modernizers in many cases appeared to accept the negative charge made on the veil by colonial rulers and agitated for its removal. Yet, as these scholars have pointed out, women's modernization in parts of the Middle East or India was not a wholesale acceptance of Western models. As Lila Abu-Lughod asks in her Introduction to a volume of essays entitled *Remaking Women: Feminism and Modernity in the Middle East*, 'How might one become modern when one was not, could not be, or did not want to be Western?'[40] Reminiscent in many ways of the idea of provincializing Europe, and of Chatterjee's notion of a modernity that was different in important ways from an European prototype while being seriously engaged with some of its founding ideals, the essays in this volume explore how anti-colonial, nationalist discourses in different parts of the Middle East attempted to create a 'national non-secular modernity' with a particular focus on women and gender. As with many other parts of the world that encountered the West through the colonial experience, in the Middle East too, 'the West and things associated with the West' were 'embraced, repudiated, and translated' in gender politics as it evolved during the late nineteenth and twentieth centuries.[41] All the contributors in the volume focus variously on debates on motherhood, women's education, marriage reform and the couple form. The results demonstrate how Islamic ideas of *adab* (norms of comportment and behaviour) came to be linked to as well as distinguished from Western ideas of bourgeois domesticity. A postcolonial history of gender relations in the Middle East demonstrates that modernity in that domain was not simply based on *taqlid* (blind imitation). Rather, feminism, as the collection goes on to demonstrate, emerges as something 'quite different' over the course of these developments from its commonplace association with questions of female individualism, choice and rights.

What, the reader may ask, is the value of studies such as these in our times? Let us close this section by considering the urgency to deepen the postcolonial historical engagement with gender by briefly discussing the long (and troubled) life of the veil in a postcolonial Europe. In her 2000 article 'Bavarian Crucifixes and French Headscarves' Leora Auslander drew attention to a controversy that rocked the French and German public spheres at the dawn of the new millennium about the legitimacy of (certain) religious signs in a 'postmodern' Europe. Auslander's was not the only scholarly account on this controversy. In 2007, the noted feminist historian Joan Scott published a monograph entitled *The Politics of the Veil*.

On 3 October 1989 the French newspaper *Libération* reported a story of three Muslim girls – Fatima and Leila Achaboun, and Samira Saidani – being expelled from school because of their refusal to remove their headscarves. The principal of the school saw the headscarf as something offensive to the principle of secularism regarded as the bedrock of the French school system. While the initial reaction to the girls' expulsion was quite critical (particularly among the Left and Islamic groups), soon these responses were overcome by a media blitz that 'systematically represented Islam as a foreign religion and the headscarf as a threat to French solidarity'.[42]

Eventually, on 15 March 2004, the French government passed a law that banned students from wearing any 'conspicuous signs' of religious affiliation in public schools. 'Although the law applied to Jewish boys in skullcaps and Sikh boys in turbans as well to anyone wearing a large cross around his or her neck,' writes Scott, the law 'was aimed primarily at Muslim girls wearing headscarfs.'[43] The other groups were included, she argues, to undercut any possible charges of discrimination. But the headscarf, veil, *foulard* and *hijab* (all words used interchangeably even though they referred to different types of female garments)

> was considered inimical to French custom and law because it violated the separation of church and state, insisted on differences among citizens in a nation one and indivisible, and accepted the subordination of women in a republic premised on equality. For many supporters of the law, the veil was the ultimate symbol of Islam's resistance to modernity.[44]

Both Auslander and Scott observe the linkages between colonial preoccupations with the veil and its persistence into the postcolonial period. They also note the reductive political equation drawn between the putative backwardness and conservatism of a community – Muslims – and an object of clothing. 'Why the veil?' asks Scott, anticipating a response that many readers will have. Her response is to argue that the veil in its colonial and postcolonial trajectory has become an 'overdetemined' signifier of all that is regarded as the 'other' of a putative 'French' culture even as the connotation of what it means to be French has undergone seismic shifts in the years that followed the era of decolonization. As discussed in the previous chapter, the end of the Algerian war led to an influx of many Algerians into France as French citizens. Yet, despite the much-vaunted ideal of French universalism whose hallmark was the unmarked citizen-subject, people of Algerian origin are still regarded as immigrants in contemporary France. Moreover, there is a facile equation made between Algerian, Arab and Muslim. In the volatile political atmosphere of a 'new' France, as a member of the European Union, the veiled Muslim woman provided a ready target of republican anxieties.

In these cross-cutting currents, many immigrant groups – Algerians, Muslims, Arabs – participated in the *foulard* controversy, sometimes supporting the wearing of a headscarf if only as an exercise that demanded recognition by the nation state. The French response to the veil, argued Scott, has to be understood as a set of anxieties emanating from a crisis of secularism, individualism, republicanism and sexuality in a changed Europe, one that we have argued in previous chapters is a new postcolonial Europe.

Within this charged setting, Scott raises a series of questions that we have seen preoccupied postcolonial theory from its inception: 'How can individuals and groups with different interests live together? Is it possible to think about difference non-hierarchically? On what common grounds can difference be negotiated?' In other words, is reconciliation possible without cultural assimilation, without all differences being made to merge into sameness? Let us close this chapter with a discussion of Leela Gandhi's *Affective Communities*, which offers a new direction in postcolonial theory by documenting what the author refers to as a 'politics of friendship' in the age of late Victorian empire. The 'minor' histories Gandhi writes about, I want to submit, offer one response towards envisioning an alternate worldview whose urgency is underscored in Scott's questions.

Postcolonial history as Utopian thought

Drawing inspiration from Ashis Nandy's *The Intimate Enemy*, Gandhi's focus in this book is on metropolitan anti-imperialists, a varied cast of characters whose individual politics and modes of dissent made them non-players in the project of either creating an anti-colonial nation state or in furthering the project of European imperialism. Gandhi also draws upon the work of previous postcolonial scholars like Edward Said, Homi Bhabha and the *Subaltern Studies* collective to demonstrate the failure of 'imperial binarism' ('us' versus 'them', colonizer versus colonized, black versus white, imperial versus national) as a project that was always doomed to failure on account of the 'irremediable leakiness of imperial boundaries'.[45] Like Said, Gandhi attempts to demonstrate through her case studies 'the contrapuntal perspective' of postcolonial thought, which is 'committed in its best moments to revealing the "overlapping territories" and "intertwined histories" of colonial encounter'.[46] At the same time, unlike the scholars mentioned above she re-engages the colonial archive to find metropolitan articulations of anti-imperialism. Unlike Burton or Paisley's feminists, who were ultimately complicit in the imperial project even as they championed the cause of Aboriginal or Indian women, Gandhi's *dramatis personae* remained avowedly anti-imperial. But they did not constitute a well-defined community as such. Their only commonality was their location in *fin-de-siècle* Victorian radical politics and their disavowal of the imperial enterprise. Following Nandy's call – that rarely does postcolonial scholarship engage with 'the numerically small but psychologically significant response of many who opted out of their colonizing society' for the cause of the colony (in her case, India) – Gandhi analyses the life and work and intellectual collaboration of/among such disparate individuals as the pre-eminent anti-colonial, Indian leader M. K. Gandhi, the missionary C. F. Andrews, the socialist, homosexual, animal rights activist and prison reformer Edward Carpenter, the late Victorian vegetarian and animal rights campaigner Henry Salt, the poet Manmohan Ghose, and the one-time extremist philosopher and nationalist Sri Aurobindo and his French–Egyptian–Jewish mystic friend Mirra Alfassa. Common to each of these individuals was their rejection of imperialism, which, argues Gandhi, they each diagnosed in their highly individualized ways 'as a peculiar habit of mind, discerning within its structures a complex analogical system relentlessly mapping hierarchies of race, culture, and civilization upon relationships between genders, species, classes etc.'[47] In this schema, she writes, recalling Frantz Fanon, any departure from the norm of

> orderliness of imperial habitation was ... an experience of profound psychic derangement: exile to the chaos of a world without taxonomy, variously in the company of sexual misfits, slaughterhouse animals, factory slaves, colonized subjects, unruly women – the wretched as it were of the earth.[48]

By bringing under the rubric of an anti-imperial politics the diverse energies of animal rights, vegetarianism, radical aestheticism, sexual dissidence, religious heterodoxy, pro-suffrage activism and socialism, Gandhi identifies the horizons of a cosmopolitan, queer politics at the turn of the twentieth century. Let me give one example from Gandhi's repertoire of what she implies by the open-ended, anti-communitarian nature of *fin-de-siècle* radical thought. In her discussion of Edward Carpenter, Gandhi argues that it was Carpenter's homosexuality that was the ground upon which his anti-imperial politics could thrive and take shape. Yet, Carpenter is regarded by latter-day British homosexual activists as someone who often evaded his own homosexuality. No doubt these criticisms found sustenance in Carpenter's own statements that he 'had never to do with actual paedestry, so-called', his chief desire being for 'love in bodily contact, as to sleep naked with a naked friend'. Gandhi argues that

> Carpenter's antiwestern polemic, and his attending affinities with Europe's subject races, can only be explained in terms of a homosexual politics whose distinctiveness accrues less from dissident 'sex acts' and more from a radical reconfiguration of association, alliance, relationality, community.

Homosexuality, in her definition, drawn from her reading of Carpenter's writings, is ultimately about a 'capacity for radical kinship'. It was this openness that made Carpenter sympathetic to the cause of animals, women, outcasts, prostitutes and workers, and a strident critic of the English imperial project in Ireland and America. It was this worldview that also paved the way for his friendship with M. K. Gandhi, another turn of the twentieth-century figure who practised 'his own peculiar brand of sexual binarism'. At a time when the British excoriated Indians for their effeminacy, and Indian nationalists of different stripes were attempting to resurrect the Indian male's hypermasculinity, M. K. Gandhi called for what may be seen as a 'queering of gender positions'.[49] He urged the nationalist worker (*satyagrahi*, literally meaning seeker of truth) to abjure from sex acts, practise celibacy and model himself on the Hindu widow. M. K. Gandhi's aspirations were often to 'mother' his companions and in the process to make himself 'God's eunuch'.[50] Carpenter and Gandhi, each in their own way, radically challenged the hierarchies of sex that were being given shape in these years by Darwin, a trajectory that culminated in Freud's conceptualization of a refusal of sex (straight or gay) as a sign of psychological ill health.

Fin-de-siècle radical utopianism was dismissed as an immature and infantile form of politics by leftist leaders and thinkers from Friedrich Engels to V. I. Lenin. But it was precisely its immaturity when measured in terms of a mature, state-sponsored political programme that made *fin-de-siècle* anti-colonial thought ripe with new possibilities. As Leela Gandhi herself notes with her signature poetic and political flourish,

> Utopianism, ... is just a matter of taste: you either want it now or you prefer to wait for it for as long as it takes to bring newness into the world. But at this time in world politics, when our solidarities simply cannot be fixed in advance ... a utopian mentality shows the way forward to a genuine cosmopolitanism: always open to the risky arrival of those not quite, not yet, covered by the privileges which secure our identities and keep us safe.

Gandhi's work signals a new turn towards queering postcolonial studies. By turning to the history of such 'minor' players in the metropole and studying their friendship with contemporaries in the colony, she demonstrates that anti-imperialism can be imagined as a project divorced from community. Anti-imperialism, in her postcolonial outlook, was a form of queer politics that worked relentlessly towards an 'anti-communitarian communitarianism'.[51] Gandhi's work is an invitation to postcolonial and gender historians to explore further these histories of non-chauvinistic critiques of imperial and nationalist hypermasculinities and to think about possibilities by which we can address the question of how to live with difference – historical, religious, sexual and cultural – in the contemporary world.

Notes

1 Frantz Fanon, *A Dying Colonialism* (New York, NY: Grove Press, 1965), p. 41.
2 Fanon, *A Dying Colonialism*, p. 47.
3 Fanon, *A Dying Colonialism*, p. 63
4 Leela Gandhi, *Postcolonial Theory: A Critical Introduction* (NSW: Allen & Unwin, 1998).
5 Gandhi, *Postcolonial Theory*, p. 83.
6 Chandra Talpade Mohanty, *Feminism Without Borders: Decolonizing Theory, Practicing Solidarity* (Durham, NC: Duke University Press, 2003), p. 23.
7 Mohanty, *Feminism Without Borders*, p. 22.
8 Cited in Gandhi, *Postcolonial Theory*, p. 84.
9 Gandhi, *Postcolonial Theory*.
10 Sara Suleri, *The Rhetoric of English in India* (Chicago, IL: University of Chicago Press, 1992), p. 273. Also see Sara Suleri, 'Woman Skin Deep: Feminism and the Postcolonial Condition', *Critical Inquiry* 18 (Summer 1992), pp. 756–69.
11 Suleri, 'Woman Skin Deep', pp. 758–9.
12 Gayatri Spivak, 'Subaltern Studies: Deconstructing Historiography', in Ranajit Guha and Gayatri Spivak (eds), *Selected Subaltern Studies* (New York, NY: Oxford University Press, 1988), pp. 3–32; Gayatri Spivak, 'Can the Subaltern Speak?', in Cary Nelson and Lawrence Grossberg (eds), *Marxism and the Interpretations of Culture* (Urbana, IL: University of Illinois Press, 1988), pp. 271–313.
13 Spivak's concerns about representation and colonial power found interesting parallels in the works of the historian/anthropologist Bernard Cohn who also wrote extensively about colonial regimes and their power over the colonized being linked intimately to the knowledge apparatus they generated. See Bernard Cohn, *An Anthropologist among Historians and Other Essays* (New Delhi: Oxford University Press, 1987).
14 This essay appeared in *Cultural Critique* 7 (Fall 1987), pp.119–56 and also in Kumkum Sangari and Sudesh Vaid (eds), *Recasting Women: Essays in Colonial History* (New Delhi: Kali, 1989), pp. 88–126. Mani's monograph on the practice of *sati* or widow burning appeared in 1998. See Lata Mani, *Contentious Traditions: The Debate on Sati in Colonial India* (Berkeley and Los Angeles, CA: University of California Press, 1998).
15 For details on the life of Bentinck, see John Rosselli, *Lord William Bentinck: The Making of a Liberal Imperialist, 1774–1839* (Berkeley, CA: University of California Press, 1974).
16 Tanika Sarkar, 'Semiotics of Terror: Muslim Children and Women in Hindu Rashtra', *Economic and Political Weekly*, Commentary (13 July 2002), pp. 2872–6; Gyanendra Pandey, *Remembering Partition: Violence, Nationalism, and History in India* (New York, NY: Cambridge University Press, 2001).
17 Cited in Mani, *Contentious Traditions*, p. 158.
18 Mani, *Contentious Traditions*, p. 159.
19 Mani, *Contentious Traditions*, p. 190.
20 Partha Chatterjee, 'The Nationalist Resolution of the Women's Question', in Kumkum Sangari and Sudesh Vaid (eds), *Recasting Women: Essays in Indian Colonial History* (New Brunswick, NJ: Rutgers University Press, 1999), pp. 233–54. A slightly different version of this essay appeared in Chatterjee's *The Nation and Its Fragments*. See Partha Chatterjee, 'The Nation and Its Women', in Partha Chatterjee (ed.), *The Nation and Its Fragments: Colonial and Postcolonial Histories* (Princeton, NJ: Princeton University Press, 1993), pp. 116–34. All citations are from the later version.
21 Chatterjee, *The Nation and Its Fragments*, p. 117.
22 Chatterjee, *The Nation and Its Fragments*, p. 121.
23 Chatterjee, *The Nation and Its Fragments*.
24 For more details on arranged marriage, see Rochona Majumdar, *Marriage and Modernity: Family Values in Colonial Bengal* (Durham, NC: Duke University Press, 2009).
25 *Marriage and Modernity* takes its cue from the postcolonial scholarship of Chakrabarty, Chatterjee and many others discussed in previous chapters to demonstrate, through a close study of matrimonial practices, how certain ideas that underpin the classical liberal or

feminist conception of the subject play out differently in a historical context outside the West. The book was inspired by my recognition of the fact that postcolonial scholarship will make an advance when it is able to give a positive name to the subject that it still describes – to speak with Homi Bhabha – as 'not quite/not white'. But this naming cannot happen without the accumulation of a body of historical analyses that refuses to simply dismiss the institution as part of an archaic tradition.

26 Anupama Rao, 'Sexuality and the Family Form', *Economic and Political Weekly* (19 February 2005), p. 717. Also see her Introduction in Anupama Rao (ed.), *Gender and Caste* (New Delhi: Kali for Women, 2003), pp. 1–47.

27 Rao, 'Sexuality and the Family Form', p. 717.

28 Antoinette Burton, *Burdens of History: British Feminists, Indian Women, and Imperial Culture, 1865–1915* (Chapel Hill, NC and London: University of North Carolina Press, 1994), p. 208.

29 Mohanty, cited in Burton, *Burdens of History*, p. 4.

30 Burton, *Burdens of History*.

31 Fiona Paisley, *Loving Protection?: Australian Feminism and Aboriginal Women's Rights, 1919–1939* (Melbourne: Melbourne University Press, 2000), p. 155.

32 Paisley, *Loving Protection?*

33 Cited in Paisley, *Loving Protection?*, p. 154.

34 Paisley, *Loving Protection?*, pp. 2–3.

35 Anne McClintock, *Imperial Leather: Race, Gender, and Sexuality in the Colonial Contest* (New York, NY: Routledge, 1995), p. 24.

36 McClintock, *Imperial Leather*, p. 31.

37 Homa Hoodfar, 'The Veil in Their Minds and on Our Heads', in David Lloyd and Lisa Lowe (eds), *The Politics of Culture in the Shadow of Capital* (Durham, NC: Duke University Press, 1997), pp. 254–5.

38 Hoodfar, 'The Veil in Their Minds and on Our Heads', p. 255.

39 Hoodfar, 'The Veil in Their Minds and on Our Heads', p. 257.

40 Lila Abu-Lughod, *Remaking Women: Feminism and Modernity in the Middle East* (Princeton, NJ: Princeton University Press, 1998), p. 14.

41 Abu-Lughod, *Remaking Women*, p. 3.

42 Leora Auslander, 'Bavarian Crucifixes and French Headscarves', *Cultural Dynamics* 12(3) (2000), p. 290.

43 Joan Scott, *The Politics of the Veil* (Princeton, NJ: Princeton University Press, 2007), pp. 1–2.

44 Scott, *The Politics of the Veil*.

45 Leela Gandhi, *Affective Communities: Anticolonial Thought, Fin-de-Siècle Radicalism, and the Politics of Friendship* (Durham, NC: Duke University Press, 2006), p. 3.

46 Gandhi, *Affective Communities*.

47 Gandhi, *Affective Communities*, p. 7.

48 Gandhi, *Affective Communities*.

49 Gandhi, *Affective Communities*, p. 63.

50 Gandhi, *Affective Communities*, p. 64.

51 Gandhi, *Affective Communities*, p. 26.

Conclusion

In the preceding pages we have analysed the impact of the diverse and contested body of ideas clustered under the rubric of 'postcolonial theory' upon the academic discipline of history. The prefix 'postcolonial' in postcolonial histories has been deployed variously by historians to designate a body of ideas, a historical period, a political and ethical stance to the world and a certain mode of thinking. The capaciousness of the category, in many respects enabling, has also invited much criticism on the grounds that it lacks precision. Some critics have even gone on to argue that the postcolonial moment is now behind us, its critical potential and relevance now swept under the tide of globalization theories. But, it should be clear that postcolonial histories of migration, race and minority rights are germane for a nuanced understanding of contemporary geopolitics. Indeed, the postcolonial historical standpoint is invaluable in understanding human diversity in the context of globalization.

The analytical schema of this book was not national. Its rationale was not to make a country-specific list of what postcolonial historians have contributed to different national histories. Rather, its aim is to analyse thematically what postcolonial perspectives have brought to the writing of history; to catalogue the purchase that postcolonial thinking has for historical work more generally. What we have seen here is not a country-by-country compendium of postcolonial writing by historians, but an analysis of the historiographical issues that postcolonial histories raise for the discipline as a whole. As historians working on different contexts use/question/recalibrate the founding assumptions of postcolonial historiography the field itself is expanding rapidly.

For example, significant areas not covered in the corpus of this book include the histories of Ireland, the former Eastern European bloc and Israel–Palestine. The latter is an area where the impact of politics is clearly felt by scholarly disciplines such as history, anthropology and archaeology. Scholars argue passionately about whether the turbulent politics of the region approximate colonial conditions. Others argue in favour of thinking about the region as simultaneously a settler-colonial and a postcolonial one.[1] The history of Ireland has similarly attracted attention from historians and other scholars sympathetic to postcolonial theory. Likewise, historians of Eastern Europe often deploy the postcolonial vocabulary of 'provincializing' Western Europe. The analyses presented in these pages are an invitation to readers to pursue postcolonial historical works coming out of these and other national contexts. Readers, I hope, will now understand clearly what features characterize particular historical works as postcolonial. What does it mean when historians working on different regions of the world across a variety of time periods describe their scholarly standpoint as postcolonial? The analysis presented in the preceding pages was an attempt to answer this question.

We began by looking afresh at what the cultural politics of decolonization has to offer to postcolonial historiography in a globalizing world. Thereafter, we turned to the writings of the *Subaltern Studies* collective to chart the rise of postcolonial history writing. This group of historians specializing in Indian history was among the earliest to produce critiques of nationalism through their active engagement with postcolonial writers like Edward Said, Gayatri Spivak and later Homi Bhabha. Crucially, they also elaborated on postcolonial history's indispensable but critical engagement with ideas that emanated from European enlightenment thinking of the eighteenth century. The account then moved on to explore the apparently anachronistic idea of medieval postcolonial history by looking at the way in which medieval studies scholars have engaged with postcolonial history and theory. The result, I showed, is far from anachronistic and enriches understanding in both the fields of medieval studies and postcolonial history.

Chapters 4 and 5 focused on Empire and postcolonial history-writing. While the analysis in Chapter 4 centred on the linkages between postcolonial and new imperial histories in the context of the British and French empires in Asia, Africa and the Caribbean, the next chapter demonstrated the yield of a postcolonial historical outlook in writing histories of settler colonies. It explored the claims of postcolonial historiography for those countries that did not experience formal decolonization movements, such as Australia, Canada and New Zealand. These were contrasted against postcolonial histories of settler states such as Algeria, closing with a discussion of the history of 'postcolonial peoples' – a category that includes ex-settlers, indigenous groups and migrants. The last chapter, on gender, race and postcolonial history, returns us once again to the ways in which postcolonial historians have been mindful of questions of historical difference in their works without either essentializing difference or erasing it.

In conclusion, I would like to submit that postcolonial historiography acquires greater salience as the inequities that mark human conditions across the world become more prominent, and as questions of justice and human rights preoccupy us ever more urgently.

Note

1 Edward Said, *The Question of Palestine* (London: Routledge, 1980) first framed the Palestinian question as a problem of the postcolonial world. For more recent accounts, see Joseph Massad, 'The "Post-colonial" Colony: Time, Space, and Bodies in Israel/Palestine', in Kalpana Seshadri-Crooks and Fawzia Afzal Khan (eds), *The Preoccupation of Postcolonial Studies* (Durham, NC: Duke University Press, 2000), pp. 311–46.

Bibliography

Janet L. Abu-Lughod, *Before European Hegemony: The World System A.D. 1250–1350* (New York, NY: Oxford University Press, 1989).

Lila Abu-Lughod, *Remaking Women: Feminism and Modernity in the Middle East* (Princeton, NJ: Princeton University Press, 1998).

Nadia Altschul, 'Postcolonialism and the Study of the Middle Ages', *History Compass* 6(2) (2008), pp. 588–606.

Shahid Amin, 'Gandhi as Mahatma', in Ranajit Guha and Gayatri Spivak (eds), *Selected Subaltern Studies* (New York, NY: Oxford University Press, 1988), pp. 288–342.

Samir Amin, *Eurocentrism* (trans. Russel Moore) (New York, NY: Monthly Review Press, 1989).

Bain Attwood, *Telling the Truth About Aboriginal History* (NSW: Allen & Unwin, 2005).

Bain Attwood and Tom Griffiths (eds), *Frontier, Race, Nation: Henry Reynolds and Australian History* (Melbourne: Australian Scholarly Publishing Limited, 2009).

Bain Attwood and Fiona Magowan (eds), *Telling Stories: Indigenous History and Memory in Australia and New Zealand* (NSW: Allen & Unwin, 2001).

Leora Auslander, 'Bavarian Crucifixes and French Headscarves', *Cultural Dynamics* 12(3) (2000), pp. 283–309.

Etienne Balibar, 'Europe: An "Unimagined" Frontier of Democracy', *Diacritics* 33(3/4) (Fall 2003) Available at http://gateway.proquest.com/openurl?ctx_ver=Z39.88-2003&xri:pqil:res_ver=0.2&res_id=xri:lion-us&rft_id=xri:lion:ft:abell:R03822140:0 [accessed 8 January 2010].

Etienne Balibar, *We, the People of Europe? Reflections on Transnational Community* (Princeton, NJ: Princeton University Press, 2004).

Homi Bhabha, *The Location of Culture* (London: Routledge, 1990).

Homi Bhabha and John Comaroff, 'Speaking of Postcoloniality in a Continuous Present: A Conversation', in David Goldberg and Ato Quayson (eds), *Relocating Postcolonialism* (Oxford: Blackwell Publishing, 2002), pp. 15–46.

Kathleen Biddick, *The Shock of Medievalism* (Durham, NC: Duke University Press, 1998).

Judith Binney, *Redemption Song* (Auckland: Auckland University Press, 1995).

Ritu Birla, *Stages of Capital: Law, Culture, and Market Governance in Late Colonial India* (Durham, NC: Duke University Press, 2009).

Carol Breckenridge, Pollock Sheldon, Homi Bhabha and Dipesh Chakrabarty (eds), *Cosmopolitanism* (Durham, NC: Duke University Press, 2002).

Antoinette Burton, *Burdens of History: British Feminists, Indian Women, and Imperial Culture, 1865–1915* (Chapel Hill, NC and London: University of North Carolina Press, 1994).

Antoinette Burton (ed.), *After the Imperial Turn: Thinking with and through the Nation* (Durham, NC: Duke University Press, 2003).

Daniel Carey and Lynn Festa (eds), *Postcolonial Enlightenment: Eighteenth Century Enlightenment and Postcolonial Theory* (Oxford/New York, NY: Oxford University Press, 2009).

Dipesh Chakrabarty, 'Conditions of Knowledge of Working-class Conditions', in Ranajit Guha and Gayatri Spivak (eds), *Selected Subaltern Studies* (New York, NY: Oxford University Press, 1988), pp. 179–230.

Dipesh Chakrabarty, *Habitations of Modernity: Essays in the Wake of Subaltern Studies* (Chicago, IL: University of Chicago Press, 2002).

Dipesh Chakrabarty, 'History and Historicality', *Postcolonial Studies* 7(1) (2004), pp. 125–30.

Dipesh Chakrabarty, 'Legacies of Bandung: Decolonization and the Politics of Culture', *Economic and Political Weekly* 40(46) (12 November 2005), pp. 4812–18.

Dipesh Chakrabarty, 'History and the Politics of Recognition', in Keith Jenkins, Sue Morgan and Alan Munslow (eds), *Manifestoes for History* (London: Routledge, 2007), pp. 77–86.

Dipesh Chakrabarty, *Provincializing Europe: Postcolonial Thought and Historical Difference* (Princeton, NJ: Princeton University Press, 2007).

Dipesh Chakrabarty, 'Aboriginal and Subaltern Histories', in Bain Attwood and Tom Griffiths (eds), *Frontier, Race, Nation: Henry Reynolds and Australian History* (Melbourne: Australian Scholarly Publishing Limited, 2009), pp. 55–70.

Dipesh Chakrabarty, 'An Anti-colonial History of the Postcolonial Turn: An Essay in Memory of Greg Dening', *Melbourne Historical Journal* 37 (2009), pp. 1–23.

Dipesh Chakrabarty, 'Europe in the World: Twenty Years after 1989', *Economic and Political Weekly* XLIV(45) (2009), pp. 23–5.

Partha Chatterjee, *Nationalist Thought and the Colonial World: A Derivative Discourse* (London: Zed Books, 1986).

Partha Chatterjee, *The Nation and Its Fragments: Colonial and Postcolonial Histories* (Princeton, NJ: Princeton University Press, 1993).

Partha Chatterjee, 'The Nation and Its Women', in *The Nation and Its Fragments: Colonial and Postcolonial Histories* (Princeton, NJ: Princeton University Press, 1993), pp. 116–34.

Partha Chatterjee, 'The Nationalist Resolution of the Women's Question', in Kumkum Sangari and Sudesh Vaid (eds), *Recasting Women: Essays in Indian Colonial History* (New Brunswick, NJ: Rutgers University Press, 1999), pp. 233–54.

Partha Chatterjee, *The Politics of the Governed: Reflections on Popular Politics in Most of the World* (New York, NY: Columbia University Press, 2004).

Sing C. Chew and Robert A. Denemark (eds) *The Underdevelopment of Development: Essays in Honor of Andre Gunder Frank* (Thousand Oaks, CA: Sage Publications, 1996).

Jeffrey Jerome Cohen (ed.), *The Postcolonial Middle Ages* (New York, NY: St Martin's Press, 2000).

Bernard Cohn, *An Anthropologist among Historians and Other Essays* (New Delhi: Oxford University Press, 1987).

Frederick Cooper, *Colonialism in Question: Theory, Knowledge, History* (Berkeley and Los Angeles, CA: University of California Press, 2005).

Frederick Cooper and Ann Laura Stoler (eds), *Tensions of Empire* (Berkeley, CA: University of California Press, 1997).

Fernando Coronil, 'Can Postcoloniality be Decolonized? Imperial Banality and Postcolonial Power', *Public Culture* 5(1) (1992), pp. 89–108.

Fernando Coronil, 'Beyond Occidentalism: Towards Nonimperial Geohistorical Categories', *Cultural Anthropology* 11(1) (1996), pp. 52–87.

Fernando Coronil, 'Latin American Postcolonial Studies and Global Decolonization', in Neil Lazarus (ed.), *The Cambridge Companion to Postcolonial Literary Studies* (Cambridge: Cambridge University Press, 2004), pp. 221–40.

Patrick Curry, 'The Historiography of Astrology: A Diagnosis and A Prescription', in K. von Stuckrad, G. Oestmann and D. Rutkin (eds), *Horoscopes and Public Spheres: Essays on the History of Astrology* (Berlin and New York, NY: Walter de Gruyter, 2005), pp. 261–74.

John Dagenais and Margaret Greer, 'Decolonizing the Middle Ages', *Journal of Medieval and Early Modern Studies* 30(3) (2000), pp. 431–48.

Roberto M. Dainotto, 'The Discreet Charm of the Arabist Theory: Juan Andres, Historicism, and the De-centering of Montesquieu's Europe', *European Historical Quarterly* 36(1) (2006), pp. 7–30.

Kathleen Davis, 'National Writing in the Ninth Century: A Reminder for Postcolonial Thinking about the Nation', *Journal of Medieval and Early Modern Studies* 28(3) (1998), pp. 611–37.

Kathleen Davis, *Periodization and Sovereignty: How Ideas of Feudalism and Secularization Govern the Politics of Time* (Philadelphia, PA: University of Pennsylvania Press, 2008).

Kathleen Davis and Nadia Altschul (eds), *Medievalisms in the Postcolonial World: The Idea of 'the Middle Ages' Outside Europe* (Baltimore, MD: The Johns Hopkins University Press, 2010).

Andrew Davison, 'Ziya Gokalp and Provincializing Europe', *Comparative Studies of South Asia, Africa, and the Middle East* 26(3) (2006), pp. 377–90.

Carolyn Dinshaw, *Getting Medieval: Sexualities and Communities, Pre- and Post-Modern* (Durham, NC: Duke University Press, 1999).

Carolyn Dinshaw, 'Margery Kempe', in Carolyn Dinshaw and David Wallace (eds), *The Cambridge Companion to Medieval Women's Writing* (Cambridge: Cambridge University Press, 2003), pp. 222–39.

Arif Dirlik, 'The Postcolonial Aura: Third World Criticism in the Age of Global Capitalism', *Critical Inquiry* 20(2) (1994), pp. 328–56.

Simon During (ed.), *The Cultural Studies Reader* (London and New York, NY: Routledge, 1999).

Frantz Fanon, *A Dying Colonialism* (New York, NY: Grove Press, 1965).

Frantz Fanon, *The Wretched of the Earth* (New York, NY: Grove Press, 1965).

Michel Foucault, *The History of Sexuality: An Introduction*, vol. 1 (New York, NY: Vintage Books, 2003).

Andre Gunder Frank, *ReOrient: Global Economy in the Asian Age* (Berkeley, CA: University of California Press, 1998).

Leela Gandhi, *Postcolonial Theory: A Critical Introduction* (NSW: Allen & Unwin, 1998).

Leela Gandhi, *Affective Communities: Anticolonial Thought, Fin-de-Siècle Radicalism, and the Politics of Friendship* (Durham, NC: Duke University Press, 2006).

Debjani Ganguly, *Caste, Colonialism and Counter-modernity: Notes on a Postcolonial Hermeneutics of Caste* (London: Routledge, 2005).

Debjani Ganguly, 'The Language Question in India', in Ato Quayson (ed.), *Cambridge History of Postcolonial Literature* (forthcoming).

Durba Ghosh, *Sex and Family in Colonial India: The Making of Empire* (Cambridge: Cambridge University Press, 2006).

David Gilmour, 'Surprises of the Empire', *The New York Review of Books* 53(17) (2 November 2006).

Julian Go, 'The Provinciality of American Empire: Liberal Exceptionalism and U.S. Colonial Rule, 1898–1912', *Comparative Studies in Society and History* 49(1) (2007), pp. 74–108.

Ranajit Guha, *Elementary Aspects of Peasant Insurgency in Colonial India* (Delhi: Oxford University Press, 1983).

Ranajit Guha (ed.), *A Subaltern Studies Reader 1986–1995* (Minneapolis, MN and London: University of Minnesota Press, 1997).

Ranajit Guha, *Dominance without Hegemony: History and Power in Colonial India* (Cambridge, MA: Harvard University Press, 1997).

Ranajit Guha, *History at the Limit of World History* (New York, NY: Columbia University Press, 2002).

Ranajit Guha and Gayatri Spivak (eds), *Selected Subaltern Studies* (New York, NY: Oxford University Press, 1988).

Catherine Hall, 'Remembering Edward Said', *History Workshop Journal* 57 (2004), pp. 235–43.

Stuart Hall, 'New Ethnicities', in David Morley and Kuan-Hsing Chen (eds), *Stuart Hall: Critical Dialogues in Cultural Studies* (London and New York, NY: Routledge, 1996), pp. 441–9.

Stuart Hall, 'The Formation of a Diasporic Intellectual: An Interview with Stuart Hall by Kuan-Hsing Chen', in David Morley and Kuan-Hsing Chen (eds), *Stuart Hall: Critical Dialogues in Cultural Studies* (London and New York, NY: Routledge, 1996), pp. 484–503.

David Hardiman, *The Coming of the Devi: Adivasi Assertion in Western India* (New Delhi: Oxford University Press, 1987).

Rachel Harrison and Peter Jackson (eds), *The Ambiguous Allure of the West* (Hong Kong: University of Hong Kong Press, 2010).

Amy Hollywood, 'Gender, Agency, and the Divine in Religious Historiography', *The Journal of Religion* 84(4) (2004), pp. 514–28.

Bruce Holsinger, 'Medieval Studies, Postcolonial Studies, and the Genealogies of Critique', *Speculum* 77(4) (2002), pp. 1195–227.

Bruce Holsinger, *Neomedievalism, Neoconservatism, and the War on Terror* (Chicago, IL: University of Chicago Press, 2007).

Homa Hoodfar, 'The Veil in Their Minds and on Our Heads', in David Lloyd and Lisa Lowe (eds), *The Politics of Culture in the Shadow of Capital* (Durham, NC: Duke University Press, 1997), pp. 248–79.

Nicholas Howe, 'Anglo-Saxon England and the Postcolonial Void', in Ananya Kabir and Deanne Williams (eds), *Postcolonial Approaches to the European Middle Ages: Translating Cultures* (Cambridge: Cambridge University Press, 2005), pp. 25–47.

Patricia Clare Ingham and Michelle R. Warren (eds), *Postcolonial Moves: Medieval through Modern* (New York, NY: Palgrave Macmillan, 2003).

Miranda Johnson, 'Making History Public: Indigenous Claims to Settler States', *Public Culture* 20(1) (2008), pp. 97–117.

Miranda Johnson, 'Struggling over the Past: Decolonization and the Problem of History in Settler Societies' (Ph. D. dissertation, University of Chicago, 2008).

Isaac Julien and Mark Nash, 'Dialogues with Stuart Hall', in David Morley and Kuan-Hsing Chen (eds), *Stuart Hall: Critical Dialogues in Cultural Studies* (London and New York, NY: Routledge, 1996), pp. 476–83.

Ananya Kabir, 'Analogy in Translation: Rome, England, India', in Ananya Kabir and Deanne Williams (eds), *Postcolonial Approaches to the European Middle Ages: Translating Cultures* (Cambridge: Cambridge University Press, 2005), pp. 183–204.

Ananya Kabir and Deanne Williams (eds), *Postcolonial Approaches to the European Middle Ages: Translating Cultures* (Cambridge: Cambridge University Press, 2005).

David Lloyd, *Irish Times: Temporalities of Modernity* (Dublin: Field Day/University of Notre-Dame, 2008).

Ania Loomba, *Colonialism/Postcolonialism* (London: Routledge, 1998).

David Ludden (ed.), *Reading Subaltern Studies: Critical History, Contested Meaning, and the Globalisation of South Asia* (New Delhi: Permanent Black, 2001).

Stuart Macintyre and Anna Clark (eds), *The History Wars* (Melbourne: Melbourne University Press, 2003).

Jamie Mackie, *Bandung 1955: Non-alignment and Afro-Asian Solidarity* (Singapore: Editions Didier Millet, 2005).

Rochona Majumdar, *Marriage and Modernity: Family Values in Colonial Bengal* (Durham, NC: Duke University Press, 2009).

Florencia Mallon, 'The Promise and Dilemma of Subaltern Studies', *American Historical Review* 99(5) (1994), pp. 1491–515.

Lata Mani, *Contentious Traditions: The Debate on Sati in Colonial India* (Berkeley and Los Angeles, CA: University of California Press, 1998).

Robert Manne (ed.), *Whitewash: On Keith Windschuttle's Fabrication of Aboriginal History* (Melbourne: Black Inc, 2003).

Anne McClintock, *Imperial Leather: Race, Gender, and Sexuality in the Colonial Contest* (New York, NY: Routledge, 1995).

Anne McClintock, Aamir Mufti and Ella Shohat (eds), *Dangerous Liaisons: Gender, Nation, and Postcolonial Perspectives* (Minneapolis, MN: University of Minnesota Press, 1997).

Walter Mignolo, *Local Histories/Global Designs: Coloniality, Subaltern Knowledges, and Border Thinking* (Princeton, NJ: Princeton University Press, 2000).

Chandra Talpade Mohanty, *Feminism without Borders: Decolonizing Theory, Practicing Solidarity* (Durham, NC: Duke University Press, 2003).

Padmini Mongia, *Contemporary Postcolonial Theory: A Reader* (London: Arnold, 1996).

Dirk Moses (ed.), *Genocide and Settler Society: Frontier Violence and Stolen Indigenous Children in Australian History* (New York, NY: Berghann Books, 2004).

Rosalind O'Hanlon, 'Recovering the Subject: Subaltern Studies and Histories of Resistance in Colonial South Asia', in David Ludden (ed.), *Reading Subaltern Studies* (New Delhi: Permanent Black, 2001), pp. 135–86.

Fiona Paisley, *Loving Protection?: Australian Feminism and Aboriginal Women's Rights, 1919–1939* (Melbourne: Melbourne University Press, 2000).

Gyanendra Pandey, *Remembering Partition: Violence, Nationalism, and History in India* (New York, NY: Cambridge University Press, 2001).

Gyan Prakash (ed.), *After Colonialism: Imperial Histories and Postcolonial Displacements* (Princeton, NJ: Princeton University Press, 1995).

David Prochaska, *Making Algeria French: Colonialism in Bone, 1870–1920* (Cambridge: Cambridge University Press, 1990).

Ato Quayson, 'Translations and Transnationals: Pre- and Postcolonial', in Ananya Kabir and Deanne Williams (eds), *Postcolonial Approaches to the European Middle Ages: Translating Cultures* (Cambridge: Cambridge University Press, 2005), pp. 253–68.

Anupama Rao (ed.), 'Introduction', in *Gender and Caste* (New Delhi: Kali for Women, 2003), pp. 1–47.

Anupama Rao, 'Sexuality and the Family Form', *Economic and Political Weekly* 40(8) (19 February 2005), pp. 715–18.

Alan Read, *The Fact of Blackness: Frantz Fanon and Visual Representation* (London: Institute of Contemporary Arts, Institute of International Visual Arts, Seattle, WA: Bay Press, 1996).

Henry Reynolds, *The Other Side of the Frontier*, new edition (Sydney: University of New South Wales Press, 2006).

Ileana Rodríguez, *The Latin American Subaltern Studies Reader* (Durham, NC: Duke University Press, 2001).

John Rosselli, *Lord William Bentinck: The Making of a Liberal Imperialist, 1774–1839* (Berkeley, CA: University of California Press, 1974).

Edward Said, 'Always on Top', *The London Review of Books* 25(6) (20 March 2003), pp. 3–6.

Tanika Sarkar, 'Semiotics of Terror: Muslim Children and Women in Hindu Rashtra', *Economic and Political Weekly* 37(28) (2002), pp. 2872–6.

Joan Scott, *The Politics of the Veil* (Princeton, NJ: Princeton University Press, 2007).

Sanjay Seth, *Subject Lessons: The Western Education of Colonial India* (Durham, NC: Duke University Press, 2007).

Sanjay Seth, 'Historical Sociology and Postcolonial Theory: Two Strategies for Challenging Eurocentrism', *International Political Sociology* 3(3) (2009), pp. 334–8.

Mrinalini Sinha, *Colonial Masculinity: The 'Manly Englishman' and the 'Effeminate Bengali' in the Late Nineteenth Century* (Manchester: Manchester University Press, 1995).

Ajay Skaria, 'The Project of Provincializing Europe: Reading Dipesh Chakrabarty', *Economic and Political Weekly* 44(14) (2009), pp. 52–9.

Andrea L. Smith (ed.), *Europe's Invisible Migrants* (Amsterdam: Amsterdam University Press, 2003).

Andrea L. Smith, *Colonial Memory and Postcolonial Europe: Maltese Settlers in Algeria and France* (Bloomington, IL: Indiana University Press, 2006).

Gabrielle M. Spiegel, 'Epater les Medievistes [Impressing the Medievalists]', *History and Theory* 39(2) (2000), pp. 243–50.

Gayatri Chakravorty Spivak, 'Three Women's Texts and A Critique of Imperialism', *Critical Inquiry* 12(1) (1985), pp. 243–61.

Gayatri Chakravorty Spivak, 'Can the Subaltern Speak?' in P. Williams and L. Chrisman (eds), *Colonial Discourse and Postcolonial Theory: A Reader* (New York, NY: Columbia University Press, 1994), pp. 66–111.

Paul Steven, 'Heterogenizing Imagination: Globalization, *The Merchant of Venice* and the Work of Literary Criticism', *New Literary History* 36(3) (2005), pp. 425–37.

Ann Laura Stoler, *Race and the Education of Desire: Foucault's History of Sexuality and the Colonial Order of Things* (Durham, NC: Duke University Press, 1995).

Ann Laura Stoler, *Carnal Knowledge and Imperial Power: Race and the Intimate in Colonial Rule* (Berkeley, CA: University of California Press, 2002).

Sara Suleri, *The Rhetoric of English in India* (Chicago, IL: University of Chicago Press, 1992).

Sara Suleri, 'Woman Skin Deep: Feminism and the Postcolonial Condition', *Critical Inquiry* 18(4) (1992), pp. 756–69.

Ngugi wa Thiong'o, *Moving the Centre: The Struggle for Cultural Freedoms* (London: James Currey, 1993).

Barbara Weinstein, 'History without a Cause? Grand Narratives, World History, and the Postcolonial Dilemma', *International Review of Social History* 50 (2005), pp. 71–93.

Gary Wilder, *The French Imperial Nation-state: Negritude and Colonial Humanism between the Two World Wars* (Chicago, IL: University of Chicago Press, 2005).

Kathleen Wilson, *A New Imperial History: Culture, Identity and Modernity in Britain and the Empire, 1660–1840* (Cambridge: Cambridge University Press, 2004).

Patrick Wolfe, 'Settler Colonialism and the Elimination of the Native', *Journal of Genocide Research* 9(4) (2006), pp. 387–409.

Robert Young, *Postcolonialism: An Historical Introduction* (Cambridge: Blackwell, 2001).

Index

Index